PACIFIC PIONEERS

The Asian American Experience

Series Editor
Roger Daniels, University of Cincinnati

A list of books in the series appears at the end of this book.

Pacific Pioneers

JAPANESE JOURNEYS TO AMERICA AND HAWAII, 1850–80

JOHN E. VAN SANT

Foreword by Roger Daniels

UNIVERSITY OF ILLINOIS PRESS

URBANA, CHICAGO & SPRINGFIELD

First Illinois paperback, 2019

∞ This book is printed on acid-free paper.

The Library of Congress cataloged the cloth edition as follows:

Van Sant, John E., 1958–
Pacific pioneers : Japanese journeys to America and Hawaii, 1850–80 / John E. Van Sant ; foreword by Roger Daniels.
p. cm. — (The Asian American experience)
Includes bibliographical references (p.) and index.
ISBN 978-0-252-02560-0 (alk. paper)
I. Title. II. Series. 1. Japanese Americans—History—19th century.
2. Japanese Americans—Hawaii—History—19th century.
3. Immigrants—United States—History—19th century.
4. Immigrants—Hawaii—History—19th century.
5. United States—Emigration and immigration—History—19th century.
6. Japan—Emigration and immigration—History—19th century.
7. Hawaii—Emigration and immigration—History—19th century.
8. United States—Relations—Japan.
9. Japan—Relations—United States.
E184.J3V3 2000
304.8'73052'09034—dc21 99-006829
CIP

2 3 4 5 6 C P 5 4 3 2 1

Paperback ISBN 978-0-252-08490-4

To my parents,
John and Eunice Van Sant

CONTENTS

Foreword, by Roger Daniels ix
Acknowledgments xi

Introduction: Transnational History, Transitions, and Worldviews 1
One Joseph Heco, a Castaway in America 21
Two *Ryūgakusei,* Rutgers, and the American Experience 49
Three Niijima Jo, Japanese Puritan 64
Four From Satsuma to Utopia 79
Five The *Gannenmono,* Eugene Van Reed, and the Emergence of Japan-Hawaii-U.S. Relations 97
Six From Aizu to Gold Hill 117
Epilogue: Japan and the United States, 1880–1924 131

Notes 137
Bibliography 171
Index 187

FOREWORD

Roger Daniels

Although the mass immigration of Japanese to the United States and Hawaii dates from the 1890s, scattered individuals and small groups began pioneering the Pacific crossing in the 1840s. The existence of these forerunners—perhaps 900 all told to the United States and a couple of hundred more to the Kingdom of Hawaii—has long been known to scholars, but it is the particular virtue of John Van Sant's *Pacific Pioneers* that he not only weaves their disconnected stories into a meaningful narrative but also uses their varied experiences to explore the beginnings of trans-Pacific cultural relationships, which would loom so large and fateful in the twentieth century. The thousand-odd travelers included castaways, students, government officials, political exiles, indentured laborers, and businessmen. Their trans-Pacific sojourns took them to a variety of sites: San Francisco; Washington, D.C.; Rutgers University in New Brunswick, New Jersey; upstate New York; Amherst, Massachusetts; Hawaiian plantations, and a short-lived colony at Gold Hill near Sacramento, California. Most returned to Japan, although a few became permanent residents.

Since the time of Marcus Lee Hansen, who began to publish in the 1920s, historians of migration have understood that the ideal positioning for such work is between the cultures that a given migration spans rather than either the launching pad or the target. Van Sant is particularly well equipped for this examination of what he calls transnational history. Raised and educated on the West Coast of the United States, he studied Japanese history and U.S. foreign relations for his doctorate and lived and worked in Japan for many years. He argues persuasively that the significance of these pioneer Japanese far transcends their precursor role.

Van Sant stresses three broad themes that form a subtext for his narrative. First of all, despite the tremendous cultural gulf between pre-Meiji and early Meiji Japan and the United States in the middle decades of the nineteenth century, most of these Japanese were able to function in both societies. Second, many of the Japanese sojourners shared a sense that the traditional *Weltanschauung* of Nippon was no longer appropriate to a nation upon whom the West had intruded. Some welcomed that intrusion and sought to instill certain Western values—including, in some instances, Christianity—into a rapidly modernizing Japan. Third, sustained contact with Japanese in the United States inspired a few Americans not only to aid the education, formal and informal, of the visitors but also to try to assist in the transformation of Japan. Van Sant tells this complex story well: it is a small but significant part of both Japanese and American history and, relatively speaking, a larger section of Asian American history.

In addition, in a time when the debate about multiculturalism and its implications forms a significant part of American sociocultural discourse, it is good to be reminded that multiculturalism did not spring up only recently. Although the word is of relatively recent vintage, the fact of multiculturalism has been a too little noticed facet of American life since the European-led invasion of the Western Hemisphere began. The experiences of these Japanese travelers is but one part of a too much neglected history.

ACKNOWLEDGMENTS

Several colleagues, friends, family members, and institutions have assisted me during the years I spent researching, writing, and revising this study.

Masao Takeda of Aizu-Wakamatsu, Japan, and Henry Taketa of Sacramento, California, initially sparked my interest in the historical relationship between Aizu, Japan, and my hometown of Placerville, California, which soon evolved into this study of the frontier era of Japan-U.S. relations. I regret being unable to complete and publish this book before these fine gentlemen passed away. Moreover, they and several local historians in northern Japan and northern California have painstakingly gathered information that proved invaluable to this study, especially chapter 6.

Glenn Anthony May, Jeffrey Hanes, and Stephen Kohl spent many hours reading earlier versions of this study while I was a doctoral candidate at the University of Oregon. Their comments, criticisms, and suggestions have made this a better and more coherent study than it otherwise would have been. Other friends and colleagues at the University of Oregon who assisted by reading and offering advice on sections of this study were Andrew Goble, Jeffrey Ostler, Bill Boyer, Sheila Broderick, Kim Loan Hill, Ellen Stroud, Stuart McElderry, Brett Walker, Richard Brown, and Leah Kirker.

The primary and secondary sources available at UCLA's University Research Library, especially its Department of Special Collections, were invaluable to this study. My thanks to Jeff Rankin and all of the curators and staff at UCLA who assisted me during the several months I spent using these resources. The Huntington Library in San Marino, California, held some important resources and awarded me a research fellowship that enabled me to complete a significant portion of this study. The interest displayed by Martin Ridge, Wilbur Jacobs, Robert Hine, and Hal Barron also aided me during the months I spent at the Huntington Library. The Griffis Collection at Rutgers University in New Jersey, curated by Ruth J. Simmons, was an important primary resource for early Japanese students in the United States. The Knight Library at the University of Oregon, including its prompt interlibrary loan service, was also quite helpful.

Others who assisted me along the way were Inez Veerkamp, Matt Sugerman, Wayne Patterson, Masanori Takeda, Chikao Koyama, Shinichi Kobayashi, Rith Crocker, Barbara Neisler, Loyd Neisler, Deborah Van Sant, and Roy Van Sant. Many thanks also to the University of Illinois Press for publishing this study.

Special thanks go to Roger Daniels. Despite his own constantly hectic schedule, Professor Daniels's early interest in the book, his reading and editing of several complete drafts, and his well-deserved reputation as an eminent scholar of Asian American and immigration history have propelled this work to publication. Special thanks also go to Karen Hewitt, Executive Editor at the University of Illinois Press, who has spent many hours working with this manuscript.

My thanks and apologies to those who have helped me but whose names do not appear. While I have benefited from the assistance, advice, and criticisms from all of the people listed above, I am ultimately responsible for any mistakes in this study.

PACIFIC PIONEERS

INTRODUCTION

Transnational History, Transitions, and Worldviews

Asians have been in the United States as early as the 1840s, when the first Chinese served as crew members aboard New England–based American whaling and trade ships plying the Pacific Ocean. Thousands of Chinese, most from the southern part of the country, arrived in California during the Gold Rush to work as miners and laborers. In the 1860s, more than ten thousand Chinese helped build the Transcontinental Railroad. After its completion in 1869, Chinese labored on farms and plantations, worked in small factories in Chinese neighborhoods, or operated their own restaurants and businesses. After five or ten years in the United States, most returned home with their earnings to pay off debts or buy farmland. But a few, especially those with businesses in urban areas, decided to remain.

Their presence, however, was greeted with discrimination, violence, and anti-Chinese legislation. For example, twenty-one Chinese were killed in a race riot in Los Angeles in 1871. Later that same decade, Dennis Kearny, the fiery leader of the San Francisco–based Workingmen's party, ended his speeches with the rousing slogan, "Whatever happens, the Chinese must go!"

Then the U.S. Congress, acting at the behest of western politicians and labor leaders, prohibited further immigration with the Chinese Exclusion Act of 1882. What happened to Chinese in nineteenth-century America, and subsequently to all Asian Americans, was part of the larger and continuing pattern of racial scapegoating: blaming nonwhites for causing or contributing to America's social, political, and economic problems.

Japanese, in contrast, began arriving in large numbers on the islands of Hawaii and on the West Coast of the United States as *dekaseginin,* or workers away from home, considerably later—not until the end of the nineteenth century, when racism against the Chinese was already firmly established. Many helped maintain the Transcontinental Railroad while others worked on farms and ranches. In Hawaii, most *dekaseginin*—both male and female—labored on sugar cane plantations. Like the Chinese, many Japanese planned to work for a few years and then return home with their savings. However, approximately half of the Japanese, a far higher percentage than that of Chinese, decided to remain in the United States and Hawaii, often to establish and operate their own farms and businesses. By 1900, just after the U.S. government annexed Hawaii, Japanese comprised nearly 40 percent (61,111) of the entire population of the islands (154,001), outnumbering not only Chinese (25,767) but also native Hawaiians (29,799).[1] Meanwhile, by 1910, Japanese outnumbered Chinese on the mainland of the United States (72,157 to 71,531).[2] Japanese would continue to be the largest Asian American group until the 1970s.

The very first Japanese, however, came to the United States much earlier. Japanese castaway sailors had washed up on Pacific shores beginning at least as early as 1830, while two that we know of, Nakahama Manjiro and Joseph Heco, spent many years in the United States during the 1840s and 1850s.* Despite this, U.S. census records indicate that the first Japanese entered the United States only in 1860 and that no more arrived until 1867, when 7 came.[3] Yet 77 members of the shogun's embassy in 1860 were not counted on census records. According to these records, the total number of Japanese who entered the United States through 1880 was only 335.[4] Sources from Japan, however, indicate that 995 Japanese were issued passports for travel to America during this same period.[5]

The discrepancy between these data and the difficulty in determining an

---

*Most Japanese names in this study are arranged in traditional East Asian order, i.e., family name first and given name second (for example, Mori Arinori). The exceptions are Japanese Americans and Japanese scholars based in the United States who use Western order for their names.

accurate count of Japanese who arrived in the United States between 1850 and 1880 are the result of three methodological problems. First, complete U.S. records on arrivals from Japan were not kept until 1869.[6] Second, throughout the nineteenth century the Bureau of Statistics did not count temporary visitors, such as officials and those on business trips, which, according to Japanese records, made up nearly two-thirds of the passports issued from 1867 to 1880.[7] Japanese sources suggest that up to 600 government officials and businessmen were not counted on American census records. The third problem is that Japanese records are based on passports issued, but not everyone who applied for and received a passport actually left Japan and entered the United States. A more accurate number of Japanese in the United States can be found in the 1870 and 1880 census reports. Fifty-five Japanese were listed on the 1870 census, the first to include Japanese residents, while the 1880 census includes 148 Japanese.[8] In light of all of the above, we cannot determine an accurate number of Japanese who entered the United States during this era. What these data do suggest, however, is that at least 600, but probably not more than 900, Japanese entered the United States between 1850 and 1880.

After 1880, the number of Japanese residents significantly increased, primarily because the Japanese government began allowing laborers to emigrate to the Kingdom of Hawaii, and many of them subsequently moved on to the mainland of the United States.[9] In 1890, the census counted 2,039 Japanese in the United States; 24,326 in 1900; 72,157 in 1910, and 111,010 by 1920.[10]

Given that overseas travel was severely restricted, expensive, and hazardous, who were these first Japanese immigrants? According to official Japanese records, about one-third each were government officials, businessmen, and students. Many of these officials were high-ranking samurai, while most students were from the middle and lower ranks of the samurai class. Many businessmen appear to have been former samurai, but existing records from Japan's Foreign Ministry also suggest that some had originally been merchants.[11] Sailors, such as Joseph Heco, were usually considered part of the peasant class, and other peasants seem to have arrived as well. Nearly all of these early Japanese residents of the United States were male. According to Japanese records, only six women traveled to the United States before 1880. However, these records are not reliable since they do not include the six women of the Wakamatsu colony counted on the 1870 U.S. census, presumably because they—and the rest of the colonists—left Japan without the permission of Meiji government officials. Nor did the Japanese records include the six women among the first group of Japanese laborers who departed

Japan in 1868 for the Kingdom of Hawaii under murky political and legal circumstances.

Because knowledge of these early settlers is unclear and conflicting, most studies of Japanese in the United States understandably begin with the mid-1880s, when Asian American communities first emerged. Nevertheless, the earliest settlers can inform our knowledge of the ways many Japanese adapted to life in their new home and of the experiences of later settlers. Contextualized within the (admittedly wide) parameters of social and political history, this study is a transnational and cross-cultural examination of the first Japanese who spent more than a year as residents of the United States or the Kingdom of Hawaii. Following Gordon Chang's transnational approach that "seeks to break from the imposed definitions of a nationally based historicism . . . to understand Asians in America as part of a growing number of internationalized people in the Pacific Rim whose lives do not fall neatly into a specific national pattern,"[12] I focus on the nineteenth-century worldview in Japan and its international relations; the relations among late nineteenth-century Japan, America, and Hawaii; and the experiences of the handful of Japanese who resided in the United States and Hawaii from 1850 to 1880.

Three interconnected themes form the basis of this study. First, despite the marked difference between the societies and worldviews of the United States and Japan, many of these Japanese were able to successfully participate in American social, cultural, and economic life. Second, as a result of the massive political and social upheaval in Japan during this era, many Japanese questioned the amalgamation of Confucian, Mahayana Buddhist, and Shinto values and beliefs that formed the basis of their worldview and became adherents of Western progress. Third, American benefactors, motivated by the nineteenth-century missionary spirit of Christianity, paternalism, and a desire to spread Western ideas in Japan, often provided crucial assistance to the Japanese who came in pursuit of education, spiritual meaning, or an improved economic situation. In addition, the laborers who arrived in Hawaii and California in the late 1860s can be seen as the vanguard of Japanese immigrants who began arriving in the 1880s and made a substantial contribution to the economic and social development of the American West and Hawaii.

It was during the first half of the nineteenth century that individual Japanese and Americans initially encountered one another, and by the mid-1850s their two governments began formal diplomatic relations. These initial encounters and the start of diplomatic relations were conditioned by their respective worldviews. For Americans, their prevailing worldview of territorial and trade expansion, often accompanied by a self-appointed mission to "civilize" those whom they had conquered by military force or by trade, emerged in the aftermath of the War of 1812, when they felt secure enough to concentrate on the tasks of nation-building without the overriding fear of Great Britain, their former colonial master. For Japanese, their worldview, which can be characterized by Tokugawa hegemony, had emerged at the start of the seventeenth century and was still firmly in place by the mid-nineteenth century.

From Shogun to Meiji: Internal Order and External Relations

By 1850, the shoguns (*shogun* is the abbreviated form of *seii tai shogun,* meaning barbarian-subduing generalissimo) of the Tokugawa family had maintained their authority for 250 years through a military government known as the *bakufu.* This remarkable accomplishment was achieved through political control mechanisms, such as an alternate attendance system that kept the immediate families of all *daimyōs*—domain lords—in the shogun capital of Edo (renamed Tokyo in 1868); a complex system of spies and inspectors who kept watch for signs of dissent; and the collective requirement that each village pay an annual tax based upon the area of the surrounding rice paddy land. As long as the *daimyō* obeyed *bakufu* rules, carried out its orders, and were not suspected of disloyalty, they were allowed to rule their own domains with relative autonomy.*

Perhaps the most important mechanism for the *bakufu*'s maintenance of social control was the adoption and implementation of a Confucian-derived hierarchical status system (known as the *shi-nō-ko-sho* system) based on heredity and function. In descending, ascriptive order, this system was composed of four status groups: samurai, peasants, artisans, and merchants. Samurai, artisans, and merchants were usually required to reside in castle towns while peasants lived in villages. The most significant division was between the samurai and their subjects, i.e., between the samurai and everybody else.

The most important samurai, of course, were the shoguns, all of whom were chosen from the three senior branches of the Tokugawa family. The shoguns ostensibly derived their authority from serving at the command of the emperor, but in reality the imperial family had not had power for centuries, and the shoguns were the de facto central governing authority. In

---

*Japan had approximately 250 domains. Most *daimyō* were categorized as either *fudai,* hereditary vassals whose ancestors were on the side of Tokugawa Ieyasu at the decisive Battle of Sekigahara in 1600, or *tozama* (outside), those whose ancestors had made the mistake of not being on Ieyasu's side at Sekigahara.

addition, all *daimyō,* their retainers, and most scholars were samurai. Comprising less than 10 percent of the entire population, samurai were considered the elite but did have their own divisions. Most significantly, the anti-*bakufu* movement of the 1850s and 1860s was primarily led by middle- and lower-ranking samurai, who in turn became the leaders and administrators of the Meiji government.[13]

The peasants were next in line according to the status system, but the gap between them and the samurai was huge. Since Tokugawa Japan was an agricultural society, the peasants, comprising more than 80 percent of the population, were the economic backbone of the country and were expected to feed the entire population through their labor. They were also obligated to pay approximately 50 percent of their crop yield (usually rice) in taxes that supported the samurai. During the course of the Tokugawa era, there was no dearth of peasant rebellions. Most were political disputes with local officials, social disputes with wealthy farmers, or economic disputes concerning taxation, poverty, and changes in the market system.

Next came the artisans, who produced and sold items made by hand, such as clothing, footwear, furniture, lacquerware, paper, swords, and armor. Since peasants were expected to be largely self-sufficient, the artisans' main customers were their fellow urban dwellers.

At the bottom of the social status system were the merchants, primarily because of the long-held Confucian tenet that money handlers were amoral, unproductive parasites living off the rest of society. "The gentleman understands what is moral. The small man understands what is profitable" is just one of many such maxims attributed to the master himself in *The Analects.*[14] Although despised during the Tokugawa era, merchants were a necessity in an increasingly commercialized society. They operated warehouses of rice, sake, and other agricultural goods; converted rice into cash or credit; loaned money to hard-pressed samurai, including *daimyō* and members of the *bakufu;* and managed other financial transactions.

As the Tokugawa era continued, merchants were gaining the most economic security while samurai were losing the most. The samurai became increasingly dependent on merchants, who acquired more and more wealth. Some impoverished samurai swallowed their pride, slipped into anonymity, and became artisans or farmers. Others became *rōnin* (masterless samurai), wandering the country disillusioned, in search of food and a fight. Although the samurai, according to Anne Walthall, had "a monopoly of political power and social prestige" because of their status, their economic power was often lower than that of merchants.[15]

In addition to this social and political order, the Japanese worldview was significantly shaped by foreign relations. During most of the Tokugawa era, these relations centered on Japan's geographic and cultural neighbors in East Asia. Yet, at the beginning and the end of that long era, the West had a major impact on the course of Japan's external relations and its conception of the outside world. In the 1630s, the newly established Tokugawa *bakufu* issued a series of edicts collectively known as the *sakoku* (national seclusion) policy that deliberately closed off the nation after more than one hundred years of unrestricted international activity. Until the 1970s scholars assumed that these seclusion edicts represented the sum total of Tokugawa foreign policy. However, Asao Naohiro, Ronald Toby, and other scholars have produced groundbreaking studies that conclusively demonstrate this long-held assumption is at best, a vast exaggeration.[16] The primary reason for this, Toby believes, is because scholars "have understated the importance of Asian affairs in Tokugawa foreign relations."[17] Throughout this long era, Chinese were allowed to reside and trade in Nagasaki. The large *tozama* domain of Satsuma was allowed, even encouraged by the *bakufu,* to trade with the Ryukyu Islands (then a quasi-independent kingdom, becoming the Japanese islands of Okinawa in the late nineteenth century).[18] Japanese residing on the island of Tsushima managed trade between Japan and Korea. The Matsumae domain in northern Japan traded with the indigenous Ainu people on Ezo (Hokkaido), and later with the Russians.[19] Moreover, the Ryukyu Islands and Korea sent diplomatic missions to Edo, usually to pay respects and offer presents to newly installed shoguns. These trade and diplomatic relations, Toby and Asao contend, were crucial elements in the internal and external legitimization of Tokugawa rule because East Asia, not the periphery of the West, was the center of Japan's geographical, political, and cultural universe.

Japan had contacts and relations with some Western powers beginning in the midsixteenth century, primarily with Portugal, Spain, the Netherlands, and to a lesser extent with Britain. Portuguese traders, accompanied by Jesuit missionaries, began arriving in Japan in the midsixteenth century, followed by Spanish traders with Franciscan missionaries. At the beginning of the seventeenth century, the Dutch and then the British came to trade with Japan.

Toyotomi Hideyoshi (1536–98), generally credited with unifying the country after a century of internal warfare, and the Tokugawa shoguns encouraged trade with the Westerners, who were usually referred to by Japanese as "southern barbarians" (*nambanjin*) because they came to Japan from a southerly direction and were obviously not from the Sino-Japanese sphere of civilization. Japan's rulers became increasingly upset at the Christian proselytizing of Portuguese and Spanish missionaries, however. Not only did hundreds of thousands of peasants convert to the Western religion, but so did some *daimyō* in Kyushu who hoped to obtain firearms and political advantages over their rivals by contacts with the Portuguese or Spanish.[20] The rulers soon realized that Christianity could become a political threat to their hegemony and governing legitimacy—or even the precursor of an invasion. They also recognized that Christianity challenged the social order of Japan, upon which their political legitimacy depended, because the Western religion placed ultimate authority in a divine God rather than in the rationalist and humanist "five relationships" of Confucianism between sovereign and subject, parent and child, husband and wife, elder and younger child, friend and friend.[21] Whereas reciprocity was an important element, the five relationships were premised on the unwavering loyalty of subordinates to superiors. Japan's political leadership, writes George Ellison, "felt that Christianity was a disease which infected their subjects with disloyalty" because it emphasized obedience to God rather than to one's temporal authorities.[22]

Toyotomi Hideyoshi, followed by the first three Tokugawa shoguns (Ieyasu, Hidetada, and Iemitsu), issued a series of edicts beginning in 1587 that prohibited the preaching of and conversion to Christianity.* Initially the edicts were haphazardly enforced, but government officials occasionally rounded up, interrogated, tortured, and executed Japanese Christians and European missionaries. The first major demonstration of the seriousness of the government's anti-Christian attitude occurred in 1597 when it executed, by crucifixion, twenty-six Christians—including six Europeans—in Nagasaki. The presence of some Christian samurai and Christian banners at the Battle of Osaka Castle in 1615, when the Tokugawa *bakufu* crushed the supporters and descendants of the Toyotomi family, did not go unnoticed. As a result, enforcement of the anti-Christian edicts intensified.[23] At his investiture ceremonies as shogun in 1623 at Edo, Tokugawa Iemitsu sent a clear and gruesome message to the assembled *daimyō* by having fifty Christians (one a European Jesuit) burned at the stake. Iemitsu also revoked Spain's trading privileges and ordered the Spanish to leave Japan. The Portuguese came under increased scrutiny and were subsequently prohibited from residing or trading anywhere in the country except Nagasaki. In 1635, the governors of Nagasaki were ordered by a *bakufu* edict to reward "any informer revealing the whereabouts of the [Japanese] followers of padres," and "any Southern barbarians who propagate the teachings of padres" were to be put in prison.[24]

The *bakufu* also became increasingly wary of Japanese with overseas ex-

---

*Hideyoshi's hegemonic reign lasted from 1582 until his assassination in 1598. Ieyasu reigned from 1603 to 1605; Hidetada from 1605 to 1623; and Iemitsu from 1623 to 1653.

periences and ideas, especially relating to Christianity, that might upset the political and social order. Therefore, the 1635 edict included maritime regulations that prohibited Japanese from journeying overseas: "Japanese ships are strictly forbidden to leave for foreign countries. No Japanese is permitted to go abroad. If there is anyone who attempts to do so secretly, he must be executed. . . . If any Japanese returns from overseas after residing there, he must be put to death."[25] The prohibition against overseas travel, not modified until the final days of the *bakufu* government more than two centuries later, explains why the few Japanese who journeyed overseas during the Tokugawa era, except for a handful of *bakufu* officials and others with special permission, did so secretly and used aliases.

Shortly after the 1635 edict, poverty-stricken peasants and *rōnin* upset at exorbitant taxation and harsh, arbitrary rule by the local *daimyō* combined forces in the Shimabara Rebellion. This massive revolt, the largest and deadliest during the Tokugawa era, pitted *rōnin* and approximately forty thousand peasants against at least one hundred thousand *bakufu* troops.[26] More significant, the rebellion embodied the spirit of a Christian-inspired protest movement because the purported leader was Amakusa Shiro (Masuda Shiro), a teenage boy believed to be an angel of God or the Messiah. The combination of Christianity with a coalition of samurai and peasants not only represented a serious internal political threat but also challenged the ideological justification of *bakufu* rule. This may explain the *bakufu*'s extremely harsh treatment of the rebels. After a long siege, all thirty-seven thousand men, women, and children inside the rebellion's headquarters at Hara Castle were slaughtered in early 1638.

There is no evidence that the Portuguese in nearby Nagasaki took part in or had any role in the Shimabara Rebellion. Nevertheless, the *bakufu* blamed the rebellion on the Portuguese and ordered their expulsion in 1639, telling the governors in Nagasaki that if any Portuguese ships returned, "the ships must be destroyed and anyone aboard those ships must be beheaded."[27] Furthermore, all other foreigners in Japan were ordered not to permit "padres and those who believe in their preaching to come aboard your ships."[28] The Portuguese were duly notified of the expulsion orders, but since they had been in Japan for nearly one hundred years, they were not ready to give up. One year after the expulsion orders, they sent a ship from Macao to Nagasaki with a delegation of sixty-one envoys to discuss the matter with Japanese officials. All the envoys were beheaded, while thirteen crew members were allowed to return to Macao to report on the obvious determination of the *bakufu* to enforce its expulsion order.[29]

Still the Portuguese did not give up. They tried again to renew their presence in Japan by sending two armed galleons to Nagasaki in 1647. Again the *bakufu* refused the Portuguese request to renew relations. The Japanese surrounded the two ships with hundreds of small vessels and thousands of troops. The Portuguese commander, Goncalo de Siqueira, perhaps influenced by the knowledge of what would certainly happen to Portuguese heads if he lost a military showdown, decided to depart the area peacefully. Portugal made no more serious attempts to renew its relations with Japan during the Tokugawa era.

The Tokugawa *bakufu* maintained its prohibition on Christianity until its overthrow in 1868. In 1868, the new Meiji government wasted no time in reminding Japanese of the anti-Christian prohibition by placing notices at the entrances of all towns and villages: "The Christian and other other evil religions are strictly prohibited."[30] An imperial decree soon followed: "The Christian religion being strictly prohibited by the law of the empire, the violation of this law is considered a serious matter. . . . Care should be taken to induce [Japanese Christians] to renounce their evil ways, and if there be any who refuse to repent, severe punishment must be inflicted."[31] In February 1873, the Japanese government finally dropped its prohibition against Christianity. As Yoshiya Abe writes, it did so "primarily as a means by which to improve its image among Western powers."[32] As will be demonstrated, the interest in the Western religion by individual Japanese who had journeyed to the United States played a significant role in the repeal of the prohibition of Christianity.

Meanwhile, the British and Dutch were interested only in trade, not in proselytizing. Acting at the request of the *bakufu,* a Dutch warship even shelled Hara Castle during the Shimabara Rebellion.[33] The British remained in Japan during this era for only ten years (1613–23), voluntarily leaving because of dismal profits. However, the Dutch, who first entered Japan in 1600, persevered and retained their presence through the Dutch East India Company throughout the Tokugawa era. The historian Grant Goodman believes that "the steady and moderate policy of the Dutch East India Company," representing a country that depended heavily on overseas trade, saved the Dutch from the fate of the Spanish and Portuguese and allowed them to be Japan's "window on the Western world" for over two centuries.[34]

Nevertheless, this was a very narrow window. Embarking from its Asian headquarters in Batavia, Indonesia, the Dutch East India Company was allowed to bring only one—sometimes two—trading ship per year to the small, artificial island in Nagasaki Harbor called Deshima. A handful of Dutch traders, hardly ever numbering more than twenty and led by the *opperhoofd* (captain) were required to live permanently only on the island. They were rarely, if ever, allowed to visit the city of Nagasaki, which was under direct *bakufu* control. *Bakufu* guards and inspectors kept the Dutch under tight security and close scrutiny. The *opperhoofd* and two or three other Dutch officials were escorted to Edo annually to honor the shogun with gifts and inform the *bakufu,* usually by a written report, of recent major developments on the Asian mainland and in the West.

The first of these Dutch reports to mention the Western Hemisphere was in 1745, while the first to mention the U.S. government was in 1809.[35] These annual reports were written in Dutch by the *opperhoofd,* then translated by a Japanese interpreter. Because there were no comprehensive Japanese-Dutch dictionaries or grammar books to consult, the accuracy of these translated reports varied considerably. Combined with the lack of effort on the part of the Dutch to learn the Japanese language, effective communication was always difficult.

In the eighteenth century, Shogun Yoshimune (who reigned 1716–45) and his influential advisor Arai Hakuseki, a Confucian scholar, took more than a passing interest in the West and began allowing the importation of Dutch books on medicine, astronomy, science, and mathematics—but not on religion or philosophy—for some samurai scholars. The study of these Western books became known as *rangaku* (Dutch learning).

In the early nineteenth century, more samurai scholars began studying *rangaku* to learn Western methods of national defense because of the increased appearance of whaling ships and threatening intrusions by Russian and British ships in Japanese waters. In addition, the *bakufu* revitalized its earlier seclusion policy with the Expulsion Edict of 1825, which read in part: "Henceforth, whenever a foreign [Western] ship is sighted approaching any point on our coast, all persons on hand should fire on and drive it off. If the vessel heads for the open sea, you need not pursue it; allow it to escape. If the foreigners force their way ashore, you may capture and incarcerate them, and if their mother ship approaches, you may destroy it as circumstances dictate."[36] In a well-known 1837 incident, the *bakufu* fired on and drove off the American ship *Morrison,* which was attempting to return three Japanese castaways. Two samurai scholars who publicly questioned the *bakufu*'s actions were arrested and eventually committed suicide.[37] Bob Tadashi Wakabayashi claims that increased study of *rangaku* by samurai scholars in the early nineteenth century, combined with intrusions by Western vessels, resulted in the development of the "revere the emperor, expel the barbarian" philosophy (*sonnō jōi*), which later served as the rallying cry for the anti-*bakufu* forces that overthrew Tokugawa rule in 1868. For example, the Mito domain Confucian scholar Aizawa Seishisai wrote in his classic work, *Shinron* (The New Thesis):

> One source of harm that has appeared of late is Dutch Studies. . . . There is no harm in Dutch Studies itself; the harm comes when some dupe with a smattering of second-hand knowledge of foreign affairs mistakenly lauds the far-fetched notions spun out by Western barbarians, or publishes books to that effect in an attempt to transform our Middle Kingdom [Japan] to barbarian ways. . . . Should the wily barbarians someday be tempted to take advantage of this situation and entice our stupid commoners to adopt beliefs and customs that reek of barbarism, how could we stop them?[38]

That a backlash against *rangaku* contributed to the anti-*bakufu* movement of the 1850s and 1860s is arguable, but "Revere the Emperor, Expel the Barbarian" was a potent ideological slogan that appealed to many.

By the middle of the nineteenth century, a handful of samurai scholars had acquired some Western scientific information, but it was a "miscellaneous collection of practical data and techniques without cohesive structure or inner meaning," according to Goodman.[39] Thus, Japanese understood relatively little about the commercial, political, technological, and industrial revolutions that had been transforming the West for the previous two centuries. Perhaps the most important reason for this, Goodman explains, is that "neither the Japanese nor the Dutch ever viewed their bilateral relationship as anything more than a mutual economic convenience. That is, there was never intended by either side to be any cultural dimension to their intercourse."[40]

Japan's knowledge of Western military and economic power on the eve of Commodore Matthew C. Perry's arrival in 1853 is summarized by the historian Conrad Totman: "Not even the best-informed *rangaku* scholar was aware of the resources that European governments and the United States could deploy in pursuit of their policies or the ideological and situational elements that sustained their aggressive behavior."[41] This may be a bit of an overstatement, but in the face of this new threat Japanese leaders were thrown into a state of confusion. Unlike in the early 1600s, when Japan had huge and powerful armies, by the midnineteenth century the West—even a middling nation such as the United States—was far more militarily powerful than Japan. The long Tokugawa era had developed an impressive culture, an urban society, a national transportation network, and a commercial economy, but its military strength had atrophied and large-scale industrialization had yet to begin. Given these weaknesses, the *bakufu* had no practical alternative to signing so-called unequal treaties on trade and extraterritoriality with Western powers following Perry's arrival.* Dissatisfied with their new world position, various anti-*bakufu* forces, led by Satsuma and Choshu domains, rallied to overthrow two and a half centuries of Tokugawa *bakufu* rule in 1868 and restore the emperor.

Although the anti-*bakufu* forces emphasized a combination of tradition, nationalism, and contempt of foreigners, by the mid-1860s their leaders were more anti-*bakufu* than anti-foreign. Once they became officials in the new Meiji imperial government, they sought to strengthen the country from within and without through Western-style industrialization. Perry's visit, Japan's forced acceptance of the unequal treaties, bombardments of Kagoshima and Shimonoseki by Western ships in 1863 and 1864, and the overthrow of the *bakufu* in 1868 had demonstrated the immediate and practical uses of Western weapons and technology.

Moreover, the nineteenth century is aptly known as the age of imperialism; propelled by the Industrial Revolution, Western powers roamed the world for new territories, raw materials, markets, and converts to Christianity. As Paul Kennedy writes in *The Rise and Fall of the Great Powers:*

> The impact of Western man was, in all sorts of ways, one of the most noticeable aspects of the dynamics of world power in the nineteenth century. It manifested itself not only in a variety of economic relationships—ranging from the informal influence of coastal traders, shippers, and consuls to the more direct controls of planters, railway builders, and mining companies—but also in the penetrations of explorers, adventurers, and missionaries, in the introduction of Western diseases, and in the proselytization of Western faiths. . . . If it eventually had its impressive monuments in the roads, railway networks, telegraphs, harbors, and civic buildings . . . , its more horrific side was the bloodshed, rapine, and plunder which attended so many colonial wars of the period.[42]

It did not take officials in the Meiji government long to realize they had to develop an industrial economy and increase the country's military power or they would likely suffer horrific consequences at the hands of Western imperialists. They immediately implemented the policy of *fukoku kyohei* ("rich nation, strong army") to address Japan's new economic and military needs.

Acquiring knowledge of Western technology and Western institutions also had a strong philosophical motivation during the late Tokugawa and early

*Holland, Great Britain, France, and Russia immediately followed the United States in making treaties with Japan in the 1850s. These treaties are collectively known as the "unequal treaties" because Japan was forced to negotiate from a position of weakness with these economically and militarily more powerful countries.

Meiji eras. In the 1840s, the samurai scholar Sakuma Shozan (1811–64) began to promote "Eastern ethics, Western science" (*Tōyō no dōtoku, Seiyo no gakugei*), a philosophy seeking to uphold Japan's traditional Confucian political and social order through the utilization of Western science and learning. Soon after the Opium War of 1839–42, Sakuma wrote in "Kaibosaku" (A Plan for Defending the Coast) that Japan should "build Western-style ships and thoroughly practice Western naval strategy" and that a system should be developed in which "men of talent would be promoted according to ability."[43] He also advocated the promotion of education for commoners so that the traditional Confucian principles of loyalty and filial piety would be understood throughout the country.[44] In the words of one of his biographers, Sakuma had concluded after the Opium War that "the West alone commanded valid science and the East alone metaphysical knowledge."[45]

In the 1850s, Sakuma promoted and expanded his philosophy in "Seikenroku" (Reflections on My Errors).[46] Sakuma wrote that "being born after the development of the study of natural science by Westerners, which was unknown to Confucius and Mencius," and "enabling our people to lead useful lives and benefitting our nation with a detailed study of the combination of Eastern ethics and Western science" were the most important pleasures for the true gentleman (*kunshi*).[47]

As a result of Great Britain's easy military victory over China during the Opium War and the threat to Japan posed by the American squadron led by Perry in 1853 and 1854, Sakuma believed that the most important thing for national defense was for "men of the world" to learn the use of firearms.[48] Moreover, Japan had to compete with the West by studying "conditions in barbarian countries," "international trade," and "the advantages and disadvantages of other nations' defenses," along with "physics, math, and technology."[49] To understand the conditions in foreign countries, it was also essential to become "familiar with barbarian languages."[50]

It is clear from "Kaibosaku" and "Seikenroku" that Sakuma's primary concern was national defense. He understood the utility and the necessity of Western science and technology for maintaining Japan's independence. His fear and hatred of Westerners, whom he normally referred to as "barbarians" (*iteki*), for using military force to push around China and Japan is obvious. Nevertheless, he became identified as a "pro-West" scholar and was murdered by anti-foreign *rōnin* in 1864. Sakuma's philosophical synthesis of "Eastern ethics, Western science" influenced many samurai during the late Tokugawa and early Meiji eras. Moreover, Sakuma's formula, with its advantages and inherent conflicts, can be seen as a paradigm of Japanese history from the midnineteenth century to the present.

Manifest Destiny and the Frontier Era of U.S.-Japan Relations, 1850–80

In the first half of the nineteenth century, the cumulative forces of expansion in population, commerce, democratic rights, and especially in territory transformed the United States. From 1803 to 1853, the nation had increased its territory by 300 percent through conquests, purchases, and diplomacy. This was the era of Manifest Destiny—the political, moral, and self-righteous philosophy of white Americans that they had the right to expand across North America at the expense of indigenous inhabitants, chiefly Mexicans and Native Americans.

The high point of Manifest Destiny came in the 1840s, when the controversy over Texas and the resulting Mexican-American War led to the U.S. acquisition of vast Southwest and Pacific territories. As soon as the war ended in 1848, news spread that gold had been discovered in California, inciting an international rush. The acquisition of these territories transformed the United States into a continent-wide empire but also "triggered the release of forces of sectional dissension."[51] Throughout the 1850s, constant political battles and short-lived compromises between the North and South over extending slavery to new territories and new states finally erupted in the American Civil War in 1861. Four years later, with at least six hundred thousand soldiers and civilians killed, the deadliest war in American history finally ended.

Immediately after the war, the federal government embarked on a massive program to renovate political, economic, and social institutions. It abolished slavery, conferred the right to vote on newly freed black men, rebuilt much of the infrastructure destroyed during the war, and established a public education system in the South. Unfortunately, Reconstruction was also plagued by scandals, controversy, and entrenched racism. Most significantly, the program clearly failed to transform the economic and social relations of the antebellum South. The Reconstruction era ended with a compromise over the disputed presidential election of 1876. In early 1877 Civil War hero and former president Ulysses S. Grant embarked on a lengthy world tour, including an extended visit to Japan.[52]

American interest in Asia had preceded Grant's visit. Although U.S. foreign relations throughout the nineteenth century were dominated by attention to Europe and Latin America, private Americans, chiefly merchants and missionaries, had already contacted China. With sealskins, sea otter pelts, sandlewood, and contraband opium in return for China ware, silks, and especially tea, American merchants had developed a trade second only to that of the British by the midnineteenth century. Immediately after its founding by Congregationalists in Salem, Massachusetts, in 1810, the American Board of Commissioners for Foreign Missions sent missionaries to China and Hawaii, decades before the U.S. government sent its first representative to China in 1832.

With regards to Japan, however, the U.S. government rather than private merchants and missionaries first established relations. Four official missions had been sent to Japan before American merchants or missionaries had established themselves in Japan. The first mission was in 1832, when the State Department sent Edmund Roberts to extend relations, especially that of commerce, to Muscat (Oman), Siam (Thailand), Cochin China (Vietnam), Borneo, and Japan. Roberts's primary objective was to negotiate trade treaties.[53] Roberts was instructed by the secretary of state to inform the leaders of these countries that "it is against the principles of our nation to build forts, or make expensive establishments in foreign countries—that we never make conquests or ask any nations to let us establish ourselves in their country as the English, the French, and the Dutch have done in the East Indies."[54] Roberts managed to negotiate treaties with Muscat and Siam, but he did not reach Cochin China or Japan on this mission. He was sent back in 1835 to exchange ratified treaties with Muscat and Siam and then to continue on to Vietnam and Japan.

Roberts's instructions for the Vietnam-Japan leg of this mission are revealing of the nineteenth-century American worldview that was interwoven with racism, Manifest Destiny, and Great Power competition: "You will, of course, accommodate yourself to the peculiar notions and customs of [Vietnam and Japan], however absurd they may be, whenever you can do to withhold such acknowledgment of inferiority as would be incompatible with the dignity of your own Government, of which you will on all occasions assert the equality with the most powerful nations of the world."[55] By this time officials and many private Americans had begun to perceive their country as a major power, particularly since it had successfully thwarted Great Britain's attempt to retake its former colonies in the War of 1812. Roberts would not have the opportunity to accommodate himself to the "peculiar notions and customs" of Japan, however, since he died of cholera in Macao before reaching the Land of the Rising Sun.

Commodore James Biddle was next to attempt opening official relations. While preparing for a mission to China in 1846, he was instructed by the State Department to "ascertain if the ports of Japan are accessible" and if the Japanese government would be interested in a trade treaty.[56] Well aware of the Dutch arrangement with the Japanese government, Biddle bypassed Nagasaki and sailed his two ships, *Columbus* and *Vincennes,* into Uraga Bay near Edo in July 1846. The two American ships were immediately surrounded by Japanese boats to prevent any attempt by Biddle and his crew to go ashore.

Biddle communicated his request to Japanese officials and a Japanese interpreter of Dutch. While waiting for a reply, he allowed many Japanese to come aboard and inspect his ships, and the Japanese supplied the Americans with food and water during the ten days the two ships were anchored in Uraga Bay. The *bakufu*'s answer to Biddle's request for establishing diplomatic relations and a trade treaty between the two countries, however, was not as accommodating: Japan "refuse[s] to trade with foreigners who come to this country . . . [and] this has been the habit of our nation from time immemorial."[57] Since Biddle's mission was more a fact-finding trip than a concerted effort to establish relations, and his original instructions ordered him not "to excite a hostile feeling, or a distrust of the government for the United States" among the Japanese, he weighed anchor and departed for China shortly after receiving the *bakufu*'s answer.[58]

Following the Mexican-American War of 1846–48, Japan became a more important ally to the U.S. government and to private business interests. Japan was geographically close to China, where the United States had already established trade relations and posted officials; Japan was close to North Pacific whaling areas frequented by New England–based ships; and, as more ocean-going ships were steam-driven vessels, securing Japan as a coal depot became an important consideration. Therefore, the government decided to send Perry to make a concerted effort to establish diplomatic and trade relations.[59]

Like Biddle, Perry sailed into Uraga Bay near Edo, the seat of *bakufu* power. Unlike Biddle, Perry sailed into Uraga Bay with four large warships. In addition to sails, two of these ships, the *Mississippi* and the *Susquehanna,* were steam frigates; fitted with coal-fired engines, they belched black smoke as they chugged up the bay.[60] The wooden hulls of all these ships were painted with a dark sealant to prevent the wood from becoming water-logged and rotten. To the Japanese, they were the "black ships" (*kurofune*).

Also unlike Biddle, Perry allowed only high-ranking Japanese officials aboard and personally spoke only with the governor of Uraga and representatives of the emperor. After Nagashima Saburosuke, the vice governor of Uraga, first informed Perry's officers that foreign affairs matters were handled only by the *bakufu* at Nagasaki and that Perry would have to go there, Perry refused. He would remain in Uraga Bay near Edo because it was the shogun's headquarters.[61] After Keyamon Yezaimon, governor of Uraga, told Perry that the Japanese would receive a letter sent by the president to the emperor only in Nagasaki, Perry demanded that a representative of the emperor accept it in Uraga or he and a force of marines would go ashore to personally deliver the letter.[62] Whether Perry was aware that the emperor resided in Kyoto, four hundred miles southwest of Edo, or meant to sail his ships down to Osaka and then march inland to Kyoto to deliver the letter is unclear. Nevertheless, the *bakufu* officials did not want a large group of armed barbarians marching around the country. They reluctantly complied with Perry's demand; Prince Toda of Izu arrived to receive the letter, which contained proposals for establishing relations between the two countries.[63]

U.S. officials had three specific objectives in seeking to establish diplomatic relations with Japan. First, they wanted the Japanese government's assurance that shipwrecked sailors—many of whom were whaling or engaging in trade with China— found on Japan's shores would be aided and protected until an American vessel arrived to retrieve them. Second, with the advent of steamships, Americans wanted to use one or more ports in Japan as coal depots. In the nineteenth century, Japan had an abundance of coal and the Americans sought to purchase this coal, along with water and other provisions, for their ships in the Asian Pacific region. Finally, U.S. officials sought to establish trade relations with Japan in the belief that commerce between the two countries would be of mutual economic benefit.[64]

American policymakers, however, were not interested in international trade simply as a means for economic benefit. Nineteenth-century Americans believed that trade with countries they considered less "civilized" would open the door to the political, cultural, and religious enlightenment of such "backward" countries and help them fulfill their self-appointed mission to bring such countries into the civilized Western community. Indeed, this common worldview explains why American diplomats, merchants, and missionaries lived and worked together in Asia, Africa, and Central and South America.

Aware that *bakufu* officials would need time to consider the proposals, which would, in effect, overturn the long-standing Tokugawa policy—though not always the practice—of limited contact with foreigners, Perry and the American fleet departed for the Ryukyu Islands and China after informing the Japanese that they would return the following year for an answer.

The *bakufu* dispatched translated copies of President Fillmore's letter to the *daimyō* and requested their views on whether Japan should accede to the American proposals. The very fact that *bakufu* officials sought out the views of the *daimyō* on such an important foreign relations matter demonstrated the government's weakness. The *bakufu* officials realized that subduing the American barbarians and their warships was going to be an extremely difficult, if not impossible, task without compromising. Many *daimyō,* who had long chafed under *bakufu* rule and realized that the *bakufu* was in a serious quandary, took advantage of this rare opportunity to shame and attack the *bakufu* by telling officials to make no compromises.

Tokugawa Nariaki, *daimyō* of Mito, advocated no compromise. Mito, although one of three domains controlled by the senior branches of the Tokugawa family, was much poorer than the other two, and many of its samurai had become disenchanted with *bakufu* leadership. Aizawa Seishisai, author of the anti-foreign and extremely nationalistic *Shinron,* was only the most prominent Confucian scholar from Mito who had questioned the *bakufu*'s commitment to maintaining Japan's political, social, and religious traditions. Many Tokugawa family members of Mito shared these views. In his response to the query from the *bakufu,* Tokugawa Nariaki listed a number of reasons for not compromising: foreigners feared Japan; the *bakufu* needed to maintain the prohibition on Christianity; trade goods from the West were worthless; and even lowly Japanese commoners considered the foreigners repulsive.[65] Moreover, he believed that Japan needed to return to the past, when strong warriors dedicated to maintaining Japan's culture and traditions dominated.[66]

Shimazu Nariakira, *daimyō* of the powerful Satsuma domain, advised the *bakufu* to stall the Americans for three years and tell them it would take that long make decisions on such far-reaching proposals.[67] During the three-year interval, Shimazu wanted the *bakufu* to appoint Tokugawa Nariaki to make military preparations that could withstand the American naval forces.[68] Similarly, Matsudaira Yoshinaga, *daimyō* of Echizen, advised the *bakufu* not to accept any proposal and to prepare for war.[69] He warned that peace would lead to Japan's becoming a colony of the foreigners.

The *daimyō* of Hikone, Ii Naosuke, was one of the few who advised the *bakufu* to compromise. Ii believed that Japan could not maintain its seclusion laws forever and should provide coal and other provisions on an emergency basis to American ships.[70] Japan could increase its international trade to include the Americans, with the Dutch acting as their agents.[71] Ii also wanted the *bakufu* to start constructing large, steam-powered merchant ships and warships. By building up Japan's strength through trade and the construction of ships, Ii believed that Japan would eventually become strong enough to reimpose its seclusion laws at a later date.[72]

When Perry returned to Japan in February 1854, he was accompanied by eight warships. While he never directly threatened to use force to secure a treaty, the presence of such firepower was an obvious factor in negotiations. *Bakufu* officials were in a bind; they would have to make an agreement with Perry despite the opposition by most *daimyōs*. After difficult negotiations, *bakufu* officials reluctantly agreed to protect shipwrecked sailors and provide the ports of Shimoda and Hakodate for depots of coal and other provisions for American vessels.[73] Nevertheless, Japanese negotiators steadfastly refused to establish trade relations. Stopping just short of threatening force, Perry sailed away from Japan with the Kanagawa Treaty, the first formal agreement between Japan and a Western country. Three years later, the first resident American diplomat in Japan, Consul General Townsend Harris, finally negotiated a formal trade agreement.[74]

To most Japanese and Americans it is Perry, not Harris, who is credited with (and condemned for) opening Japan to the West. Moreover, Perry is also credited with (and condemned for) ushering in the final stage of Tokugawa *bakufu* rule: the *bakumatsu* era (literally, "end of the *bakufu*"), which lasted from 1853 to the overthrow of the last Tokugawa shogun in 1868. Ii Naosuke, who was promoted to the position of *tairō* (regent) to negotiate the trade treaty with Harris and to bring order to an increasingly unstable internal political situation by cracking down on the most dangerous opponents of the *bakufu,* became the most prominent victim of the anti-*bakufu* and anti-foreign coalition when he was assassinated in 1860. Perry and Harris may have succeeded, in the American view, in opening Japan to the West, but Sakuma Shozan, Ii Naosuke, and other Japanese paid for that success with their lives.

Between the Perry mission of 1853–54 and Grant's visit in 1879, American officials paid relatively little attention to Japan. The crisis over slavery in the 1850s, the Civil War, and Reconstruction diverted their attention from many foreign relations issues. Japanese officials, however, paid comparatively more attention to the United States than to any other foreign country. After all, Americans had negotiated the first diplomatic treaties between Japan and the West. In 1860, the shogun sent a delegation of high-ranking officials to the United States to ratify the Treaty of Amity and Commerce and meet with American officials, including President James Buchanan. In 1871, the Meiji government sent an even higher-ranking delegation of officials, led by Prince Iwakura Tomomi, to the United States and Europe. The Iwakura mission failed in its primary task to revise the unequal treaties of the 1850s, but its delegates carefully studied American and European political, economic, and social institutions with the objective of adopting and adapting what would be useful in modernizing Japan. Within this transitional context of history and worldview, the first Japanese journeyed across the Pacific to the United States.

ONE

Joseph Heco, a Castaway in America

In early March 1851, a San Francisco newspaper reported the following: "We learn from Capt. Jennings of the barque *Auckland,* which arrived in this port yesterday . . . that about 500 miles off the coast of Japan he fell in with a Japanese junk, which was completely waterlogged. The crew, consisting of seventeen persons . . . are now on board his vessel. They had been fifty days on the wreck, and were in great distress. . . . No communication, of course, has been had with them, but they appear exceedingly grateful for the assistance and kind treatment received from the Captain."[1] While this was not the first time Japanese sailors had washed up on the Pacific shores of North America, this was by far the largest number of Japanese who had been in the United States at one time.

The youngest, Hikozo, remained in America for eight years before returning to Japan. He went to school, worked at a commercial trading firm, converted to Catholicism, met American presidents, became a citizen, and adopted the name Joseph Heco.* When he returned to Japan in 1859, he probably

*His given name was Hikozo. It is not known how he came to be called Heco. Probably the American sailors who rescued him called him Heco as a nickname. In Japanese writings, Heco is sometimes called Hamada Hikozo (the family name is taken from his hometown).

had more firsthand knowledge of the United States than did any other Japanese. In certain ways, he can be seen as a symbol for Japan's growing interest in and knowledge of the West in the midnineteenth century.

Castaways

The first Japanese to set foot in North America were sailors.[2] Typhoons, southerly winter winds, and the *kuroshio* (black current) sometimes pulled Japanese coastal shipping vessels and fishing boats far out into the Pacific Ocean. Without compasses and the knowledge of celestial navigation, these sailors were entirely at the mercy of the weather and the sea. According to a nineteenth-century study, at least sixty Japanese vessels were pulled out into the Pacific Ocean from 1617 to 1875.[3] It can be safely assumed, however, that the overwhelming majority vanished without a trace and their crews perished at sea.

A few fortuitous castaways were rescued by passing European and American ships, but even fewer were returned to Japan. At least three Japanese castaways are known to have been briefly on the Pacific Coast of North America before being returned to East Asia, but only Nakahama Manjiro spent a significant period of time in the United States before Joseph Heco's sojourn in the 1850s.*

In 1841 Manjiro, then fourteen years old, and Toraemon, Denzo, Jusuke, and Goemon were blown out to sea on their fishing boat during a storm.[4] Although they managed to land on a small island (probably Torishima) after drifting for one week, their boat was destroyed on the rocks during the landing. A few months passed before they were rescued by a passing American whaling ship. After completing six more months of whaling the captain, William Whitfield, left Toraemon, Denzo, Jusuke, and Goemon on Hawaii and offered to take young Manjiro back with him to Fairhaven, Massachusetts, for an education. Manjiro agreed, and the American ship reached Massachusetts in early 1843. Manjiro spent four years in Massachusetts, where he attended public school, studied English and mathematics, and was apparently quite adept at learning navigation and sailing.

Manjiro returned to Hawaii after spending time aboard another whaling vessel. Jusuke had died of illness, and Toraemon married a native Hawaiian woman and decided to remain on the island. Manjiro, Denzo, and Goemon

---

*Not a hereditary samurai, Manjiro had only his given name until his return from the United States, when the *bakufu* elevated him to honorary samurai status and awarded him the family name of Nakahama (from his village name of Nakanohama on Shikoku Island). Americans referred to him as "John Manjiro" and "John Mung."

then arranged for a whaling vessel headed to the north Pacific to drop them off in the Ryukyu Islands. From there the returning castaways were escorted under guard to Satsuma. Because the seventeenth-century prohibition against allowing Japanese to return from overseas was still formally in effect, they were confined and questioned at length by Satsuma and *bakufu* officials about their experiences overseas. The officials' major concern was whether any of the men had become Christians. Denzo and Goemon had significant contact with American missionaries in Hawaii, and Manjiro had attended church services with the Whitfields in Massachusetts, so the concerns seemed justified. One and a half years after they had come ashore in the Ryukyu Islands, Manjiro and his companions finally convinced wary Japanese officials that they had not converted to Christianity and that their knowledge of the outside world would not cause social or political disruption. Ten years after they were believed to have perished at sea, Manjiro, Denzo, and Goemon finally returned to their village of Nakanohama on Shikoku Island.[5]

Manjiro soon began teaching mathematics at a school sponsored by Tosa domain; then he was employed by the *bakufu* government; and he may have been a behind-the-scenes advisor to the *bakufu* during its negotiations with Perry in 1854.[6] Manjiro also accompanied the shogun's legation to the United States in 1860 (although he, Fukuzawa Yukichi, and others returned by way of Hawaii after spending only a few weeks in San Francisco). He went again on a government mission to the United States and Europe in 1870, during which he took a side trip to Fairhaven, Massachusetts, to visit his American friends and benefactors.

In spite of his knowledge of the United States and the West, Manjiro's influence with the *bakufu* government and the succeeding Meiji government was surprisingly limited. One reason may be that he was not a hereditary member of the samurai class (though the *bakufu* elevated him to the status of honorary samurai), and both *bakufu* and Meiji government officials were hereditary samurai. However, the primary reason was that officials distrusted him because of his foreign experience. To them, he had been contaminated by living among the overseas barbarians for far too long. Joseph Heco would experience this same sense of distrust.

Manjiro is rarely mentioned in nineteenth-century writings, but soon after his death in 1898 several works of both fact and fiction were written about him, including children's books, stressing that Manjiro was a role model of *gaman* (perseverance, courage) and a bridge between Japan and America. Although he never wrote a memoir of his overseas experiences, Manjiro became the most famous—and certainly the most romanticized—of all Japanese castaways.

Memoirs, History, and Joseph Heco

At the same time Manjiro returned to Japan, Joseph Heco's overseas sojourn began. Heco wrote extensively of his experiences and impressions of a world virtually unknown to Japanese in the 1850s and 1860s. In 1863, using his Japanese name, Hikozo, Heco published *Hyoryuki* (The Account of a Castaway).[7] Three decades later he produced a two-volume memoir entitled *The Narrative of a Japanese.*[8] Autobiographies have the capacity "to illuminate lived experience and social realities," as James Goodwin explains, but they are also problematical because they are "subject to social, and ultimately historical, permutation and recombination."[9] This is especially true of those written for publication. Nevertheless, these memoirs are valuable sources in that they reveal how one Japanese described what was for him the new world of America and the West. After only a few pages the reader of these memoirs begins to see Heco as a human being caught in what was then an unusual, even fascinating, setting between East and West.

Although we do not know exactly why *Hyoryuki* was published, Heco wrote in the preface that he hoped the book would "be profitable in learning about the conditions in foreign countries."[10] It is also possible that political and ideological factors played a role in the publication—and writing—of this memoir. Yet, in the text Heco did not indicate a strong interest in the political ideologies of the era, and although he was personally acquainted with officials in the American and Japanese governments, his employ for both was brief.

The nature of the writing offers other difficulties. Part of this memoir is in the form of diary entries Heco apparently began to write soon after his ship was cast adrift. Like most diarists, he did not write entries every day, and significant portions of the memoir are based on recollections after his return to Japan in 1859 and before the book's publication in late 1863. Because Heco was only thirteen years old when his journey to America began and was not of the samurai class, he had not learned to write very well in Japanese. To construct his memoir in a language and style that would be understandable to other Japanese, Heco stated that he "consulted with a friend" while writing *Hyoryuki* for publication.[11] Unfortunately, except that the person must have been Japanese, we know nothing of this unnamed friend. It is certainly possible that this friend embellished and edited *Hyoryuki,* but we do not know the extent of this work. In other words, like memoirs published today that are ghostwritten or "as told to," *Hyoryuki* was not exclusively the work of its author/subject.

It is a little surprising that *Hyoryuki* was published at all because intense anti-foreign tensions dominated Japan in the first half of the 1860s in the conflict between the *bakufu* and the anti-*bakufu* forces. As one who had resided overseas for many years and lived and worked with foreigners in Japan, Heco had been explicitly threatened by anti-foreign *rōnin.*[12] These *rōnin* sought to prove their loyalty to tradition and the emperor through threats and violent attacks upon foreigners and Japanese with connections to Westerners, who they believed had thrown Japan into political, social, and economic turmoil. In a February 1861 diary entry, Francis Hall, an American merchant and Heco's neighbor in Kanagawa, wrote that Heco had been warned that he was "expos[ing] himself to the fate of [Henry] Heusken," the secretary and interpreter of the American legation in Edo murdered by *rōnin* the previous month.[13] In a diary entry dated September 16, 1861, Heco wrote, "For the past six or eight months I had been frequently warned by the native authorities of Kanagawa and Yokohama to be careful of myself. They cautioned me not to ride out on the Tokaido, or to any place at all distant from the Foreign Settlement, inasmuch as it was a well-ascertained fact that several *rōnin* deemed me worthy of their attention. . . . Their warnings had of late waxed far too frequent for my comfort."[14]

The consequence of such threats was caution and circumspection in his memoirs. For example, the author of *Hyoryuki* is listed only as Hikozo on the book and the obviously non-Japanese name Joseph Heco does not appear. Moreover, Heco omits two significant personal details from *Hyoryuki:* his conversion to Christianity in 1854 and his American citizenship, granted in 1858. Since Heco included these details in *Narrative of a Japanese* thirty years later and they were verified by independent sources, he may have deliberately omitted them from *Hyoryuki* out of fear for the anti-*bakufu* forces of Satsuma and Choshu, who were still anti-foreign in both word and deed in 1863, and of the anti-foreign *rōnin* roaming Japan. In addition, he may have feared the *bakufu*'s reaction to his Christianity and American citizenship. Converting to Christianity was still prohibited in Japan, and it is hard to imagine that the *bakufu* would have accepted a Japanese who changed his national allegiance. Despite these omissions, *Hyoryuki* is proximate to Heco's sojourn in America, and as the only Japanese we know of who resided in the United States throughout most of the 1850s, his first memoir is a valuable source for an examination of early Japanese in America.

In 1892, the first volume of *Narrative of a Japanese* was published in Yokohama; the second followed three years later. The first volume covers much the same ground as *Hyoryuki,* but adds details. The second volume covers Heco's life from 1864 to 1890. Unlike *Hyoryuki, Narrative of a Japanese* was initially published in English and apparently was intended for a foreign audience. Nearing sixty years of age and suffering from arthritis at the time of publication, Heco had become a reflective middle-aged man who, like many Japanese in the 1890s, was no longer certain about the benefits of Westernization. It is possible that he decided to publish this later set of memoirs solely for financial reasons, but their retrospective tone suggests a desire to secure his place in posterity. By 1890, Heco had long been forgotten by Japanese and Americans, and perhaps he wanted to remind people of his unusual and fascinating life.

Like for *Hyoryuki,* Heco had help with the production and publication of *Narrative of a Japanese.* James Murdoch, a scholar, journalist, and adventurer then teaching in Tokyo, edited the volumes. Originally from Scotland, Murdoch had a talent for learning languages and earned a master's degree in classical languages at Aberdeen University. He was appointed to the position of assistant professor of Greek at Aberdeen, but soon thereafter left to teach in Australia. Then he became a journalist, traveling to South America, China, and finally Japan, where a friend helped him gain a teaching position in Kyushu. He moved on to Tokyo and was teaching at Tokyo University when he edited Heco's memoir. In the mid-1890s, Murdoch began intensively studying the Japanese language in preparation for what would become his major work, *A History of Japan,* published in three volumes between 1903 and 1926. He later moved to Kagoshima, married a Japanese woman, and then returned to Australia, where he taught at the University of Melbourne until his death in 1921.

In the introduction to the first volume of *Narrative of a Japanese,* Murdoch wrote that he was presented with "eight thin but closely-written notebooks" in the spring of 1892 and was requested to "extract from them all that was of more than purely personal interest and . . . see to the publication of the same."[15] He implies, but does not directly state, that Heco gave him the notebooks.[16] According to Murdoch, the first two notebooks were of Heco's childhood, his experience as a castaway, and his life in America during the 1850s and early 1860s. Murdoch, with his knowledge of Japan and his experience as a journalist, may have revised and rewritten Heco's notebooks more than he let on.

With the exception of Heco's alleged meeting with President Abraham Lincoln in March 1862, the significant facts of his life in the United States in the 1850s and the first few years back in Japan in the 1860s can be verified by independent sources, but silences in the narratives indicate they are a less than complete portrayal.[17] For example, although few passages blatantly maximize Heco's positive characteristics and accomplishments, we learn practically nothing about failures and negative characteristics. Large chronological gaps mar the second volume and are presumably the result of Heco's tiring of writing diary entries while becoming more involved in business activities.

The narratives, then, are at once tantalizing and problematic glimpses into two worlds. Like many Japanese students who followed him to the United States, Heco can be seen as a symbol of Japan's growing interest in the West. Unlike them, however, he appears to have been motivated to learn about America and the West for personal rather than patriotic reasons. Heco was in many ways representative of early Japanese residents in the United States between 1850 and 1880, but he was certainly not representative of most Japanese of the same era. If used judiciously, Heco's memoirs, combined with independent sources whenever possible, can provide us with an illuminating representation of the experiences of one of the first Japanese who lived in the United States.

From Hamada to San Francisco

Heco was born in 1836 and raised in the village of Hamada (then known as Banshu) near Kobe.[18] His natural father, a farmer, died when Heco was one year old. His stepfather and older brother were sailors who transported goods and passengers around the Inland Sea and along the Pacific coast. Heco's stepfather and brother sometimes traveled as far as Edo. Heco heard their travel adventure stories and yearned to explore beyond the comfortable environs of his hometown. But, as he later wrote, "I don't suppose that . . . I even dreamt of the existence of other lands, or if I did, it was to pity the Barbarians who . . . came each year or so to Nagasaki to trade with us."[19]

Except for sailors, samurai accompanying their *daimyō* to and from Edo, and those with enough money for temple-and-shrine sightseeing tours, many Japanese probably did not travel further than a few miles from their hometowns during the Tokugawa era. Finances were not the only restriction, since travel permits from *bakufu* officials were required. While scholarship suggests that *bakufu* officials flexibly interpreted travel restrictions and that travel among commoners within Japan may have been more prevalent than previously believed, there is no reason to expect that Heco ever ventured far from Hamada.

In *Narrative of a Japanese,* Heco reported that his stepfather was in Edo delivering goods from his junk when Commodore James Biddle and his ships *Columbus* and *Vincennes* sailed into Uraga Bay in July 1846. His junk was one of hundreds pressed into service by the *bakufu* as a guard boat surrounding the strange, huge ships.[20] Heco recalled that his stepfather often told him the story of this adventure, including the fear he felt during his encounter with the barbarians from the West.[21]

Heco reports that his mother was extremely concerned about his safety and did not permit him to go on his first sea voyage until he was fourteen. He accompanied his older brother while he took sightseers to temples and shrines around the Inland Sea.[22] Upon his return, Heco excitedly told his mother about the voyage and the wondrous sights he had seen, including the magnificent *torii* gate at Itsukushima Shrine. She still worried about his safety and apparently did not want him to go on any more voyages. According to Heco, a few days later his mother suddenly became ill and died.

His mother's death was undoubtedly a wrenching blow to young Heco, but the tragedy broke the child-parent obligation emphasized in Confucianism's ethical worldview and freed him to accompany his stepfather and brother on their sea voyages. He immediately joined his stepfather on a trip to Edo. Two ships were to deliver sake and other goods to coastal cities and finally to Edo, where they would pick up other merchandise and return to Osaka and Kobe. Heco was with his stepfather on board the *Sumiyoshi Maru* until the two ships stopped to wait out a storm south of Ise. There crew members of the *Eiriki Maru,* a new, 240-ton ship, persuaded Heco's stepfather to let the boy join them for the remainder of the voyage to Edo.[23] The *Sumiyoshi Maru* had been delayed while doing business along the coast, so the *Eiriki Maru*'s crew took Heco to visit the city while they waited. Edo had a population of nearly one million at the time, but there was "absolutely no trace of intercourse with foreigners," and Yokohama was still an "insignificant fishing hamlet."[24] Because the *Eiriki Maru* was obligated to return to Kobe, the ship departed Edo with Heco on board around October 20, 1850, before Heco's stepfather had arrived.[25]

Coasting near the same area where they had waited out a storm on the voyage to Edo, the *Eiriki Maru* was suddenly blown out to sea by a storm. To lighten the pitching ship, the crew cut the heavy mast and threw some of its cargo of barley and peas overboard. Heco now regretted having left his stepfather's ship and reflected on his late mother's concerns for his safety.[26] His fear increased when he heard the crew chanting, "Namu Amida Butsu, Namu Amida Butsu . . ." (save us, o merciful Buddha). In *Hyoryuki,* Heco revealed that he and the crew prayed to both Shinto and Buddhist deities.[27] In *Narrative of a Japanese,* however, he specified that he prayed only to Shinto deities, which may have reflected the emphasis on Japan's native religion in the 1880s and 1890s. He claimed that he vowed to the Shinto gods that if they spared his life, "and in their gracious mercy permit me to set foot on dry land once again, I would never more set out in a ship while I lived."[28]

Like all ships built in Japan during the national seclusion era, the *Eiriki Maru* was not designed for ocean travel. By order of the *bakufu,* only ships designed for coastal trade and transportation were permitted to be built. These ships had open sterns, large square rudders, and no keels.[29] Furthermore, the *Eiriki Maru* had no compass. In these circumstances, compounded by the missing mast, the crew's chances of piloting back to Japan were virtually nil.

The ship drifted with the current east across the Pacific. Fortunately, the crew had taken on a cargo of foods at Edo and had enough water to last for months. Aboard a newly constructed, relatively large vessel with ample provisions and water, Heco and the crew of the *Eiriki Maru* were fortunately well prepared for the danger and tedium of drifting on the Pacific.

On or about the fiftieth day of drifting, the *Auckland,* a New England trading ship, sighted the stricken vessel about five hundred miles east of Japan and rescued all aboard. Heco and his shipmates were initially alarmed at the huge, black vessel that could stop and turn around in midocean with its sails.[30] Nevertheless, after being so long at sea and "worried solely about the problem of life and death, . . . the happiness of all of us was indescribable," Heco recalled.[31] On board the *Auckland* was a crew of eleven: Captain Jennings, two officers, six crewmen, a cook, and a cabin boy. To Heco, "the appearance of the officers and men was all alike" and was exacerbated by their beards and uniform of flannel shirts and pants.[32] The rescued Japanese remained wary and fearful of the "rough and odd" but "kind and attentive" crew throughout the voyage.[33]

Only the cook looked different from the others. He had a shaved head with a long queue and wrote *gam saan* (literally, "gold mountain," meaning California) in Chinese characters for the Japanese.[34] To Heco the cook appeared "like our own people," but he surprisingly claimed that neither he nor any of his countrymen realized the cook was Chinese. Given that by 1850 only Japanese who lived in or around Nagasaki had probably ever seen Chinese, Heco's claim is plausible, but to recognize characters as Chinese but not the person who wrote them is unlikely.

After the Japanese boarded, Captain Jennings and one of his officers attempted to show them the ship's location on a large map spread out in the captain's cabin. In *Hyoryuki,* Heco recalled that "the third officer of the foreign vessel spread out a map of the world, and with sign language, indicated that this ship was an American ship, and was one that was returning from China to a place in America called *Kyarihonia* [California]. We got the general drift of what he wanted to say. Then he taught us the names of the countries on the map."[35] In *Narrative of a Japanese,* however, the officer

> pointed out a large tract of land and said "America," and at the same time pointed to the ship. From this we understood that the vessel belonged to that country. The next country he pointed to was a small spot; he said "Japan" and "Jeddo" [Edo] and pointed at us. This we did not understand exactly, but supposed that he meant this to be our country, although the name he used was wrong, for we never knew our country by such a name, and the spot on the chart seemed altogether too small for *Dai Nippon* since we were told and taught to believe that our country was large.[36]

In addition, this later account includes Heco's claim that he and a few of his fellow castaways recognized the name "Ah-me-ri-ka" because of the arrival of the *Columbus* and *Vincennes*.[37] Details may have been added to make *Narrative of a Japanese* more interesting to the foreign audience for which it was intended, and the term *Dai Nippon* (Great Japan), common among the more nationalistic decades of the 1880s and 1890s, marks the passage as a later construction.

The Japanese were astonished at the technology of the *Auckland*'s design and construction. The 32-point compass and numerous sails were particularly fascinating.[38] They were also amazed that the much larger *Auckland* had a crew of only eleven, while the *Eiriki Maru* had a crew of sixteen.

The castaways did not care for some of the food offered to them, especially meat and butter. According to Buddhist beliefs, anything from four-footed animals was spiritually and physically unclean. Heco first hid the bread with butter given to him and later threw it overboard. However, he heartily drank up soup made from beans, fried bread, and—unknown to him at first—salted meat.[39] When he discovered the soup he enjoyed contained meat, he recalled the saying, *shiranu ga hotoke* (that which is done in ignorance has no harm).[40] He also claimed to have asked the gods to forgive him for the sin of eating unclean food.

Heco observed that although they were not forced to eat meat, his shipmates lost their cultural and religious aversions to eating it not long after being rescued. Sweet potatoes, yams, hard tack, and coffee rounded out the provisions on the American ship, and the Japanese brought an ample supply of rice with them when they transferred from their stricken vessel to the *Auckland*.[41] One Japanese crew member purportedly told Heco the Japanese proverb *go ni haitte wa, go ni shitagae* (when you are in the country, do as they do in the country).[42] Heco and his fellow castaways seem to have used such proverbs to rationalize their adaptation to the culture and lifestyle of nineteenth-century America.

However, when Heco published *Hyoryuki* in 1863, Japan was at the height of the "revere the emperor, expel the barbarian" movement. Its ideology emphasized the traditional ways of Japan, reverence for the emperor, and resistance to foreigners and foreign ways. Apparently concerned about how his adaptation to American culture and lifestyle would be interpreted back in Japan, Heco did not include his meat-eating episode aboard the *Auckland* in *Hyoryuki.*

In addition to a change in diet, Heco began wearing foreign clothes, which "were much warmer than my own garment, besides being more convenient for working."[43] And, in what was probably an attempt to make the Japanese boy look like a Western boy, an American crew member cut off Heco's top-knot. As it was the distinctive hairstyle of most Japanese males until the 1870s, Heco claimed that the sudden and unwanted removal of his topknot "vexed me sorely" and prayed for forgiveness for the "unwittingly committed" sin.[44] Nevertheless, he kept the Western hairstyle for the rest of his life.

Even though they adopted certain Western cultural habits aboard the American vessel, the Japanese retained their fear of the ship's crew, especially after witnessing the cook killing a pig for food. One of Heco's elders even suspected that if the *Auckland* ran out of food, the foreigners would devour their Japanese passengers.[45] The Japanese would be unable to confirm this suspicion, however, because the *Auckland* reached San Francisco before the ship's provisions had been depleted. The ship arrived on March 3, 1851, forty-two days after picking up the castaways. In all, the Japanese had spent nearly one hundred days at sea and were eager to see land.

They were likely unprepared for San Francisco. The 1848 discovery of gold in northern California had already transformed the former Mexican coastal village of Yerba Buena into the largest city on the Pacific Coast. By the time Heco and his fellow castaways arrived, nearly thirty thousand French, German, English, Irish, Chilean, Mexican, Chinese, Hawaiian, Yankee, and Southerner settlers had crowded the booming port city and gateway to the gold mines. According to the historian Roger Lotchin, "There has probably never been a more thoroughly uprooted city population than that of San Francisco" in the late 1840s and 1850s.[46] As Heco and his shipmates were escorted around the city, they were amazed at the broad streets (some paved with stones), sidewalks, spacious houses built of brick and wood, shops with large glass windows displaying goods, saloons, horses, carriages, nonstop construction of buildings and streets, and bustling people.

Heco did not return to Japan for over eight years. By his own choice, he learned English, received an education, and entered business. In what can be defined as a patron-client relationship that would repeat for many early Japanese residents of the United States, Heco was assisted by some Americans who seemed to take a paternal or fraternal liking to the eager, hard-working sojourner from mysterious and virtually unknown Japan. His primary benefactor was Beverly C. Sanders, a businessman from Baltimore and, from 1852 to 1853, the U.S. Customs collector at San Francisco. In all, Heco spent approximately three years in San Francisco and five years in the East, primarily in Baltimore. As Heco was probably the only Japanese residing in America throughout most of the 1850s (he also made a return visit in late 1861 and early 1862), his transnational and cross-cultural encounters provide a unique perspective on American life during this period.

The Education of a Japanese Castaway

Young Heco began learning English in San Francisco from Thomas Troy, a crewman aboard the U.S.S. *Polk,* where the U.S. government lodged the castaways until they could be returned to Japan.[47] According to Heco, Troy had been fascinated with Catholic school stories of St. Francis Xavier's experiences in sixteenth-century Japan and took a great interest in Heco and the other Japanese.* Troy evidently told Heco that it would benefit him and his country if he learned English.[48] At the time, Heco was so young that he probably did not comprehend this rationale, but he was keen on studying the foreign language anyway. Using spelling and reading books, he studied English with Troy whenever possible.

The other Japanese resisted learning English and counseled Heco against it. They told him that if he went back to Japan speaking a foreign language, he would be thrown in jail and suffer serious punishment, "the exact details of which they were not certain of."[49] Heco was frightened by the admonitions of his elders, but he was also eager to learn, so he continued to study.

Heco's prospects for receiving an education were boosted tremendously when he was befriended by Beverly Sanders. Leaving his wife, Elizabeth, behind, Sanders had journeyed to San Francisco in 1850 in the hope of profiting from the booming port city.[50] He became part-owner of a steamship, helped found the San Francisco Gas Company, and established the Sanders and Brenham Bank with former San Francisco mayor Charles Brenham.[51] Sanders, Brenham, and others also established the Russian-American Company, which brought ice from Alaska—then part of Russia—to San Francisco.[52] In 1852, Brenham, chairman of California's Whig Central Committee, helped Sanders gain the lucrative post of U.S. Customs collector for San Francisco, a position he held for less than a year because of the November

*One of the founders of the Jesuit order, St. Francis Xavier lived in Japan from 1549 to 1551. He was among the first Catholic missionaries allowed in the country.

Joseph Heco. (Chikamori, *Josefu Hiko*)

1852 Democratic presidential victory.[53] As a "public officer, merchant, citizen, or neighbor," reported the *Daily Alta California,* Sanders held "a high place in the esteem of his fellow citizens."[54]

In the summer of 1852, a ship arrived in port with a rescued Japanese castaway aboard who was taken to be interviewed by Sanders. As Heco knew some English by this time, he was brought to the office to translate for Sanders, whom he had never met.[55] After this encounter, Heco amicably parted from Troy and agreed to help Sanders with office work.

In a letter to Heco composed in 1858, Sanders asserted that he was motivated to befriend, educate, and sponsor the fifteen year old because of a "parental feeling" he felt when they first met.[56] In a letter to California senator William Gwin that was subsequently published in the *Washington, D.C., Evening Star,* Sanders, however, maintained: "I took Heco under my protection, and soon discovered that he was much superior in general intelligence to his race generally, and determined to educate him; thinking he might some day be very useful, both to his own country and to mine."[57] As a businessman and customs collector, Sanders was undoubtedly aware of government plans to send a diplomatic mission to Japan. Indeed, in the very same San Francisco newspaper article that announced the arrival of Heco and his fellow Japanese castaways in 1851, the writer opined that the rescue of the Japanese and their safe return home by way of the U.S. Navy "would seem to afford a good opportunity for attempting to open intercourse with Japan."[58] The nineteenth-century American vision of Manifest Destiny along with the Gold Rush inspired entrepreneurs such as Sanders to journey to the new Pacific state in search of business opportunities. Since Sanders was already interested in business opportunities in the Russian territory of Alaska, Japan may have been equally appealing.

As for Heco, he later wrote that he wanted "to avail myself of this chance of receiving an education."[59] Staying with and doing office work for a well-off patron who was willing to pay for his education was certainly a plausible explanation for making this decision. Whether the desire for education was the only reason for Heco's decision is impossible to know. As a non-samurai, Heco was certainly aware that his educational prospects in Japan were limited. He may have also looked upon Sanders as a father, as demonstrated by his unlimited admiration and affection for him. Heco's stepfather in Japan spent most his time working, so he grew up under the parental guidance of his mother and perhaps desired a male guide.

Heco's formal education began in the fall of 1853 after Sanders resigned his post and returned to Baltimore.[60] Sanders sent Heco to a Catholic school with fifteen instructors and approximately 150 students. "My studies lay in learning to spell, write, and cipher, and in reading some religious books," Heco recalled.[61] The school's world atlas, he noticed, did not contain a map of Japan.[62] He described the instructors, some of whom were Catholic priests, as "exceedingly kind," and he apparently got along well with the other students.[63] He attended this school for about six months.

Sanders and he returned to San Francisco in the fall of 1854, and Heco reported that he attended school in the Bay Area for one and a half years. Unfortunately, neither memoir includes a description of the school. Then in February 1855, a financial panic began in San Francisco and swept many banks and businesses into bankruptcy, including the Sanders and Brenham Bank. Sanders was also removed from his leadership position at the Russian-American Company as a result of the company's financial difficulties.[64] By 1856, he could no longer afford to send Heco to school. In all, Heco received two and a half years of formal education in the United States, in addition to the year spent learning English from Thomas Troy.

Sanders managed to get Heco a position as an office assistant at Macondary and Company, a commission house in San Francisco that received consignments from all over the world.[65] Unfortunately, Heco wrote disappointingly little about what he actually did during his one and a half years there. Presumably, he performed office chores and ran errands as he previously had done for Sanders. However, he did make some revealing comparisons between Japanese and American business practices soon after he returned to Japan. He observed that a large commercial house in Japan required many workers, but Macondary and Company utilized machines to reduce human labor. The workers at Macondary and Company worked "without idleness," there were no "empty formalities," and the salaries were "ample."[66] In sum, Heco was "perfectly satisfied" with his position at the firm.[67] Heco's work experience at Macondary and Company apparently proved to be fruitful: he spent most of his life back in Japan as a successful businessman.

In addition to education and business, Heco expressed an interest in technology. In *Hyoryuki,* he included his drawings of a steamship, a "steam carriage"—or train engine—an artificial leg, a telegraph, and a steel bridge.[68] His first experiences with the telegraph and the train are particularly indicative of the Japanese perception of Western technology in the midnineteenth century. After arriving in New York by ship from San Francisco in the fall of 1853, Sanders sent a telegraph message two hundred miles to his family in Baltimore. He explained to Heco that there would be a reply in a few minutes. In *Hyoryuki,* Heco reported that he "could not take to be true" Sanders's explanation, but after the reply was received, he "could only marvel."[69] Thirty years later, Heco recalled his disbelief somewhat differently: "For how could a message run along a wire faster by far than a bird could fly?"[70] His response to the telegraph's receipt had also changed: "I believed that his words were true."[71] The difference between these two versions is not substantial, but does demonstrate that someone revised the more proximate account.

Although the first railway in Japan was not constructed until 1872, Heco's first train ride was in 1853, immediately following his first encounter with a telegraph. Of this first journey on a New York train bound for Baltimore, Heco recalled in his 1863 memoir: "Getting in and watching the farmers plowing in the fields near the tracks, I felt like a flying bird; and though I was unable to observe the scene clearly, it was not because the jolting of the carriage was violent for one could even write."[72] Thirty years later, he remembered the ride a little differently: "We took our seats . . . and while we sat there the engine began to snort and puff and the car to move. It moved slowly at first but presently it sped along so rapidly that what we passed could not be distinctly seen, while the train itself vibrated and undulated like a snake chased in the water."[73]

Heco's drawing of a "steam carriage." (Hikozo, *Hyoryuki: Floating on the Pacific Ocean*)

In the nineteenth century, the units of space and time as traversed by means of human and animal muscle power were compressed into smaller, more precise units by the technological advances of steam power and electricity. While Heco was one of very few Japanese who set foot in the United States during the 1850s, his perception of velocity, the visual blurring of the landscape, and the ability to read and write while the train was in motion were common to nineteenth-century descriptions by Americans and Europeans.[74]

Race Matters

In addition to telegraphs and trains, Heco had never encountered *kokujin* (black people) before he arrived in the United States.[75] His perceptions are unique because very few Japanese in the 1850s had seen blacks.[76] In *Hyoryuki,* Heco reported that a few days after first arriving in San Francisco, the shipmaster from the *Auckland* took him sightseeing around the city, where he saw "black men, raising loud cries, [who] were driving horses which were being made to pull carriages. . . . The black men looked as though a mixture of soot and oil had been rubbed on their faces."[77] Furthermore, Heco "was a child of thirteen, so I was frightened. I clutched the shipmaster's hand, drew close to him and could not separate myself from him."[78] Thirty years later in *Narrative of a Japanese,* Heco repeated a nearly identical version of this encounter but added that he had been frightened because he had been taught folktales that black, red, and white demons inhabited Hell.[79] Consequently, when he saw the black wagon drivers in San Francisco, he thought Hell was nearby. As Heco was from Japan, an almost racially homogeneous country in the midninteenth century, his reported reaction of fear is believable, especially since he had remained wary of his white rescuers, but its later rationalization is questionable.

He eventually overcame his fear to express an idiosyncratic, sympathetic view of slavery. In his 1863 memoir, Heco wrote that blacks did not mind working on hot, humid plantations in the American South because they were "products of a tropical land."[80] He believed the South was "desirous of stopping slavery" and had even discussed compensation for slaves right before seceding from the Union.[81] Moreover, he believed that the American Civil War was rooted "in religion," especially with "English ecclesiasts" (presumably abolitionists) of the North, who viewed slavery as against the will of God.[82]

During the summer of 1854, Heco spent five weeks on a plantation a few miles south of Baltimore owned by Elizabeth Sanders's mother. In his later memoir, he condescendingly portrayed the thirty to forty slaves on the plantation as "the most healthy and cheerful people I ever saw. Their ways and manners were exceedingly funny; their dances in the evening used to interest me especially."[83]

Heco's perceptions were almost certainly influenced by those of his benefactor, whose family was from the border state of Maryland, owned a plantation with slaves, and served as a colonel in the Confederate Army.[84] In addition, Heco later expressed considerable admiration for Lt. John Brooke, an officer in the Confederate Army and the captain of a U.S. Navy survey mission that helped return Heco to Japan in 1859. And in 1857 Sanders introduced Heco to California senator William Gwin, who was later jailed during the Civil War on suspicion of treason because of his southern background.[85] When Heco stopped in Hawaii on his return trip from the United States in 1862, the *Honolulu Friend* reported that his sympathy was "unmistakably with the North in the great struggle," which was likely wishful thinking, since Heco never deviated from his views.[86] Written many years apart, both *Hyoryuki* and *Narrative of a Japanese* conspicuously represent his views as similar to those of his benefactors, who were white southerners. Despite these influences and Heco's stay in the United States throughout most of 1850s, his memoirs do not indicate that he understood slavery as the most salient moral, political, and economic issue of the decade.

Meanwhile, Heco's East Asian neighbors began arriving in the United States in large numbers during the Gold Rush. By the end of 1852, there were as many as twenty thousand Chinese miners and laborers in California, nearly all of whom disembarked at San Francisco. By the time Heco departed San Francisco for his return voyage to Japan in 1858, there were over thirty thousand Chinese in California—nearly 10 percent of the state's population.[87] For centuries Japan had borrowed and adapted Chinese traditions, and China had been allowed to continue its trade with Japan during the era of national seclusion, yet Heco's only comment about the Chinese in San Francisco evidences no respect: They were "a greedy and cringing race, and to make money will submit to any treatment," he wrote in *Narrative of a Japanese*.[88]

While Heco's derision and ignorance of the Chinese is surprising given the two countries' history, it should not be surprising that, after spending years among middle- to upper-class white businessmen, politicians, and their families, he would adopt many of their attitudes and prejudices. Adopting the attitudes and even prejudices of American benefactors would become a common characteristic of many Japanese during the frontier era of U.S.–Japan relations.

Heco the Catholic

Another attitude Heco adopted was his benefactors' religion. Both Thomas Troy and Beverly Sanders were Catholic, and Heco had attended Catholic school and Catholic church services with the Sanders family in Baltimore. Elizabeth Sanders, whom Heco depicted as "very ardent in the matter of religion," wanted him baptized as a Catholic. The Sanders family took him to the Cathedral of the Assumption of the Blessed Virgin Mary in Baltimore in the fall of 1854 for that purpose.[89] After a priest questioned Heco on his religious beliefs, he read a list of names from which the Japanese castaway was to chose his Christian name. Heco claimed that he chose Joseph because it sounded "so pleasant."[90] He was led to an altar, baptized with Holy Water, and christened with his new name.

Heco's memoirs do not indicate that he was ever an ardent follower of Christianity, and, indeed, his knowledge of Christianity appeared to be both superficial and quirky. In *Hyoryuki*, for example, he indicated that there were only two Christian sects in America, one whose priests were celibate and one whose priests had wives.[91] In addition to "encouraging virtue and punishing evil," priests were teachers of reading, writing, math, and other subjects.[92] He nonchalantly described the Christmas holiday for his fellow Japanese as "the birthday of a saint who taught the way of man by means of religious teachings."[93] More telling is his brief and matter-of-fact description in *Nar-*

rative of a Japanese of the Japanese government's crackdown on Christians in the Nagasaki area. More than one thousand Japanese Christians—most of whom were Catholics—were uprooted from their homes and forced to move to cold, inhospitable areas of northern Japan. While the foreign community strenuously complained about these actions to the Japanese government, Heco expressed no concern.[94] Furthermore, there is no indication that Heco attended church services during his years in San Francisco. It appears, then, that Heco agreed to be baptized not as a result of developing a personal interest and faith in Christianity, but because he felt a sense of obligation to accommodate to the wishes of his benefactors.

Although Heco included drawings of a Catholic priest and a church and a few pages on religion in *Hyoryuki,* he did not mention his baptism. He appears to have omitted this significant personal detail for two reasons. First was the personal fear of being attacked by anti-foreign *rōnin.* These were not idle threats. Among those murdered were Henry Heusken, the secretary and interpreter to the American Minister Townsend Harris, in 1860, and Denkichi, a castaway on the *Eiriki Maru* who worked as an interpreter for the British legation, in 1861. Public acknowledgment of Heco's Christian baptism would certainly increase his visibility to the *rōnin.*

Second, converting to Christianity had been prohibited by the *bakufu* since the early seventeenth century. Since Heco had become an American citizen by the time he returned to Japan, he was protected from legal action by the Japanese government by extraterritorial law. Nevertheless, the Japanese government could make his life and business difficult, which they did with many Japanese and foreign Christians, even after the prohibitions against Christianity were repealed in 1873. Thus, Heco (or the unnamed friend who assisted him) may have omitted any direct reference to his Christianity in the 1863 memoir due to prudent and serious concerns about his personal safety and potential problems from a government long opposed to the Western religion.

Meeting the "Chief Man of the Nation"

In the fall of 1853, Sanders took Heco to the White House to meet the president. According to Heco, Sanders described Franklin Pierce to him as the "King of America" and the "Chief Man of the Nation."[95] Because Heco was the first Japanese to meet an American president, some writers have assumed that he was "nervous about the formality" of the occasion.[96] In fact, there is no indication that Pierce, Sanders, or Heco were aware this was the first encounter between a Japanese national and an American president.

Heco's drawing of a church. (Hikozo, ***Hyoryuki: Floating on the Pacific Ocean***)

Heco reported in *Hyoryuki* that after shaking hands with him and Sanders, Pierce told Heco that he would be useful to America and Japan if he learned "to write, study, and do sums."[97] Sanders and Pierce then had a discussion of trade relations with Russia while Heco gazed out the window at the Potomac River.[98] He doubted that Pierce was the most important official of the American government:

> Why does my old gentleman [Sanders] tell me such stories? What does he mean by saying that this man is the "Chief of the Nation?" The appearance of everything here seems against the truth of his words. Only the building is large and fine, being of marble, and there are also iron railings. . . . But there is no grand gate, no guard of soldiers, not even police on the outside. And as the rooms of office, they are furnished with silk curtains and cushions on the chairs, but beyond that there is nothing to warrant the idea that they are those of such a great man as the "Chief of the Nation" should live in. And again the dress of the man—just a plain black suit quite apiece with the one my old gentleman wears. And yet he tells me this is the Greatest Man of the Nation! What can he mean?[99]

Heco could not believe Pierce's position because in his home country, "even the smallest district official has more pomp and splendor about his person than this man has!"[100] Far from feeling nervous or awestruck, Heco was both surprised and unimpressed.

Four years later, Heco was taken to meet President James Buchanan and Secretary of State Lewis Cass by Senator William Gwin. Gwin hoped to get Heco an appointment with the State Department, as he believed Heco could be an asset to U.S.-Japan relations if he returned to Japan as an employee.[101] As was Sanders, Gwin was well aware that Heco could contribute to trade relations between the two countries, which would certainly benefit the Pacific port city of San Francisco. For example, a few days before Heco and Gwin's meeting with Cass and Buchanan, the *Washington, D.C., Evening Star* opined: "We are . . . most anxious that no stone should be left unturned to commence the work of driving the American commercial opening wedge into Japan as soon as possible."[102] Obviously at the urging of Gwin (and probably Sanders), the newspaper also recommended that Heco, "an extraordinary youth[,] . . . be made diplomatically of service to the interests of American commerce" in Asia.[103] Heco was treated cordially by Cass and Buchanan, but they said they could not give him a diplomatic post with the State Department at that time since all vacancies were filled and no appropriation was available to create a position for him.

Heco briefly described President Buchanan as "a large-built old man of 70. One of his eyes was affected. He was dressed in a black suit, and held his head on one side."[104] As with Pierce, Heco was not impressed with Buchanan. However, he no longer doubted the occupant of the White House was the "Chief Man of the Nation."

Later, when Heco returned to America for a few months in late 1861 and early 1862, Sanders arranged for him to meet Secretary of the Navy Gideon Welles and Secretary of State William Seward so that he could apply for the post of U.S. naval storekeeper in Kanagawa, Japan.[105] After a couple of meetings, Seward appointed Heco as the official interpreter of the American consulate in Kanagawa, a post Heco previously held but had formally resigned from in February 1860 to pursue business interests. Heco was disappointed because the interpreter post paid significantly less than did naval storekeeper.[106]

Then a significant, but problematic episode appears in *Narrative of a Japanese.* Just before Heco returned to Japan, Seward allegedly took him to meet President Abraham Lincoln, whom Seward apparently described as "our Tycoon."[107] *Taikun,* often romanized in the nineteenth century as "tycoon," is a Japanese word that literally means "great ruler" and referred to the shogun. Whether Seward meant to refer to Lincoln as having the same all-powerful status as Japan's shogun is unclear. It is even possible that Seward used this reference sarcastically, as he may have still been smarting from Lincoln's victory over him for the Republican party's presidential nomination two years earlier.

In *Narrative of a Japanese,* Heco described his March 12, 1862, meeting with Lincoln:

> We entered the President's office and found him seated in an arm chair tilted back on to its two hind legs, with his ancles [*sic*] crossed over each on the desk in front of him and his spectacles up on his forehead. . . . The President stretched out a huge hand, saying he was glad to meet one coming from such a far-off place as Japan. He shook hands with me very cordially, and then he made a great many inquiries about the position of affairs in our country. . . . The President was tall, lean, with large hands, darkish hair streaked with grey, slight side-whiskers and clean shaved about the mouth. He was dressed in a black frock coat. It was said that he was a most sincere and kind person, greatly beloved by all those who came in contact with him.[108]

Unlike his meetings with Pierce and Buchanan, Heco's meeting with Lincoln was not included in *Hyoryuki,* the most proximate memoir to his sojourns in America. The account of his 1861–62 trip to the United States, mostly in the form of diary entries, appears only in the first volume of *Narrative of a Japanese,* published thirty years later.[109] In his biography, *Abraham Lincoln: The War Years,* Carl Sandburg reports the same meeting between Heco, Seward, and Lincoln, but his main source of information appears to be Heco's *Narrative of a Japanese.*[110]

On the surface, Heco's depiction of meeting Lincoln seems plausible enough. When he and Seward entered the office, Lincoln was listening to an army officer complain about his superior; Lincoln told the officer that he was "long-winded" and dismissed him; Lincoln then got out of his chair, shook hands with Seward and Heco, and asked Heco questions about Japan; some more people came into the office, apparently for a scheduled meeting; Heco then left.[111] We can infer from Heco's description that he spent no more than ten minutes in the president's office, and perhaps five minutes in conversation with Lincoln, who had then been president for one year. Still, its absence from *Hyoryuki* and the apparent lack of independent sources leaves some room for doubt. It is possible that Heco or Murdoch concocted this meeting to make *Narrative of a Japanese* of more interest to a Western audience.

Heco's meetings with Pierce in 1853 and Buchanan in 1857 predated the first meeting between Japanese diplomats and an American president in 1860. If Heco actually met Lincoln in 1862, then he is the only native Japanese known to have done so. Even so, his reactions match those of later Japanese. Constant themes of Heco's descriptions of his meetings with presidents are his lack of awe and nervousness and his lack of understanding the rare opportunities of gaining access to a head of state. Moreover, his expressed reactions of surprise and disappointment at what he considered to be the relatively common attire and lack of pomp and formality of the president was echoed by Japanese diplomats of the shogun's embassy in 1860 and the Iwakura mission of 1871–72.

An American Citizen

It is not surprising that Heco, who lived in the United States between the formative ages of fourteen and twenty-three, would adopt certain characteristics, habits, beliefs, and even the prejudices of his American benefactors and friends. He also adopted America as his country of citizenship.

Before Heco left for California to join a U.S. Navy survey expedition that would return him to Japan, Sanders took him to the U.S. District Court in Baltimore, where Heco became a naturalized American citizen on June 30, 1858.[112] Unknown to Heco, Sanders, and District Court Judge William Gill,

Heco was the first native of Japan to become an American citizen. He was probably the only Japanese to receive American citizenship for decades.

As Heco was born in Japan and both of his parents were ethnically Japanese, how did he become an American citizen when one of the prevailing requirements for citizenship was to be "a free white person"?[113] Secretary of State Hamilton Fish asked this same question in 1875 to John Bingham, the American minister to Japan and a former judge.[114] Bingham replied that it was a "judicial question" concerning "how white the alien must be to constitute him a white person."[115]

The "free white person" requirement contained in the 1790 and 1824 Naturalization Acts was originally designed to exclude Africans and Native Americans from citizenship. The government neglected to exclude Asians because there were virtually none in the United States until the 1850s. State and local governments enacted anti-Chinese laws as early as 1852; however, congressional legislation and federal court decisions did not begin to exclude Asians from gaining citizenship on the basis of the "free white person" requirement until the 1870s.[116] Some Japanese were able to gain American citizenship as late as 1906, when the U.S. attorney general ordered federal judges to stop issuing naturalization papers to Japanese applicants. According to a special report on the 1910 U.S. census, 420 Japanese had obtained naturalized American citizenship.[117] In 1922, the U.S. Supreme Court conclusively decided that Japanese were excluded from obtaining naturalized American citizenship because they were not black—blacks obtained the right of citizenship in 1870—and were not "white persons."[118] Heco's naturalization papers clearly stated he was "a native of Japan," yet, Judge Gill apparently decided that he met all requirements for citizenship—including that of being "a free white person." It appears, then, that Heco was granted American citizenship in 1858 in part because a person of Japanese ancestry had yet to be legally defined as "non-white."[119]

Sanders claimed in 1857 that Heco had a "desire to become an American citizen," but whether Heco made this decision of his own free will or felt obligated to accede to the wishes of his benefactor is unclear.[120] What is clear is that after he returned to Japan Heco demanded and expected to be treated as an American citizen by both the American and Japanese governments for the remainder of his life.[121]

Although Heco omitted reference to his American citizenship in *Hyoryuki,* friends and acquaintances in Japan must have known he was a Japanese native but an American citizen. Certainly the Japanese government and the foreign community were aware of this. For a few years he worked full-time or part-time for the American government, and he lived in the foreign section of Kanagawa. As with his Christian baptism, Heco probably felt it was not prudent to publicly acknowledge his American citizenship.

Soon after being granted American citizenship, Heco was elated at the opportunity to return to Japan with a U.S. Navy survey expedition led by Lt. John Brooke.[122] Yet, it was with great sorrow that he parted from Beverly Sanders. Now twenty-two years old, Heco and his "old gentleman" had developed a strong father-son relationship.[123] Heco paid farewell visits to the Sanders family and other friends and then started for home aboard the *Fenimore Cooper* in the fall of 1858.[124] When the ship was delayed in Honolulu, Heco transferred to the *Sea Serpent,* a clipper ship bound for Hong Kong and Shanghai.

Aboard the *Sea Serpent* was Eugene Van Reed, whom Heco had first met in San Francisco in 1853 and considered a friend.[125] Heco had known Van Reed's parents and sisters in San Francisco and had visited his relatives in Pennsylvania.[126] Heco taught Van Reed some Japanese and, as a result, Van Reed was one of the few foreigners in Japan during the *bakumatsu* and early Meiji periods who could communicate in Japanese.[127] Just before Heco left for Japan, he and Van Reed had a portrait taken together in San Francisco.[128] Van Reed's early connection to a Japanese American would play an important role for later immigrants.

Eugene Van Reed and Heco. (Jonas, "Foreign Influence")

After a nine-year absence, Heco returned to Japan on June 18, 1859. American Minister Townsend Harris and Consul General Eben Dorr hired Heco as the interpreter at the American consulate in Kanagawa.* In this post, he helped plan for the shogun's embassy that traveled to Washington, D.C., in 1860 to ratify the Treaty of Amity and Commerce. He was also aboard the U.S.S. *Wyoming* during the Battle of Shimonoseki in July 1863 when American, British, French, and Dutch ships bombarded Choshu domain in response to that domain's firing on foreign ships passing through the Shimonoseki Straits.[129] In addition to his services as an interpreter, he kept American diplomats, merchants, and other foreigners in Yokohama well informed about the latest maneuverings and shifting alliances among the *bakufu,* the anti-*bakufu* forces, and the imperial court during the turbulent 1860s.[130]

During his first few years back in Japan, Heco lived in the foreign section of Kanagawa next door to Francis Hall, who was a partner in the American trading firm of Walsh, Hall, and Company. Hall and Heco became close friends, and Heco seems to have been popular with both the foreign community and the Japanese people in the Yokohama area. His advice and services as interpreter were widely sought by foreigners and Japanese. However, Heco did not always get along well with the American diplomats he worked for. Soon after the American consulate in Kanagawa opened in July 1859, he nearly got into a fight with Consul General Dorr after a heated discussion, but Van Reed intervened before any punches were thrown.[131] Hall and Heco were once reprimanded by Harris when the two spent an extra night in the still-restricted Edo.[132] Heco was upset that Seward turned him down for the lucrative post as manager of the U.S. Navy warehouse in Kanagawa. Later Heco was turned down for a post at a new bonded warehouse by the American chargé d'affaires.[133] And he was furious that Harris and Dorr refused to help him get a foreign currency exchange allowance even though they were receiving substantial exchange allowances from the Japanese government.[134] He reportedly resigned his post as official interpreter in the fall of 1863 to devote full attention to his business as a commercial agent, but his rocky relationships with Harris and Dorr and his failure to gain more lucrative government posts certainly contributed to his decision.[135]

Heco spent most of the rest of his life as a commercial agent and business entrepreneur in Yokohama, Nagasaki, Kobe, and Tokyo. He started one of the first Japanese newspapers, the *Kaigai Shimbun* (Overseas Newspaper),

*The American Legation (embassy) was located in Edo, where Harris carried out his official duties. In addition to Kanagawa (Yokohama), there were American consulates in Hakodate and Nagasaki.

in 1864.[136] Perhaps because of his knowledge of foreign economics, Heco was recruited by Inoue Kaoru to work for the Finance Ministry in the early 1870s.[137] He was employed in this post for about two years, and according to one source, he was used primarily as an interpreter for a British *yatoi* (foreign expert) hired by the ministry.[138]

Nevertheless, Heco had a stronger connection to the Japanese government than his relatively brief stint in its employ would indicate. He reported in *Narrative of a Japanese* that in late 1866, some young samurai from Choshu came to him in Nagasaki to consult about the governments and other institutions of the United States and Great Britain. These Choshu samurai included Ito Hirobumi, Inoue Kaoru, and Kido Koin, all three of whom would later become major political figures in the Meiji government.[139] He also reported that he became Choshu's business agent the following year.[140] As Choshu domain had expressed an active interest in learning about the West and Western technology since the early 1860s, it is not at all surprising that samurai from the domain would have sought out Heco, who had as much experience and knowledge of the West as virtually any other Japanese and had just moved to nearby Nagasaki. Coincidentally or otherwise, Heco's friend Van Reed had become a business agent for Satsuma domain at about the same time.[141] Yet, as with Van Reed's relationship to Satsuma, Heco's relationship to Choshu seemed to have more to do with business interests than with any ideological or political interests.

A Japanese American

After living in Kanagawa, Nagasaki, and Tokyo throughout most of the 1860s and early 1870s, Heco moved to Kobe and established a commercial trading firm specializing in the export of tea. While he concentrated on business activities, he occasionally did some work for the American consulates. In 1877, at the age of forty, Heco married eighteen-year-old Matsumoto Choko. He returned to Tokyo in 1888, where he remained until his death nine years later.

Despite his apparent success as a businessman dependent on foreign markets, his American citizenship, and his diplomatic contribution as an interpreter, Heco began to question the impact of Westernization on Japan by the mid-1880s. In a January 1886 diary entry, he wrote that he was disillusioned because "Japanese seem to have gone crazy over foreign things."[142] Three years later, he complained that "the introduction of so-called foreign civilization seems to occasion a sad falling-off in the old politeness and strict etiquette of the Japanese people."[143] Such comments suggest a middle-aged man infused with nostalgia, but they also reflect the emphasis on tradition and conservatism of Japan in the 1880s and 1890s.

Heco's place in the history of Japan and America had come relatively early in his life. By remaining in America, he was able to develop his language and business skills and learn about Western social and political institutions. Unlike other Japanese who followed him to America, who were samurai primarily motivated by a patriotic desire to strengthen Japan as a modern nation-state, Heco's motivation appeared to be more personal than patriotic. He had no direct political or ideological interests dependent on the outcome of the turmoil between the *bakufu* and the anti-*bakufu* forces during the 1860s. Nor does he indicate in either memoir that he was ever motivated by a national desire to strengthen Japan through "Eastern spirit, Western science," "rich nation, strong army," or "civilization and enlightenment," the primary Japanese philosophies of the period. While he was a skilled interpreter and knowledgeable liaison, he never expressed a desire to be the bridge between Japan and America that his American benefactors had hoped for.

Despite these differences, and his unique situation of being virtually the only Japanese we know of who resided in the United States throughout most of the 1850s, Heco's reported experiences were in some important ways similar to those of later Japanese who followed him to America during the frontier era of U.S.–Japan relations. Primarily, his ability to adapt to the transnational and cross-cultural challenges of nineteenth-century America was dependent upon personal ambition, determination, and a patron-client relationship with a benefactor willing to support his interest in Westernization. As a result, Heco gained access to education, to business, and to middle- and upper-class American society. For the next few decades, many Japanese who followed him to America traveled a similar journey.

TWO

Ryūgakusei, Rutgers, and the American Experience

Reverend John Ferris of the Dutch Reformed Church in America returned to his office at the Board of Foreign Missions in New York City after running an errand one day in the fall of 1866 to find two young men waiting for him "who appeared to be Chinamen."[1] They presented Ferris with a letter of introduction from Reverend Guido Verbeck, a teacher and missionary for the Dutch Reformed Church in Nagasaki. Verbeck had taught English to the two young men and helped arrange for their secret departure from Nagasaki. When Ferris asked them why they had come to the United States, they replied that they wanted to learn how to build "big ships" and "big guns" to keep Japan independent of the Western powers.[2] Ferris took the two men to New Brunswick, New Jersey, where they studied at Rutgers Grammar School before enrolling in Rutgers College.

The two young brothers were Yokoi Saheita and Yokoi Daihei of Kumamoto, nephews of Yokoi Shonan, a nationally known advocate of opening Japan to the West and a top official to the *daimyo* of Echizen. Yokoi Shonan believed that Japan would have to "enter the international comity of nations and participate in trade and friendship," and establishing cordial relations with the United States was the place to start.[3] The purpose of establishing such relations was to promote the "rich nation, strong army" philosophy (*fukoku kyōhei*) and Sakuma Shozan's juxtaposition "Eastern ethics, Western science" (*Tōyō no dōtoku, Seiyō no gakugei*).[4] Yokoi first advocated "rich nation, strong army" as a domainal policy for Echizen, but the Meiji government adopted it as a national policy in the early 1870s. Although Yokoi was a renowned Confucian scholar devoted to maintaining Japan's traditions, his supposedly pro-West views attracted the attention of anti-foreign *rōnin.* In 1863, they attempted to assassinate him; in 1869 they succeeded.

Yokoi's nephews were among the first Japanese *ryūgakusei* (overseas students) to attend colleges in the West. Except for the castaways Joseph Heco and Nakahama Manjiro, there is no evidence that any Japanese had studied abroad for hundreds of years before the 1860s. Geography, and the national seclusion edicts of the early seventeenth century precluded that possibility. Under pressure from Western countries that insisted on more trade and contact with Japan, in late 1866 the *bakufu* formally established a passport system that permitted Japanese to study overseas.[5] However, because of increased turmoil between the *bakufu* and its domestic opponents until 1868, few were able to take advantage of this legal opportunity, although some left the country secretly.

In the 1860s, individual *daimyōs* and the *bakufu* were primarily motivated by a desire for information on Western weapons in their sponsorship of overseas students. Thus, the Yokoi brothers were sent to learn about "big ships" and "big guns" by their uncle and *daimyō* Matsudaira Yoshinaga of Echizen. Foreign merchants—especially Americans—were of greater assistance than overseas students in procuring Western weapons and ships for both the *bakufu* and its opponents, but the first *ryūgakusei* had two important influences on the course of events in the 1860s. First, they were able to inform their superiors of the huge technological distance between Japan and the West. Combined with the bombardments suffered by Satsuma and Choshu from European and American ships in 1863 and 1864, this information had a sobering effect on the opposition movement's anti-foreign virulence.[6] It is no coincidence that the two most powerful domains in opposition to the *bakufu,* Satsuma and Choshu, sent the most students to the West in the 1860s.[7] When the samurai (and after 1871, former samurai) from Satsuma and Choshu became leaders of the new Meiji government, they adopted "rich nation, strong army" as a military and commercial policy designed to protect Japan's independence from Western powers.

Second, from 1868 to the end of the 1870s, the new Meiji government and individual students believed Westernization to be the solution—even a panacea—for Japan's modernization. In addition to the military, scientific, and commercial emphasis of "rich nation, strong army," many Japanese were interested in examining and, if possible, adapting Western political and social institutions to advance "civilization and enlightenment" (*bunmei kaika*). A few Japanese were even interested in Christianity despite the prohibitions against conversion. As a result of their transnational and cross-cultural educations and experiences, the first *ryūgakusei* were crucial in expanding Japan's knowledge of the West.

Go West, Young Man

Many Japanese who went overseas to study in the 1860s did not have *bakufu* permission, so they used aliases. Ishizuki Minoru and James Conte have painstakingly uncovered 153 Japanese who went abroad as students during the *bakumatsu* era, at least 60 of whom were not given permission or sponsorship by the *bakufu* government.[8] Of the 33 students who went to the United States, only 3 received *bakufu* permission. The rest were surreptitiously sent by their *daimyō* or were privately sponsored.[9] Most early *ryūgakusei** went to England, France, or the United States, but from 1869 to 1879 the United States became the favored destination.[10] Of the 884 study passports issued by the Japanese government during this decade, 293—33 percent—were for Japanese headed to the United States.[11] Nearly 200 of the 293 study passports issued for the United States were granted in 1870, 1871, and 1872.[12] However, we cannot assume that everyone who received a passport actually left Japan. While estimates vary slightly, my research indicates that at least 200 but no more than 250 Japanese took courses at colleges in the United States from the 1860s to 1880.[13]

A primary factor for promoting overseas study was Article 5 of Emperor Meiji's Charter Oath of 1868: "Knowledge shall be sought throughout the world so as to strengthen the foundations of imperial rule."[14] Despite this imperial support, government policies for overseas education remained disorganized until the 1880s, reflecting a hurried and fluctuating process of nation-building. Several times the government changed its procedures for issuing study passports, selecting overseas students, and funding their work. In addition, the Iwakura mission of 1871–72 discovered that many *ryūgakusei* were doing poorly in their studies. There were also complaints that most

*In this chapter, I use the term "early *ryugakusei*" to indicate those Japanese who journeyed overseas primarily for the purpose of college-level education in the 1860s and early 1870s.

government-sponsored slots were given to students from Satsuma, Choshu, Hizen, and Tosa—the four domains in control of the early Meiji government. As a result of these problems, the high costs of government sponsorship, and a reemergence of anti-Western sentiment among some Japanese officials, all government-sponsored students were ordered home in 1873. Some privately sponsored students, however, managed to remain in the United States to complete their education.

But this does not mean there was no coherent philosophy, motivation, or practical objective for overseas study other than a naive desire for Western knowledge. Commodore Perry's expedition, Japan's forced acceptance of the unequal treaties with Western powers, the bombardments of Kagoshima and Shimonoseki, and the overthrow of the *bakufu* in 1868 demonstrated the immediate and practical uses of Western weapons and military technology.

Another motivating factor for overseas study was the promotion of Westernization by Fukuzawa Yukichi. In "Gakumon no Susume" (The Encouragement of Learning), Fukuzawa wrote that "Heaven never created a man above another nor a man below another," so regardless of hereditary background, those "who strive to be educated and are capable of reasoning will earn rank and riches."[15] Fukuzawa's advocacy of "civilization and enlightenment" through the nearly wholesale adoption of Western social and cultural practices inspired many Japanese to read translations of Western books, learn English from foreign teachers in Japan, and, for those with enough money and determination, study overseas. Yet, "Gakumon no Susume" was not published until 1872, and only one of Fukuzawa's works (*Things Western, Seiyō Jijō*) was published before 1868. In addition, nearly all *ryūgakusei* during this era were from the hereditary samurai or nobility. While Fukuzawa's influence on education and *ryūgakusei* of the Meiji era as a whole is beyond dispute, his influence on early *ryūgakusei* was thus probably limited.

Perhaps the most influential motivating factor among the early *ryūgakusei,* which predated both "rich nation, strong army" and "civilization and enlightenment" by more than a decade, was the philosophy and policy advocated by Sakuma Shozan, "Eastern ethics, Western science," which sought to uphold Japan's traditional Confucian political and social order through the utilization of Western science and learning. On the surface, such a combination appears contradictory, but Sakuma did not think so. In his study of political consciousness during the *bakumatsu* era, the historian H. D. Harootunian writes: "Sakuma saw no conflict between his concept of an ethical civilization and the acceptance of Western knowledge, which he understood as a natural concomitant of Neo-Confucianism that would inflict no damage on its governing principles. . . . The principles of ancient sages and Western empirical skills were one and the same thing. Neither was limited to a special country or culture [and] . . . both were accessible to all peoples in all times."[16] Sakuma's theorem appealed to loyalists devoted to restoring the emperor's "traditional" powers and to the *bakufu* who warned of the inevitable necessity of compromising with the West. From China's defeat by Great Britain's superior navy and weaponry in the Opium War (1839–42) until his assassination by anti-foreign *rōnin* in 1864, Sakuma expounded on the need for "Eastern ethics, Western science" through private letters, memorials to the *bakufu,* and in his autobiography, *Seiken Rōku* (Reflections on My Errors). Following W. G. Beasley's view that Sakuma was "the most famous advocate of study of the West" during the *bakumatsu* era, I believe it is evident that "Eastern ethics, Western science" was a major motivating factor for students journeying overseas in the late *bakumatsu* and early Meiji eras.[17]

What previous studies of early *ryūgakusei* fail to point out, however, is that the dichotomy between "Eastern ethics" and "Western science" acted as "a barrier against any serious concern with Western social and political ideas."[18] Expressing an interest in Christianity or political democracy, for example, was often seen as a threat to the traditional, Confucian relationship between ruler and subject. Despite the conflicting policies regarding overseas study during the *bakumatsu* and early Meiji era, Japan's vulnerable political position, Fukuzawa's campaign for Westernization, and especially Sakuma's philosophy of "Eastern ethics, Western science" provided more than enough motivation for overseas study for the early *ryūgakusei.*

The United States at first glance, however, does not seem like the logical choice for such study. In the mid- to late nineteenth century, England, Germany, and France were certainly more impressive military powers than was the United States, and the Netherlands had been the only Western country allowed contact with Japan during the two centuries of national seclusion. Moreover, *rangaku* (Dutch studies) was the original fount of Western knowledge for Sakuma and Fukuzawa—the prophets of Western learning in *bakumatsu* and early Meiji Japan. Nevertheless, the early *ryūgakusei* and their sponsors often chose the United States over other Western countries.[19]

First, it was easier and cheaper to get to the United States, especially after the Pacific Mail Steamship Company began regular monthly service from Yokohama, Kobe, and Nagasaki in 1867.[20] From these three ports, San Francisco could be reached in less than a month. After the Transcontinental Railroad was completed in 1869, it was possible to travel by rail from San Francisco to the East Coast, where nearly all colleges in the United States were located at that time.

Second, it was cheaper to live in the United States than in Europe. Government-sponsored *ryūgakusei* received money only part of the time they were overseas, as did those Japanese who were privately funded. Regardless of their funding source, most students had to rely on American benefactors for at least part of their educational sojourn. Despite the samurai and noble class background of most early *ryūgakusei,* money was a major, constant concern.

Third, American missionaries and teachers in Japan influenced and assisted many prospective *ryūgakusei.* Japanese wanting to learn of the West sought out a foreign teacher if possible, and this was often an American missionary. These missionaries usually taught only English and science, since teaching Christianity was prohibited by law until 1873.[21] It was not uncommon, however, for missionaries to circumvent the law by using the Bible as a text for English-language study. These Americans saw it as their duty to uplift "heathen" peoples—meaning non-Christian, nonwhite, and, therefore, uncivilized peoples—to the spiritual glory and technological progress of Christian civilization.[22] One way to fulfill this duty was to assist young Japanese in attending American colleges, most of which still had strong church affiliations.

Fourth, Japan had a closer relationship with the United States than with any other foreign country between 1853 and the late 1870s.[23] After the revolution against the shogun, Japanese saw themselves living in a "new" country, much as those in the United States did after their own revolution.[24] The Japanese viewed the imperial powers of Great Britain, Germany, France, Russia, and the Netherlands as old regime countries who posed a military threat to Japan, while the United States, despite Perry's intrusion in 1853, was not seen as a military power with imperialist motives. Moreover, Americans in Japan, including those working for the Japanese government, comprised the largest group of Westerners living in the country during the 1860s and 1870s and thus had more personal contact with Japanese than did the nationals of any other Western country.[25]

To Rutgers

Near the end of his life, William Griffis, a prolific author, minister, and Rutgers alumnus, wrote, "New Brunswick was the original Mecca and Rutgers the Holy Place" for Japanese students in America.[26] Griffis's statement, if not his grandiose metaphors, is supported by statistics. Of approximately 250 Japanese college students in America between the 1860s and 1880, at least 38 attended Rutgers College or its affiliated Rutgers Grammar School for at least part of their studies.[27] Fourteen of the 40 or so Japanese who studied in New Brunswick formally enrolled as regular students in one of Rutgers College's two divisions, Scientific and Classical.[28] Four graduated from Rutgers College, 2 of whom were elected to Phi Beta Kappa.* Many of the early *ryūgakusei* who began at Rutgers completed their studies at other colleges in America, as did Kanda Naibu, who stayed at Rutgers less than one year and later graduated from Amherst College.[29] Others finished their education in Japan. For example, Hatakeyama Yoshinari attended Rutgers College for three years before completing his studies at Tokyo Kaiseigakko (later known as Tokyo University). An examination of student biographies indicates that over half of the 40 Japanese who attended either Rutgers College or Rutgers Grammar School graduated from Rutgers College, some other college in the United States, or one of the few colleges in Japan.[30]

Of the 55 Japanese listed in the 1870 U.S. census, 10 lived in the New Brunswick area and were students at Rutgers.[31] As small as this number is, the only larger group of Japanese in the entire country at the time was 22 colonists from Aizu in Coloma, California. New Brunswick may not have been overrun by Japanese students seeking Western knowledge, but Rutgers was certainly the favorite American institution of higher education.

Twelve of the formally admitted, full-time Japanese students at Rutgers College during the 1860s and 1870s enrolled in the Scientific Division.[32] The science curriculum concentrated on agriculture, chemistry, and especially engineering. To advance to these areas, students had to fulfill requirements in arithmetic, algebra, geography, and English grammar.[33] Only 2 Japanese enrolled in the Classical Division, probably because it required courses in Greek, Latin, English literature, and philosophy—a formidable linguistic challenge. Other Japanese studied English and math at Rutgers Grammar School (equivalent to a modern high school) and were allowed to sit in lecture classes at the college.

Rutgers was chartered in 1766 as the eighth college in Great Britain's North American colonies. Though its charter was granted by King George III, Rutgers (then known as Queen's College) was established as an affiliate of the Dutch Reformed Church. By the time the Yokoi brothers enrolled in 1867, Rutgers had become a state college of New Jersey. Nevertheless, it remained affiliated with the Dutch Reformed Church of America, and during the 1860s and 1870s, nearly all faculty and staff were church members. In

*The four graduates were Kusakabe Taro (1870), Hattori Ichizo (1875), Kudo Seiichi (1878), and Matsudaira Tadanari (1879). Kusakabe and Matsudaira were the two Phi Beta Kappa students.

addition, some of the faculty, including William Griffis, were ordained ministers. The college had a full-time enrollment of approximately 50 students in the 1860s and 1870s.[34]

Many of the Japanese who attended Rutgers in the 1860s and 1870s were guided there by American missionaries and teachers in Japan affiliated with the college. The first of these guides was Guido Verbeck, a native of Holland, a naturalized American citizen, and an ordained minister in the Dutch Reformed Church of America who taught English and science in Nagasaki from 1859 to 1868 before moving to Kanagawa and working for the Meiji government as a *yatoi*. Since Verbeck could speak Japanese and was fluent in English and Dutch—the most widely known foreign language in Japan until the end of the *bakumatsu* era—he was in a unique position to influence Japanese about the West. In 1863, the governor of Nagasaki asked him to teach English at a language school. Verbeck's basic texts were the U.S. Constitution and the Bible.[35] A couple of years after sending the Yokoi brothers to Rutgers in 1866, Verbeck helped other Japanese students go overseas.

William Griffis was another guiding influence. While on the Rutgers faculty in the 1860s, he taught the Yokoi brothers, two sons of Prince Iwakura Tomomi, Kusakabe Taro—the first Japanese to graduate from Rutgers College (he was awarded his degree posthumously)—and a few other Japanese students before he left for Japan.[36] He described these early *ryūgakusei* as "equals of American students in good-breeding, courtesy, and mental acumen."[37] Then, from late 1870 to 1874, he taught in Fukui prefecture (formerly part of Echizen domain) and Tokyo. During his sojourn in Japan, he helped a number of students enroll at Rutgers and other colleges in America. His experience with *ryūgakusei* in America, his service as a teacher and missionary in Japan, and his prolific writings on all things Japanese made Griffis one of the most knowledgeable Americans about Japan in the nineteenth century.

Along with Verbeck and Griffis, David Murray, an administrator and a professor of mathematics with an interest in methods of education, helped direct Japanese students to Rutgers College. Murray participated in many of the Japanese extracurricular activities.[38] When Mori Arinori, Japan's chargé d'affaires in Washington, wrote to several education leaders soliciting their advice on "advancing civilization in the East," the president of Rutgers College chose Murray to respond. Murray emphasized the universal education systems of the United States and Germany because "it is cheaper to educate the people than to govern them uneducated."[39] He stressed the need for Western technology and learning and, consciously or otherwise, appealed to Japan's growing sense of nationalism: "Education in a nation means standing and influence among the powers of the earth; it means well-trained officers and soldiers to defend it in times of war; it means ships, and steamboats, and railroads, and commerce; it means cultivation of science, and philosophy, and art; it means the development of a national literature in which the best thought, the inner life, and outward achievements of the nation, shall be embodied."[40] Murray's advice so impressed Mori and other Japanese officials that he was asked to join Japan's new Education Ministry as a special advisor.[41] In this capacity, Murray had an enormous influence on the development of Japan's education system between 1873 and 1879.*

The Diversity of the American Experience

Soon after Mori became Japan's chargé d'affaires in Washington, D.C., in 1871, he solicited *ryūgakusei* already in America to write essays on subjects of interest to them. They responded with comparative essays on science and technology, education, gender, and religion. Given the critical tone of some essays, it is apparent that these student-writers were not aware their essays would be published for an American audience. Nevertheless, they were included the following year in *The Japanese in America,* coauthored and coedited by Charles Lanman and Mori.[42] While all *ryūgakusei* vastly expanded their knowledge of the West, these essays, plus material from the Griffis Collection at Rutgers University, demonstrate the diverse impacts of their American education and experience.

As Joseph Heco did, these students praised American ingenuity. "The world," wrote Inoue Ryoichi, "is indebted to the Americans for the steamboat, telegraph, and many other useful inventions. It may be broadly asserted that whatever had a practical application was studied and improved by them."[43] However, Inoue also believed that the emphasis on practicality had a strong negative impact: it made people too "money-loving" and unappreciative of the arts and philosophy.[44] Americans "should pay more attention to philosophy and the fine arts [because] admirers of wealth," he believed, "are merely practical and inconsistent people."[45] Making a cross-cultural analysis of technology that closely resembled Sakuma's philosophy of "Eastern ethics, Western science," another student felt the "social stagnation and utter decline" of Asia required the "wakening power" of the steamship, railway, and telegraph from the West.[46]

*Other Americans connected to Rutgers College who influenced and guided Japanese students to New Brunswick were the missionaries James Ballagh, Edward Clark, Robert Brown, and Martin Wyckoff as well as Robert Pruyn, a Rutgers alumnus and the American minister to Japan from 1862 to 1865.

Another subject of interest to the all-male *ryūgakusei* was gender relations. One of Griffis's own students was shocked to discover that a Western woman supposedly treated her husband "like a servant."[47] Such a relationship was clearly wrong because "a husband had a right to treat his wife as a maid."[48] Furthermore, this student believed that women who rode horseback in front of men were "very impolite," and the "narrowness of the waists of women" was worse than the shaved eyebrows and blackened teeth of Japanese women.[49]

Others had a different view of gender relations, particularly with the topic of coeducation. Most American colleges were still exclusively male, but many *ryūgakusei* studied at coeducational grammar and preparatory schools before beginning their college studies. Takato Shioji believed coeducation was a positive experience because men and women complemented each other. If men and women were educated by the same schools, the same professors, and the same books in the same classrooms, "the saucy mischievousness of the boys will be tempered by the gentle politeness of the girls, and the fancy and timid-weakness of the girls will take on the primitive simplicity and determined steadiness of the boys; and, at last, a moderate, accomplished, and unblemished virtue and culture will be attained by both sexes."[50] However, he was concerned about the moral consequences of coeducation, lest it make "young gentlemen and ladies too intimate, and occasion objectionable associations."[51] As nearly all early *ryūgakusei* were samurai and interacted almost exclusively with middle- and upper-class Americans during their educational sojourn, it is probably no coincidence that this Japanese student's view of coeducation closely resembled that of his American counterparts.

Mori echoed the belief that coeducation had complementary influences on men and women and advocated its adoption in Japan.[52] Due in part to the experience of *ryūgakusei,* the Education Ministry implemented coeducation as a national policy in the early 1870s.[53] In addition, when the members of the Iwakura mission arrived in the United States in late 1871, they brought along five Japanese girls to live and study in America.[54] Three eventually became the first Japanese women to attend and graduate from American colleges.*

On the controversial subject of Christianity, three writers were laudatory—Takato, Kanda Naibu, and Niijima Jo, writing anonymously—while three others were overwhelmingly critical—Inoue, Toyama Masakazu, and Hayashi

---

*At the time of their arrival in the United States, Tsuda Umeko was eight years old, Nagai Shigeko was ten, and Yamakawa Sutematsu was twelve. Tsuda graduated from Bryn Mawr while Nagai and Yamakawa graduated from Vassar in the 1880s. All three became advocates of education for women in Japan. Tsuda, the daughter of Tsuda Sen, a prominent progressive scholar in the early Meiji era, founded what is now known as Tsuda Women's University.

Tadasu. In a short autobiographical account, Niijima undoubtedly chose to remain anonymous because he announced that he came to America to pursue his "long-cherished idea of becoming a missionary in Japan."[55] Takato praised God for "creating all things and beings" and for giving complementary forms and character traits to men and women.[56] Kanda studied at Rutgers and became a Christian before transferring to Niijima's alma mater, Amherst College in Massachusetts. He described Christmas as "the birthday of Jesus Christ, who came to this world to save sinners."[57]

Meanwhile, Toyama, Inoue, and Hayashi were so critical of Christianity that Lanman issued a warning that they held beliefs "wide of our cherished notions."[58] Although he spent some time at Rutgers before studying law at Harvard, Inoue castigated hypocritical Americans who "consent to pay their pew tax, and to be bored by an occasional sermon on Sunday for appearances sake; but . . . their real god is no Almighty God, but the almighty dollar."[59] Toyama, who studied in England before moving to the University of Michigan, where he received a master's degree in 1876, sarcastically noted that he visited a Catholic church with "two other Japanese pagans." Its priest was "a man . . . who knows perfectly well how to convince the ignorant people like the Irish."[60] In another essay, entitled "Raid on the Missionaries," Toyama opined that "the ignorant have been always the same superstitious, bigoted, and credulous people, no matter whether they are Roman Catholics or Protestants. Thus, although the Swedes and Scotch are the oldest Protestants, yet the superstition and bigotry among their ignorant people has scarcely been surpassed by those of the Spanish or Irish."[61] Toyama's disdain for Christianity in all its forms, combined with his obvious racial prejudices, appears more indicative of a comprehensive antiforeign sentiment than simply a disbelief in Christianity. Few Japanese of the nineteenth century had Toyama's overseas experience, but many shared his sentiments.

These *ryūgakusei* resided in the United States during the Reconstruction Era, a period of controversies about slavery, massacres of American Indians, and acrimonious debate over immigrants, especially Chinese and Irish. One might expect Japanese students, who observed the apparent hypocrisy among American Christians, to comment on these prevailing racial issues in the country that had declared "All men are created equal" as a "self-evident" truth. Surprisingly, only Toyama complained of the "oft-repeated outrages committed upon the Chinamen by the people of the United States."[62] One explanation for this omission is that *ryūgakusei* interacted almost exclusively with middle-class, white, Anglo-Saxon Americans and seemed to have adopted many of their beliefs and prejudices. In addition, these first Japanese encountered only relatively minor discrimination directed toward themselves.

Rutgers *Ryūgakusei* Alumni

Due to their experience in the industrialized West and their study of its political, economic, social, and scientific institutions, the *ryūgakusei* were highly sought after (though not always admired) by a government and a nation undergoing the process of modernization.[63] Many obtained influential positions in government, business, or education after their return to Japan.

Matsumura Junzo, Hatakeyama Yoshinari, and Yoshida Kiyonari were with a group of Satsuma samurai who arrived in England in 1865 and later joined the Brotherhood of the New Life, a Christian utopian colony in upstate New York before studying at Rutgers. After one year, Matsumura entered the U.S. Naval Academy at Annapolis.[64] He graduated from the regular course of studies in 1873 and was commissioned as a captain in the Imperial Navy upon his return to Japan. In 1882 he was promoted to rear admiral, and ten years later to vice admiral.[65] He played a major role in expanding Japan's navy from a handful of ships used primarily for coastal defense into a formidable naval force that helped defeat China in 1895 and Russia ten years later.

Hatakeyama studied at Rutgers College for three years before he left to accompany the Iwakura mission as an interpreter. When he returned to Japan in 1873 after an absence of eight years, the Japanese government hired him to work in the ministries of the interior, foreign affairs, and education. He also became the director of Tokyo Kaiseigakko (later known as Tokyo University) and expanded its Western curriculum. He returned to the United States in 1876 to assist with Japan's exhibit at the Centennial Exhibition in Philadelphia. He died of tuberculosis while returning to Japan from Philadelphia.[66]

Yoshida first studied at University College in London, briefly at the Monson Academy in Massachusetts, and then at Rutgers College before returning to Japan to join the new government. He first served in the Finance Ministry, where he helped negotiate a much-needed $12 million loan from the United States and Europe in 1871. A few years later, he transferred to the Foreign Ministry and succeeded Mori as Japan's top diplomat in Washington. Well liked and well connected in Washington, he persuaded Congress to return America's portion of the Shimonoseki indemnity fund to cash-strapped Japan.* Yoshida also arranged for Ulysses S. Grant's visit to Japan in 1879 and accompanied Grant and his wife, Julia, during their two-month stay.[67] Grant's visit delighted and impressed his Japanese hosts because they believed it significantly expanded their country's international reputation.

---

*The Shimonoseki indemnity was a series of reparation payments made by Japan to Great Britain, the United States, Holland, and France as compensation for Choshu domain's attacks on foreign ships passing through the Shimonoseki Straits in 1863 and 1864.

Of all the early Rutgers *ryūgakusei,* however, Hattori Ichizo of Yamaguchi (formerly part of Choshu domain) appears to have been the most active during his years in New Brunswick. He entered the Scientific Division in 1871, excelled in his studies, and graduated four years later, delivering a commencement speech in Japanese.[68] Especially involved in extracurricular activities, Hattori was elected secretary of the sophomore class and then vice president of his senior class.[69] He also participated in the literary society and the natural history society and was an associate editor of the monthly *Rutgers College Targum.*[70] Probably the first Japanese to demonstrate an interest in what would later be regarded as the American pastime, Hattori served as vice president of the Rutgers College Base Ball Association during his junior year.[71] Upon his return to Japan in 1875, Hattori started work at Tokyo University, first as the vice director of the language school, and then rising to the vice presidency of the university and dean of the Law Department.[72] Around 1890, he left education and served as governor of Iwate, Hiroshima, Nagasaki, and Hyogo prefectures from 1891 until at least 1903, when he became a member of the House of Peers, the upper house of parliament.[73] No doubt Hattori's Choshu connections lead to some of these government positions, but his academic skills and versatile talents also enabled him to contribute to Japan's modernization.

Not all Rutgers *ryūgakusei* contributed their unique skills and experiences so visibly to Japan's modernization. The Yokoi brothers, for example, assumed aliases to disguise their identities. Daihei, the older brother, was known as "Numagawa," while Sahei, the younger one, was called "Sentaro Ise." Reverend John Ferris brought the two Japanese to New Brunswick, but had some trouble finding a rooming house for them because "other boarders threatened to leave if they were taken into the house."[74] He found rooms for them with "two excellent Christian ladies" who cared for the Yokoi brothers "as they would for their own children."[75] The two studied at Rutgers Grammar School for two years before Daihei returned to Japan on account of illness.[76] He helped establish a Western-style school in Kumamoto and sent students to Griffis in Fukui in the early 1870s.[77]

Sahei studied first at the Rutgers Grammar School and then at Rutgers College for a total of three years. He was among the first Japanese selected to attend the U.S. Naval Academy in 1869.[78] During his short stay in Annapolis, he wrote to Maria Van Arsedale, his landlady in New Brunswick, that "all the professors and also the midshipmen have been very kind to us" and he felt "quite contented."[79] Unlike Matsumura Junzo, however, Yokoi was unable to pass the entrance examinations. Dejected at his failure, he returned to Japan and reportedly died soon afterward.[80]

From the perspective of Japanese government officials, even worse than the failure of some individual *ryūgakusei* to contribute to Japan's modernization was that some brought back a belief in Christianity. In 1870, Japan's Foreign Ministry even reminded American diplomats that the government was "desirous that their people be instructed in arts and sciences . . . instead of being instructed in religion."[81] From the perspective of many Japanese officials in the new Meiji government, Christian *ryūgakusei* went beyond the boundaries of "Eastern ethics, Western science" and were a potential threat to the Confucian social and political order.

It does not appear that Japanese students were forced to convert to Christianity by missionaries in Japan or by the colleges they attended in America. Some, however, probably converted out of obligation to their American benefactors. The normally optimistic Griffis later expressed his chagrin that "far fewer than we could wish became personally identified with Christianity."[82] Furthermore, on both a national and a personal level, it was easier to adopt and adapt practical knowledge from the outside—i.e., Western science and technology—than an abstract, outside cultural belief such as Christianity. Nevertheless, some Rutgers *ryūgakusei* did become Christians, and a few even became missionaries who disseminated Christianity into Japan during the Meiji era.[83]

With the exception of five who are buried at Willow Grove Cemetery in New Brunswick, nearly all Rutgers *ryūgakusei* of the 1860s and 1870s returned to Japan. Matsudaira Tadaatsu, however, did not return. Matsudaira Tadaatsu and his brother Tadanari arrived in the United States with the Iwakura mission and began their studies at Rutgers in 1872.[84] After a couple of years, Tadaatsu transferred to Harvard, graduating in 1877. When Tadanari finished his studies in 1879, their father ordered them home. Upon his return, Tadanari obtained a post in the Foreign Ministry. Tadaatsu, however, refused to return reportedly because he desired to put his training in civil engineering to practical use in the United States.[85]

Tadaatsu began working as an engineer with the Manhattan Elevated Railway. While working in New York, he invented the "trigonometer," an instrument enabling surveyors to make quick and accurate calculations.[86] His invention attracted press attention, and as a result, he received and accepted an offer to work as a surveying engineer for the Union Pacific Railway in Wyoming Territory, Idaho, and Montana. He worked in the American West for nearly three years and then moved to Bradford, Pennsylvania. In 1884, he was appointed city engineer of Bradford.[87] He was almost certainly the first Japanese national to hold a civil post in the United States.

He held this position for nearly four years, during which time he married a white woman named Sampson and had two children. After he contracted tuberculosis, Tadaatsu and his family moved to Denver in an attempt to restore his health. He made some maps for the Colorado state government before he died in November 1888.[88] Unlike many *ryūgakusei* who put their education to work by contributing to the Western-style industrialization of Japan, Matsudaira Tadaatsu made his contributions in the United States.

These Rutgers alumni, as well as the rest of the early *ryūgakusei,* then, made "ambitious and earnest reformers, in sympathy with progress and education," as William Griffis notes.[89] They certainly contributed significantly to Japanese Westernization, but they were not wholly responsible for "political reforms" and the abolition of "social abuses," as Griffis claimed in *The Mikado's Empire,*one of the most informative and best-selling books on Japan in the nineteenth century.[90] Along with foreign teachers in Japan, the translation of Western books into Japanese, and the ideas of Sakuma Shozan and Fukuzawa Yukichi, early *ryūgakusei* contributed to Japan by utilizing their cross-cultural experiences and Western knowledge for the promotion of modernization. They were also the vanguard of later *ryūgakusei* who journeyed to the United States in more substantial numbers beginning in the 1880s. Furthermore, their ability to adapt to American society and their pursuit of an education in the United States during the formative era of U.S-Japan relations contributed to the expansion of relations between the two countries.

THREE

Niijima Jo, Japanese Puritan

On July 19, 1864, the merchant ship *Berlin* left the northern Japanese port of Hakodate for China. The ship was subjected to the usual search for contraband by Japanese customs officials the previous evening. Undetected by these officials, however, was a twenty-one-year-old Japanese stowaway. Captain William Savory of Salem, Massachusetts, had agreed to take the Japanese stowaway to Shanghai and arrange for his passage to the United States.[1] In Shanghai, the young man boarded the *Wild Rover,* commanded by Horace Taylor of Chatham, Massachusetts, and owned by Alphaeus Hardy and Company of Boston. Captain Taylor asked the young man's name, to which he replied, "Neesima Shimeta." The name was apparently too difficult for Taylor to pronounce and so he told the young man, "I shall call you Joe."[2] Niijima willingly adopted the English name Joseph and later changed his Japanese given name from Shimeta to Jo.*

*During his lifetime, Niijima Jo and his American friends usually spelled his family name "Neesima" in English. The most accurate transliteration from Japanese *kanji* characters to roman letters, however, is "Niijima."

Niijima Jo would become the most influential Japanese Christian of the nineteenth century. He transformed himself from a frustrated, duty-bound samurai into a fervent, uncompromising, Puritan missionary during his nearly decade-long sojourn in the United States. Niijima was a "Puritan" in two senses of the term: he became a religious descendant of the Puritans who colonized New England in the seventeenth century and were known as Congregationalists by the nineteenth century and he was an advocate of a strict moral code. He then put his American education and strong Christian beliefs to work in an effort to, in his view, spiritually modernize Japan through Christianity.

During his time in America, Niijima regularly corresponded with his benefactors.[3] It is highly unlikely Niijima intended his letters to be published and they are, of course, subjective sources of his experiences, but I believe they are credible sources for two reasons. First, after he returned to Japan in late 1874, he remained just as puritanical and driven to spread Christianity throughout his native country as he had been in the United States. Second, the basic facts of his experiences in the United States have been verified by scholars such as Irwin Scheiner and Watanabe Minoru.[4] Scheiner interprets Niijima's experiences within the development of Protestant Christianity in Meiji Japan, while Watanabe considers him a major Japanese cultural figure. Both scholars devote some attention to Niijima's experiences in America, but they are primarily concerned with his activities and religious beliefs after his return to Japan. I represent and interpret Niijima as one the earliest Japanese residents of America who came searching for a Western, scientific education and for Christian, spiritual education, which he believed to be the foundation of strong nations and of civilization itself.

Frustrations at Home, Desires Abroad

Alphaeus Hardy sent for the Japanese stowaway soon after the *Wild Rover* returned to Boston. Hardy was a well-to-do businessman, a leading member of the American Board of Commissioners for Foreign Missions (an organization of the Congregational Church that sponsored overseas missionary work, especially in Asia and Africa), and a trustee of Amherst College.[5] Captain Taylor told Hardy beforehand that Niijima was interested in Christianity and in receiving an education in the United States. Although Niijima had been tutored in English for a few months in Hakodate and spent one year aboard two ships among English-speaking sailors before arriving in Boston in the fall of 1865, Hardy had difficulty understanding the young Japanese man at their first meeting.[6] Hardy sent Niijima to the Boston Sailor's Home and instructed him to explain in writing his reasons for leaving Japan and coming to the United States. In a grammatically garbled yet revealing statement that took one month to compose, Niijima expressed his frustrations over the lack of opportunities as a duty-bound samurai and his decision to abandon his status—and even his life—to pursue Western education and Christianity.[7]

Niijima was born in 1843 at the Edo residence of *daimyō* Itakura Katsuakira of Annaka domain (now part of Gunma prefecture). His father was Itakura's chief clerk. In addition to studying his native language, like most young samurai, Niijima studied Chinese and the Confucian classics. He became interested in Western knowledge and studied Dutch with a Japanese instructor by the time he was a teenager. However, Itakura and Niijima's own family disapproved of his studying Dutch. Niijima wrote to Hardy that they laughed at him and even beat him for this.[8]

One day in the early 1860s, Niijima went to Edo Bay and saw a large Dutch warship. "While I look upon her," he recalled, "one reflection came down upon my head: that we must open navy, because the country is surrounded with water, and if foreigners fight to my country, we must fight with them at sea."[9] In other words, Niijima claimed that he had suddenly arrived at the same conclusion many other samurai had: Japan could maintain its independence and protect itself from the Western military powers only by using Western technology. Niijima had undoubtedly seen Western warships in Edo Bay, but it is doubtful that he suddenly arrived at this conclusion. Kawanishi Susumu has suggested (though not conclusively demonstrated) that Niijima learned of the importance of Western science and technology from friends and acquaintances from Annaka domain.[10] Regardless of how Niijima came to such a conclusion, his statement to Hardy indicates that by 1865 he realized that Western science would be needed to maintain Japan's independence.

Meanwhile, he apparently realized that the presence of Western foreigners in Japan was having another serious consequence. Ever since the unequal treaties of the late 1850s the "price of everythings got high, [and] the country got poorer than before, because the countrymen don't understand [how] to trade with foreigners."[11] *Bakufu* officials were well aware of this situation and complained to the U.S. government that "prices of articles of general consumption are daily advancing, owing to extensive exportation to foreign countries."[12] American officials in Japan agreed that foreign merchants were damaging the Japanese economy. Townsend Harris, the first American minister to Japan, estimated that the prices of export articles in the Edo and Yokohama areas had risen more than 300 percent from 1859 to 1861.[13] To protect the country from Western military and economic power, Niijima wrote, "We must go to foreign countries, we must know to do trade, and we must learn foreign knowledge."[14] Clearly, Niijima's views on Japan's relationship with the West during the *bakumatsu* era closely resembled those of many samurai familiar with the ideas of Sakuma Shozan and Yokoi Shonan.

Bakufu officials were more cognizant of Japan's position in the world and less obstinate than Niijima realized. From 1862, as we have seen, they permitted small numbers of loyal samurai to venture overseas as students to gain technical knowledge. They understood the connection between Western technical knowledge and strengthening Japan. Indeed, by the early 1860s, the philosophy of "Eastern ethics, Western science" was so influential that Sakuma himself was an advisor to the *bakufu*.

Niijima did what he could to arm himself with Western knowledge. After learning the rudiments of the Dutch language, his *daimyō* reluctantly allowed him to attend the naval school run by the *bakufu* in Edo. Here Niijima learned physics, astronomy, and mathematics. In addition, he read books on Western history and religion as well as fiction, including a Japanese translation of Daniel Defoe's *Robinson Crusoe*.[15]

As the story of a young Englishman who embarks on a trading voyage but winds up marooned on an island for more than two decades, *Robinson Crusoe* whetted young Niijima's appetite to learn of the West. "It created in me a desire to visit foreign lands," Niijima later wrote.[16] However, Sukehiro Hirakawa's observation that *Robinson Crusoe* "induced him to become a Christian" is questionable.[17] *Robinson Crusoe* includes an abundance of Christian introspection, but the material had probably been excised in the Japanese translation Niijima read. Moreover, Niijima himself never mentioned the religious perspective of *Robinson Crusoe*. Nevertheless, *Robinson Crusoe* certainly demonstrated Niijima's "yearning for information about foreign affairs."[18]

Another book Niijima mentioned was a Chinese translation of Elijah Bridgeman's *Historical Geography of the United States*.[19] After reading it several times, Niijima wrote, "I was wondered so much as my brain would melted out from my head, picking out President, Building, Free School, Poor House, House of Correction, and machine working, etc."[20] Niijima reported to Hardy that he was impressed by the system of American government as compared to that of the shogun: "I thought that a governor of our country must be as President of the United States. And I murmured myself that, O Governor of Japan! Why you keep down us as a dog or a pig? We are people of Japan. If you govern us you must love us as your children. From that time I wished to learn American knowledge."[21] Niijima's wide-eyed enthusiasm for "American knowledge" was frustrated by travel restrictions: Edo was still off-limits to foreigners (except certain diplomats) and Japanese needed *bakufu* permission to enter the foreigners' section in nearby Kanagawa and Yokohama. Thus, he was apparently unable to find someone to teach him more about America.

The most influential book Niijima read before his departure for America was a Chinese translation of the Christian Bible he discovered at a friend's house.[22] Cognizant of the edicts against Christianity in Japan, he read the Bible at night to avoid detection. "I understood God at first," Niijima wrote to Hardy, "and he separated the earth from firmament, made light upon the earth, made grass, trees, creatures, fowls, fishes. And he created man in his own image, and made up a woman, cutting a man's side bone. After he made up all things of universe, he took a rest. That day we must call Sunday or Sabbath day. I understood that Jesus Christ was Son of Holy Ghost, and he was crossed [crucified?] for the sins of all the world; therefore we must call him our Saviour."[23] The sabbath became so important to Niijima that he soon refused to travel on it.[24] John 3:16 became his favorite Bible verse: "For God so loved the world that he gave his only begotten Son, that whosoever believeth in him should not perish, but have everlasting life."[25] After his first encounter with the Bible, Niijima began learning English from a Japanese teacher in Edo and planned to go to the open port of Hakodate to find someone who could teach him both English and the Bible.[26] Niijima's reported reaction to his initial encounter with the Bible suggests that he essentially converted himself to Christianity before leaving Japan.

Why did Niijima, a young samurai, embrace the forbidden religion of the West? In the mid-1880s, he explained to the American Board of Commissioners for Foreign Missions that samurai,

> being far better educated than any other class[,] . . . are more susceptible to Christian truth. Being strictly trained to faithfulness to their feudal masters, they will be more faithful to the Master of masters, if He is clearly known to them. . . .
>
> Yea, this may be the people, whom God has chosen from the beginning to be the foremost cross-bearers to lead their fellow countrymen to that blissful eternal city.[27]

In other words, Niijima believed the structural similarities between the two disciplines could allow the traditional samurai faith to be transferred to the Christian faith.

Similarly, Irwin Scheiner interprets samurai's (and former samurai's) conversion to Christianity as a replacement for the time-honored, East Asian ethical value system and worldview of Confucianism.[28] During the political and social turbulence of the bakumatsu and early Meiji eras, many samurai saw Confucianism as a failure. Confucianism had confined them to a frustrating hierarchy of values and obligations. With the collapse of the *bakufu* regime and the samurai world, Confucianism became increasingly untenable. As a result, some samurai grasped the forbidden religion of the powerful West as a viable worldview that gave political, social, and psychological meaning to their existence.[29]

One major interpretive element of Scheiner's study, however, is questionable. He argues that "the young samurai who were to convert were clearly opposed to the political trends of the time" and were opposed to the Satsuma- and Choshu-dominated central government.[30] As we have seen, several *ryūgakusei* from Satsuma and Choshu either converted to Christianity or attended Christian-affiliated schools and colleges. In the 1880s, the central government became noticeably less tolerant of Christianity and cracked down on political dissenters, some of whom were Christian converts. But many young samurai of Satsuma and Choshu who witnessed the collapse of the old order in the 1860s were nearly as likely as were their political opponents to transfer their loyalties for *daimyō* and family to God and Christianity.

As for Niijima, he reported to Hardy that his reading material and especially his desire to learn about Christianity alarmed his family and *daimyō*. His family refused him permission to go to Hakodate. Committing a serious transgression against Confucian loyalty and obedience, he gathered some clothes and books and left for Hakodate anyway. While awaiting a ship to take him to the West, Niijima studied Christianity and English from Nicolai Kasatkin, a Russian Orthodox priest, in exchange for reading and teaching the *Kojiki* (Record of Ancient Matters).[31]

Niijima's explanation of the reasons behind his departure so moved Alphaeus Hardy and his wife, Susan, that they became Niijima's life-long friends and benefactors. Niijima spent most the following nine years (1865–74) in Massachusetts—the heart of New England Puritanism—and the Hardys paid for all of his living and education expenses. The correspondence between them shows that Niijima regarded the Hardys as parents, and they regarded him as a son.[32] Niijima referred to them as "my fostering parents" and usually referred to himself in English as "Joseph Hardy Neesima."

A Puritan Education

Hardy soon enrolled Niijima at Phillips Academy in Andover, Massachusetts, a preparatory school for well-to-do families. Niijima concentrated on improving his English skills and also studied natural science and mathematics. Hardy arranged for him to board with Mary Hidden and her brother David in their farmhouse just outside Andover. In a letter to a Japanese friend who helped him escape from Hakodate, Niijima confided that the Hiddens treated him "as one of their own family, and I am very much enjoyed to stay here."[33] During his time in the United States, Niijima wrote over forty letters to Mary Hidden, more than to anyone else except the Hardy family. The correspondence between Niijima and Mary Hidden is typically about daily activities and other mundane matters, with no hint of romance, probably because Hidden was twenty-four years older than Niijima. One can surmise, however, that Mary Hidden, in addition to Susan Hardy, filled a maternal void for Niijima, whose own mother was far away and whom he would not see again for many years. For Mary Hidden, who appears to have been confined to the farmhouse by the necessity of taking care of her chronically ill (possibly disabled) brother, the young Japanese samurai-turned-Christian probably enlivened an otherwise dreary existence. Also living at the Hidden farmhouse were Ephraim Flint and his wife, Orilla. Flint was a local high school teacher and a student at the Andover Theological Seminary. He often helped Niijima with English, mathematics, and other academic subjects, while Orilla taught Niijima about Christianity and the Bible.[34]

In the fall of 1867, Niijima entered Amherst College. Ephraim Flint wrote to Professor Julius Seeyle that Niijima had studied English, was a "fine mathematician," and "a most faithful and diligent student of the Bible."[35] During his four years at Amherst, Niijima studied Latin and Greek and was especially interested in geology and botany.[36] He tutored his roommate, William Holland, in Japanese, while Holland helped him with Greek. Niijima and Holland also spent many hours exploring western Massachusetts for its variety of plants and rocks. Although his primary interest was religion, Niijima majored in science.

Even though he had come to the United States during an era of scientific and religious controversy over Charles Darwin's theory of biological evolution—the *Origin of Species* first appeared in 1859—there was little chance that Niijima's scientific studies would detract from his fervent, new-found religious belief. Throughout the nineteenth century, Amherst College was staunchly dedicated to preserving the Puritan faith. Indeed, its founding in 1821 was in reaction to the perceived "apostasy of Harvard," which had begun welcoming Unitarian students and faculty a few years earlier.[37] Geographically removed from the secular and Unitarian influences of Boston and eastern Massachusetts, the people of Amherst and western Massachusetts were adamantly Yankee and Puritan. According to Otis Cary, Niijima's edu-

Niijima Jo. (Davis, *Maker of New Japan*)

cation "happened to be in the most direct and typical orthodox Congregational tradition which New England could offer."[38]

Furthermore, his mentor at Amherst College, the philosophy professor and ordained minister Julius Seeyle, inundated his classes with Puritan ethics, evangelical religion, and Calvinist theology.[39] Attending Amherst in the mid-1880s, Uchimura Kanzo described Seeyle as a "venerable man" who "believed in God, in the Bible, and the power of prayer to accomplish all things."[40] Seeyle's Puritan credentials propelled him to the presidency of the college in 1875. As a result of this intellectual and religious atmosphere, Niijima's Christian faith became more focused, uncompromising, and Puritan at Amherst.

For example, in April 1868 he received the first message from his family since his departure from Japan four years earlier. Niijima Tamiharu asked his son to return to Japan because of the civil war between the Satsuma- and Choshu-led forces and the shogun's *bakufu*. The townspeople of Edo, including Niijima's family, feared an attack by the anti-*bakufu* forces. Furthermore, Niijima's mother was ill, supposedly because of her son's long absence.[41]

Niijima refused to return home. He told Susan Hardy, "God is present everywhere, so I trust He will take care of her [his mother]," and he did not wish to be killed in "such a barbarous war." Instead, he wanted to prepare "to battle against Satan, taking the helmet of salvation and the sword of the Spirit, which is the word of God."[42] Significantly, when faced with a conflict between his traditional, East Asian worldview of obligations and responsibilities and his new worldview of an absolute faith in God and Christianity, Niijima chose the latter.

His faith was also evident during an unexpected encounter in November 1867 with two Japanese students attending Monson Academy preparatory school, also in Massachusetts.[43] Since this was the first time that Niijima had met any of his countrymen in over three years, it was disconcerting at first for him to speak in Japanese. But, he reported, he was soon speaking his native language "better and faster than they did."[44] Niijima was obviously glad to see his countrymen after such a long period in the West. He showed them around Amherst and the college and stayed up late at night talking with his visitors. Yet, he was apparently concerned more with their religious beliefs than with anything else. He asked them to read about Christ's resurrection in the twenty-eighth chapter of Matthew, he explained the doctrine of the Trinity, and he prayed for them. In a letter to Orilla Flint, he proudly claimed victory: "They found their sins; they found also the way where they meet their Master. They have humble and beautiful spirits, just as little children. . . . I am thankful that God bless my countrymen so much, and I hope the time will soon come for Gospel to bear fruit in the barren and unmatured land."[45] In this chance meeting, Niijima seemed more interested in proselytizing than socializing—a pattern he maintained for the rest of his life.

During his sojourn in the United States, Niijima's religious views, including his determination to bring Christianity to Japan, were fittingly expressed in a lengthy letter he wrote at Amherst to an American acquaintance at Princeton Seminary. In Niijima's view, Buddhism, the religion of the Japanese "uneducated class," was "degraded idol worshipping." Educated Japanese believed in Confucianism, which contained good ethical instructions, but "did not have the power to change hearts." Niijima judged the "moral character" of Japanese to be "rather low," though a "little higher than that of Chinese." Nevertheless, he believed the moral state and spiritual faith of the Chinese were progressing because Christianity was being brought to them by missionaries.[46]

Niijima had a strong desire to bring Christianity to Japan after preparing himself in America. He told his Princeton acquaintance, "I feel always sad when I think of my countrymen, and I am willing to submit myself entirely to the will of God. I think it is his will that all nations should know him."[47] And in remarks that he probably never expressed to his benefactors, all of whom were involved in missionary efforts, he criticized Americans for not doing enough to Christianize Japan. Americans were willing to give money for missionary efforts, he wrote, and were interested "to hear something about the heathens."[48] But they were not willing to separate themselves from their families and bring the gospel to Japan and other "heathen lands."[49] In the margin of the last page of this letter, Niijima asked rhetorically, "Is there anyone who is willing to go to Japan to save the people from perishing?"[50] Aware that his criticism might upset some missionaries, he asked his Princeton acquaintance to keep the letter private.

Niijima was graduated from Amherst College in July 1870. For the commencement ceremonies, he was asked to give an oration in Japanese.[51] Language studies were a vital component of a college education in nineteenth-century America, so it was not uncommon to demonstrate this linguistic ability by speeches in foreign languages at commencement. Indeed, Niijima's speech was not the only foreign language speech that day. The salutary address was in Latin, and another commencement speech was in German.[52] Niijima's speech, however, was obviously the first of its kind at an American college's commencement ceremony. One newspaper reporter wrote that the novelty of the speech caused the audience to applaud "as heartily and judiciously as though every word had been thoroughly understood."[53] The most significant distinction of Niijima's graduation was overlooked at the time, however. He and Kusakabe Taro of Rutgers College were the first Japanese students to graduate from an American college.

During the following summer Niijima considered becoming a naturalized American citizen. Since Christian missionary work was still legally prohibited in Japan, friends advised him to become an American citizen because it would afford him U.S. consular protection when he returned to his native country.[54] But Niijima decided not to do so, as he believed it would seriously weaken his influence with his fellow Japanese.[55]

To prepare himself for missionary work in Japan, Niijima entered the Andover Theological Seminary in the fall of 1870 and spent four years there. His most important experience during these years, however, was with officials of the new Japanese government. Soon after Mori Arinori was posted to the United States as Japan's top diplomat, he sought out Niijima and the Hardy family.[56] Mori offered to have the Japanese government reimburse the Hardys for all the money they had spent for Niijima's education and living expenses.[57] Because Niijima believed that he would then be obligated to the Japanese government, he asked Hardy to refuse. Mori also asked Niijima to return to Japan to help establish a school system based on the American one. Niijima favored such a plan, but refused to work for the Japanese government because he believed it would hinder his religious work.[58] Despite Niijima's rebuffs, Mori provided him with a Japanese passport and persuaded his superiors in Tokyo to grant official permission to the former stowaway to remain in the United States to complete his studies.[59]

In February 1871, Niijima agreed to meet with Mori and Education Commissioner Tanaka Fujimaro of the Iwakura mission, then in Washington, D.C.[60] Before departing for Washington, Niijima told Ephraim Flint he would "stand up for Christ before the heathen embassy" of Japanese officials.[61] As Niijima's English skills had substantially improved during his years in America, Mori offered him a position as Tanaka's interpreter during the commissioner's tour of schools and colleges in the eastern United States. Niijima initially turned down the offer. Moreover, his haughty behavior may have irritated the officials. He pompously told Tanaka that he had never received government funding, nor would he accept such funding because he refused to become a "slave" to the Japanese government.[62] He emphasized that he was not associated with the twelve other Japanese students who had been summoned to Washington at the same time. He went to great pains to stay physically apart from these students and refused to participate in their discussions.[63] In a letter to the Hardys, he explained this behavior as his method of remaining "a free man in Christ."[64] Undeterred, Tanaka still wanted him as an interpreter. Niijima finally agreed after making it clear he was doing so as a favor and that he expected to be paid for his services.

Soon after Tanaka began his tour of schools in the eastern United States, he asked Niijima to accompany him to Europe for the same purpose. Tanaka, Mori, and other Japanese officials agreed to his every demand and treated him only with courteousness and respect. Yet Niijima imagined that Tanaka might "possibly lay a snare to catch and take me back to Japan" as the government's "slave."[65] Mori, Hardy, Seeyle, and others had to convince Niijima that there was no such scheme. Reluctantly, he agreed and took a one-year leave of absence from Andover Theological Seminary to assist Tanaka and the Iwakura mission.[66] After recuperating from a bout of rheumatism in Germany, Niijima returned to Andover in 1873 and graduated the following year. At the graduation ceremonies, Niijima gave a commencement speech in English about his mission entitled "The Preaching of Christ in Japan."[67]

Throughout 1874 Niijima prepared to return to Japan with the support of the American Board of Commissioners for Foreign Missions (ABCFM).

Established in 1810 in Salem, Massachusetts, the Congregational ABCFM sent missionaries to convert the peoples of Africa and Asia to Christianity. In a testimonial statement, Niijima told the ABCFM he had been raised "in the faith of Buddhism, and was also instructed in the moral precepts of Confucius. Afterwards the former became offensive to me and the latter were unsatisfactory."[68] He related the story about how he had come across a Chinese translation of the Bible and claimed that he immediately knew God "from the hour I read his word."[69] He offered himself as a missionary in Japan for "the need of my country, and love for perishing souls."[70] To questions from the ABCFM on the importance of Christian doctrines, Niijima replied that "the leading doctrines of the Scriptures are: the existence of one true God, inspiration of the Scriptures; the Trinity; the decrees of God; the freedom of the will; the total depravity of man; the atonement; regeneration; justification by faith; the resurrection of the dead; [and] the final judgement."[71] Assured of Niijima's sincerity and theological beliefs, the ABCFM immediately appointed him a corresponding member of their Japan mission. In this capacity, Niijima preached his first sermon in May 1874 in Lexington, Massachusetts. The subject was John 3:16, Niijima's favorite Bible verse.[72] He had previously spoken many times at many churches, but this was his first formal sermon.

In September he was formally ordained as a Congregationalist minister.[73] A few Japanese had been ordained as Catholic priests in the late 1500s and early 1600s before the national seclusion edicts prohibited Christianity, but Niijima appears to be the first Japanese minister of a Protestant denomination.

While preparing to return to Japan, Niijima traveled to Plymouth, Massachusetts, and saw "that famous Rock and a few relics of the Pilgrim fathers."[74] He also attended the annual meeting of the ABCFM in Rutland, Vermont, and announced his desire to establish a Christian college in Japan.[75] However, the ABCFM—which included his benefactor, Alphaeus Hardy—thought the plan too ambitious. According to Hardy's son Arthur, the ABCFM was expanding its missions throughout the world at the time and felt it had to first concentrate its resources on evangelical work in Japan before undertaking major—and much more expensive—projects, such as building a Christian college.[76]

Niijima departed Boston for San Francisco by train in mid-October 1874. A fellow passenger purportedly told him there was no sabbath west of the Mississippi River, but Niijima refused to travel on the Christian day of rest.[77] He spent one Sunday at Green River, Wyoming, among some frontier settlers. He tried to speak of Christianity, but found them to be "white heathens" who were primarily interested in swearing and drinking.[78] He also met some Chinese laborers "living like pigs."[79] Seizing the opportunity to proselytize, he told them about the "Christian truth" until two replied, "We believe . . . Jesus Christ is our Saviour."[80] He regarded the non-believing Chinese as "dirty, ignorant, and degraded" gamblers.[81]

His remarks on these Chinese workers were reminiscent of those he had made after an encounter three years earlier with Chinese workers at a shoe factory in North Adams, Massachusetts. Aware of the prejudicial impact of a widely reprinted poem by Bret Harte, he reported to Susan Hardy that he did not want to be mistaken for a "heathen Chinee" while in North Adams.[82] In a sweeping generalization, he added that Chinese were content simply with "accumulations of the almighty dollar" while Japanese were "craving after the knowledge and ideas of the Western civilization."[83] As anti-Chinese prejudice among Japanese was not significant until the first Sino-Japanese War of 1894–95, Niijima's encounters with Chinese in America suggests, as do those of Joseph Heco and some *ryūgakusei,* that he had adopted some of the prevailing racial prejudices white Americans.

Niijima's other notable experience during his transcontinental railway journey was an encounter with Mormonism. He stopped at Salt Lake City—the Mormon capital and major supply center for those headed to the Pacific West—to meet with Brigham Young. Young, unfortunately, was ill, but Niijima was able to spend some time with Orson Pratt, one of the Twelve Apostles of the Church of Jesus Christ of Latter-day Saints. According to Niijima, Pratt led him on a tour of the tabernacle, a Mormon school, Salt Lake City Hall, and other sights.[84] Niijima was impressed with Pratt. He regarded the apostle as "the ablest theologian and preacher among the Mormons. He answered all my questions very obligingly."[85] Niijima was not impressed with Mormonism, however. When Pratt asked Niijima if he was interested in preaching Mormonism, he replied, "I should preach the Gospel which I find in the New Testament and nothing else."[86] "I know what Mormonism is," he wrote to Seeyle, "and am glad that I am not one of them."[87] Although he spent most of a day with Pratt, it is doubtful Niijima learned much about Mormon life and theological beliefs. In his letters to Hardy and Seeyle, Niijima did not object to any specific aspects of Mormonism, such as the controversial practice of polygamy. Yet, with widespread controversy concerning Mormonism in nineteenth-century America, and given Niijima's propensity to criticize those with different religious beliefs, his admiration for Pratt and tame criticism of Mormonism is rather surprising.

In San Francisco, Niijima boarded the Pacific Mail Steamship Company's *Colorado* bound for Japan. During the passage across the Pacific, he judged his fellow passengers' "chief aim for this life" by whether they observed the sabbath.[88] On December 6, 1874, Niijima returned to Japan, ten and a half years after he had secretly left as a stowaway. He was elated to see his parents and other family members after such a long separation. Instead of settling down and catching up on lost time, however, the first thing he did upon arrival at his parents' home was burn all their Buddhist and Shinto religious objects. He began his Christian missionary work by preaching to his family.[89]

Niijima's Legacy: Doshisha and the Expansion of Christianity

Niijima immediately began preaching to other families, eventually traveling around the country to speak to groups of Japanese interested in Christianity or America.[90] Within one year of his return, he founded a Christian school in Kyoto, the historic capital of traditional Japan. He named the school Doshisha, meaning an association of "one mind" or "one common purpose."

At first the school consisted of a handful of students who met in Niijima's living room. The central government's prohibition on Christianity had been repealed in 1873, but anti-Christian regulations issued by the local Kyoto government, protests from Buddhist priests, and less-than-enthusiastic support from the ABCFM nearly turned the struggling school into a short-lived failure.[91]

With some behind-the-scenes assistance from Tanaka and Mori, a determined Niijima kept the school alive. By 1880, Doshisha had a theological department, a collegiate department, and a girls' school. In 1888 the school became Doshisha University. By 1890, a preparatory school, a hospital, and a nurses' training center had been added, and the university consisted of twenty buildings. Furthermore, there were 740 students—498 of whom claimed to be Christians—at Doshisha by 1890.[92] More than one hundred years later, Doshisha has long been recognized as one of Japan's premier private universities. Niijima died of rheumatism on January 23, 1890. Three days later, over four thousand people attended the funeral in Kyoto honoring the memory of this dogmatic, Puritan Christian in a country where Confucianism, Buddhism, and Shinto dominated the moral and religious beliefs of the vast majority of Japanese.[93]

Niijima Jo's lengthy and successful adaptation to nineteenth-century American society was due in large part to the American benefactors who provided him with financial and moral support in the hope that the young Japanese would help spread the word of God to his native land. Through this support and his own determination, Niijima was transformed from a frustrated young samurai bogged down by the traditional obligations and responsibilities of his class into a fervent Christian missionary. His early interest in "Eastern ethics, Western science" led him to question the efficacy and even the morality of the traditional East Asian worldview of Confucian ethics and Buddhist religious customs. Although this transformation was probably not as sudden as he had depicted, he did become a determined missionary who sought to expand Christianity in nineteenth-century Japan because it would lead, he believed, to the spiritual modernization of the nation.

FOUR

From Satsuma to Utopia

Sameshima Naonobu and Yoshida Kiyonari returned to London in the spring of 1867 from their first trip to the United States and excitedly told their fellow Satsuma *ryūgakusei* about meeting a charismatic Christian leader whom they called "Faithful." "Faithful" was Thomas Lake Harris, the Father, Primate, and Prophet of the Brotherhood of the New Life. According to one account, Harris had a profound, uncanny effect on his two Japanese visitors. When he preached to them in New York, one cried. The right arm of the other began to tremble and continued to do so for weeks afterward. Sameshima and Yoshida said they had physically felt God's presence inside their bodies through Divine Respiration. Before meeting Harris, they regarded Christianity as just one among many absurd superstitions of the West. Afterward they read the Bible, prayed to God, and felt themselves drawn closer to the Heavenly Father—and Harris.[1]

Sameshima, Yoshida, and seventeen other young samurai from Satsuma who studied English, Dutch, and Western military technology in Kagoshima and Nagasaki had been selected by their *daimyō* and secretly sent to England in 1865 to expand their knowledge of Western science and technology and learn what they could of Western society.[2] During the spring and summer of 1867, thirteen returned to Japan while six journeyed to the United States and became members of the Brotherhood of the New Life—a Christian, spiritualist community—and participated in the nineteenth-century utopian quest for individual and social perfection. So began one of the more bizarre cross-cultural encounters between Japan and the West in the nineteenth century.

Although utopian communities may not have had a direct, significant impact on the vast majority of Americans—or Japanese visitors—this does not mean Americans were indifferent to utopian ideas. For example, Edward Bellamy's *Looking Backward,* an 1888 novel depicting a utopian Boston in the year 2000, was one of the most popular and influential works of nineteenth-century American literature.[3] Utopianism was clearly part of the social fabric of the country.

Searching for Perfection in Nineteenth-Century America

Inspired by the predominantly Protestant, evangelical revival known as the Second Great Awakening of the late eighteenth and early nineteenth centuries, reform movements, new religions, and utopian communities multiplied dramatically in nineteenth-century America. Oneida Community, Amana Society, Shakers, Aurora Community, Harmony Society, Zoar, and Brook Farm were among the approximately one hundred utopian communities that either began or began to flourish between the Revolution and the Civil War. According to the historian Ronald Walters, utopian communities were truly radical because they "aimed at creating a totally new order rather than improving the old one," as did reform movements and most new religions.[4] Because of their radical goals, however, utopian communities were not very popular and, with some noteworthy exceptions, lasted only a few years at most. The Harmony Society and Amana Society (Society of True Inspiration) lasted between eighty and one hundred years, while the Oneida Community lasted for thirty-three years. The Shakers, who first arrived in America in 1774 from England and are formally known as the United Society of Believers, still have a handful of members in Sabbathday Lake, Maine.

Almost all these societies took as their role model Thomas More's sixteenth-century imaginary island of Utopia, an ideal, flawless society governed entirely by reason.[5] According to Robert V. Hine, the nineteenth-century incarnations were composed of "a group of people . . . attempting to establish a new social pattern based upon a vision of the ideal society and who have withdrawn themselves from the community at large to embody that vision in experimental form."[6]

The creation of utopian communities in America was motivated by two fundamental forces. First, as a reaction against established religious institutions and the sinful influences of society, religious ideals drove fellow believers to live in association with one another.[7] Some communities were originally European separatist and pietist groups seeking refuge from dominant churches. For example, the Harmony Society, Amana, and Zoar were originally German separatist groups whose members desired to live according to their belief in "primitive Christianity," while the Shakers began as a small, sectarian society in Manchester, England. Furthermore, nearly all religious utopias formed around a charismatic leader whose heterodox theology served as the foundation of the community.[8]

Second, many utopian communities were founded as a secular reaction to the "mechanization, overcrowding, and poverty" that developed as a result of industrialization.[9] People attracted to secularist utopias sought refuge from the dehumanization of the factory system and capitalist competition. Seymour R. Kesten distinguishes this group of utopias devoted to "secure happiness in this world" from religious utopias, which "sought eternal joy in the next world."[10] However, like their religious counterparts, members of secular utopias lived and worked in association with fellow believers.

The line of demarcation between religious and secular utopias was not always clear, especially for those utopian communities that endured. The Brotherhood of the New Life, for example, gradually became less religious and more secular after its move to California in the mid-1870s, while the Oneida Community, Amana, and the Shakers included commercial enterprises that exist to this day. Whether religious or secular, utopian communities "promised a stable, morally perfect environment in which a person could find meaning and serve the cause of human uplift. Things did not always work that way, but the prospect was an appealing one in a time of great uncertainty and change."[11] The motivation for joining a utopian community obviously varied from individual to individual. However, to serve the cause of human uplift, to find meaning in oneself, and to create a new, ideal society, one had to take a great leap of faith in joining the "morally perfect environment" of a utopian community.

In return for personal and economic sacrifice, utopian communities offered the idealized values of human perfection, the spirit of brotherhood, order, unity of mind and body, experimentation, and group coherence.[12] Yet, a combination of personal conflicts, family pressures, financial difficulties, loss of faith, and especially the unattainable, radical goal of replacing the existing social order resulted in the departure of many adherents from utopian communities, which, in turn, led to their demise. Nevertheless, utopian communities did have an impact on their adherents that is difficult to estimate. Those who joined a utopian community and failed to find contentment or direction in their lives may have left more disillusioned than ever before. The self-discipline required for maintaining one's faith, for performing labor, and for obeying the rules necessary for sustaining the order of the community, however, undoubtedly contributed to the success of many former utopians.

Thomas Lake Harris and the Brotherhood of the New Life

Thomas Lake Harris (1823–1906) had both the aura and the credentials of a patriarchal leader of a nineteenth-century Christian utopian community. Tall and thin, with a flowing beard attached to a stern, messianic face, he usually dressed in formal black clothes. Before establishing the Brotherhood of the New Life in 1860, his life had taken some curious turns. He grew up as a strict Calvinist, yet Harris became a Universalist pastor in his early twenties. He also became a devotee of spiritual clairvoyance and then cofounded a religious utopia in Mountain Grove, Virginia, which he and his followers designated the original Garden of Eden. By the late 1850s, Harris had become a self-appointed leader of American Swedenborgianism. The Brotherhood of the New Life was founded upon Harris's adaptation of this philosophy.[13]

Emanuel Swedenborg (1688–1772) spent the first half of his life attempting to prove the existence of God through science.[14] After receiving a divine revelation in 1743, which Swedenborg claimed, "opened my sight into the spiritual world and enabled me to converse with spirits and angels," he sought to authenticate the Bible through a mixture of theology and spiritualism.[15] Harris's biographers defined his esoteric theology as a similar system of "revelation from angelic spirits" in which "further revelations could follow and out of which a spiritual science would grow."[16] Like the Swedish scientist and mystic who was his inspiration, Harris believed there were three levels of reality: physical, spiritual, and celestial.[17] Through hypnotic trances, Harris communicated with the celestial and spiritual worlds.

Harris's theology encompassed two doctrines. First, God was both male and female, "the Divine Woman one with the Divine Man, Christa one with Christas—the Divine Twain-One," as he explained it.[18] Because of God's nature and lack of need for sexual union, humans could reclaim the original, unspoiled world and personally draw closer to God through chastity: "God is the Infinite Chastity."[19] Harris claimed to have been chaste since

1855, and, according to one scholar, "there is no serious evidence against his word."[20] Celibate marriage was permitted for his followers, and most evidently followed this doctrine since few residents of Brotherhood of the New Life colonies produced children.[21]

Second, "Divine Respiration" would save people from the corrupt environmental and social influences of the physical world. In a one-hundred-page treatise on the subject, Harris wrote that for true believers, "[God's] breath may enter us. We then breathe again, respiring in God, and as He gives Himself in the warm, inflowing life, we experience the facts of a Supersensual Existence; the Living One demonstrates His direct presence by direct inbreathing force."[22] Divine Respiration could be experienced through prayer. In addition, the experience was dependent upon the sense of "self-abnegation and self-surrendery" of the applicant.[23] Sameshima Naonobu and Yoshida Kiyonari undoubtedly comprehended little of Harris's esoteric theology during their first encounter with him in New York. However, they reportedly felt "some change in their breathing, as if He filled their lungs, and they have at times a certain fluttering or trembling of the heart, as if their whole system were touched by the influence of His presence in them."[24] Such a physical sensation may well have been the result of nervousness, fear, or admiration, but they believed it to be the presence of Divine Respiration.

Shortly after Sameshima and Yoshida returned to England from America, Harris arrived in London to meet with his publisher and British adherents of the Brotherhood of the New Life, including Laurence Oliphant. Son of a wealthy Scot, Oliphant was a part-time journalist, part-time politician, and full-time adventurer in the physical and metaphysical worlds. Thirty-eight years old in 1867, he had visited or lived in Europe, the Middle East, India, North America, and Asia. Six years earlier he was appointed first secretary of the British Legation in Edo. He served in this post for less than one week before anti-foreign *rōnin* broke into the legation and nearly hacked him to death.[25] After recovering from his wounds, Oliphant returned to England and was elected to Parliament. He befriended the nineteen Satsuma *ryūgakusei* after they arrived in 1865 and told them about Thomas Lake Harris, whom he had met a few years earlier.[26]

Harris's visit to England in the spring and summer of 1867 came at a time of financial difficulty for the Satsuma *ryūgakusei* studying in that country. They had been taking courses at University College, London, and traveling in Europe since their arrival.[27] By the spring of 1867 they were running out of money. Harris offered free passage to the United States, room, board, and additional education to any who would join his Brotherhood of the New Life colony in New York.[28] Of the nineteen Satsuma students, six accepted—Mori

Arinori, Matsumura Junzo, Hatakeyama Yoshinari, Yoshida Kiyonari, Sameshima Naonobu, and Kanaye Nagasawa.

Scholars have emphasized financial need, the desire for more Western education, Mori's increased interest in the United States, and Oliphant's influence in their decision to join the Brotherhood of the New Life.[29] They may also have been simply mesmerized by an unorthodox, yet charismatic religious leader. In addition, their search for Western science and knowledge had expanded into a search for new values, new meanings, and spiritual refuge from the turmoil of the *bakumatsu* era.

Commodore Matthew Perry's forceful entry and demands for a treaty in 1853 had thrown Japan into a state of political and social turmoil. A large, powerful, *tozama* domain from the south, Satsuma was one of two domains that led the challenge against what it regarded as the *bakufu's* capitulation to barbarians. In 1863, British warships bombarded Kagoshima—Satsuma's capital and home of most of the Satsuma students who would journey to England.

By 1867, after two years in England, these students realized that *bakufu* control in Japan was nearing an end, as was their traditional worldview. To them, "Eastern ethics, Western science" was no longer a satisfactory policy, especially since their interests had expanded to include the cultural and social spheres of Western knowledge. At nearly the same time as Niijima Jo and some other *ryūgakusei* had become interested in Christianity, these samurai sought spiritual meaning and refuge in the Brotherhood of the New Life.

According to a lifelong adherent, Harris believed that "the old Princely Nobility of Japan" were well disposed to promoting Divine Respiration.[30] "He earnestly entertained this hope mainly because in the old Shinto religion and traditions the worship of the Divine Mother [Amaterasu] is the central most inspiring influence; who from Her high alter, Fusiyama [Mount Fuji] . . . rules supremely over the hearts of all the Japanese people."[31] Whether the Japanese who joined the Brotherhood of the New Life understood this supposed connection between Harris's Divine Mother (who also embodied the Divine Father) and the Shinto goddess Amaterasu, the legendary creator of Japan, is unknown. It is likely, however, that the Japanese made this connection to Harris, and it thus represents their own effort to understand Harris's esoteric theology. Furthermore, nearly all of the Japanese who joined the Brotherhood of the New Life were samurai from Satsuma, a leading domain that represented itself as the champion of Japan's traditional values and beliefs.

Furthermore, Harris's conception and practice of Divine Respiration bears a resemblance to *zazen,* the silent meditation practice of Zen Buddhism. In *zazen,* one sits cross-legged, with straight posture and regulated breathing, and empties the mind (*mushin*) of all thoughts with the goal of attaining personal peace and enlightenment. Harris and his adherents believed that Divine Respiration—attaining a state of self-abnegation—could be physically felt during prayer at his church services or suddenly felt while at rest.[32] Some religious scholarship claims that in addition to this outward resemblance, "the paths of Christian mysticism and Zen meditation concur with each other on many points of experience."[33] Although Zen Buddhism had "an enduring spiritual influence" in Satsuma since the sixteenth century, we do not know for certain whether the *ryūgakusei* practiced it or noticed any resemblance between *zazen* and Divine Respiration.[34] A related item of suggestive evidence is provided by Oliphant, who wrote to a friend that Divine Respiration was "quite demonstrative" among the Japanese members of the Brotherhood of the New Life.[35]

Another possible metaphysical connection is provided by Wallace Winchell's intriguing comparison of Harris's esoteric mysticism to that of Tibetan Buddhism.[36] Harris's belief in angelic spirits, such as the Divine Mother, is comparable to the "projective mysticism" of the thirteenth-century Tibetan poet and saint Milarepa.[37] And, like Zen, Tibetan Buddhism is a form of Mahayana Buddhism. These comparisons led Winchell to conclude that "Orientals felt at home" in the Christian, utopian community of the Brotherhood of the New Life.[38]

These connections are more suggestive than demonstrative, but there is no doubt that Harris had a tremendous influence upon the Satsuma students from the start of their relationship. This influence was paternal, asymmetric, and spiritual. Yet, the Japanese also influenced Harris. We can discern this influence in an essay entitled "Japan: How a Nation May Enter the Divine Path," which Harris wrote shortly after he met the Satsuma students in England. In it, he declared he had "solved the problem of Japan": "The policy is this: that [a] Damio will declare himself neutral and a peacemaker in all Japanese conflicts. He will accept the New Life; take the advanced Japanese who are receiving the truths and establish a Military College! He will concentrate the entire revenue to the one end of organizing a Japanese Divine Army."[39] Harris also wrote that he planned to form a Brotherhood of the New Life community in Japan, where he would "devote all the powers for the regeneration of the Japanese individually and Japan collectively, making it an open breathing people."[40] Furthermore, he claimed,

> I have penetrated to the internal morals of the court of Satsuma, and I am disgusted with the brutality, the arrogance, and the dishonesty of the older politicians. They are scoundrels, having no love of their country

> and professing politics as so-called Christians profess religion. The hope of Japan is in the young men. The old feudal system of Japan is rotten at the heart and very weak. . . . From the general wreck and ruin of Japan some province must be saved if possible; this being reorganized will serve as a nucleus for the resurrection of the nationality.[41]

This unpublished essay represents Harris's first written thoughts on Japan. His "solution" obviously originated from his new Japanese adherents. At this time Satsuma was fighting to overthrow the shogun and the *bakufu* government—the "old feudal system"—by claiming the emperor as its leader. These anti-*bakufu* forces were led by young, middle- and lower-rank samurai. Harris's "solution" for Japan thus reflected Satsuma's own political and military campaign to overthrow the *bakufu* and establish a new Japan anchored by the emperor.

Life at Brocton Colony

First located in Wassaic and then in Amenia, New York, the Brotherhood of the New Life colony had just moved to Brocton, New York, when Mori, Matsumura, Yoshida, Sameshima, Hatakeyama, and Nagasawa arrived in August 1867. The 2,000-acre Brocton Colony, located on the shores of Lake Erie, was within the region of western New York state known as the burned-over district, so-called for its evangelical hub of religious forces and social movements that swept the United States in the first half of the nineteenth century.

The principal profit-making business of the colony was its winery. Hundreds of acres were planted with Salem grapes. The colony's massive, arched-stone wine cellar could hold up to fifty thousand gallons of wine.[42] Its wines became popular throughout the eastern United States and England. The colony also had a dairy farm, a steam grist mill, a restaurant, a general store, a nursery, a hotel, and a printing shop.[43]

At its height, the Brocton Colony had nearly two hundred resident adherents, with perhaps two thousand nonresident adherents in the United States, Scotland, and England.[44] Herbert Schneider and George Lawton provide a partial membership list that includes descriptions of social and economic status, regional background, religious affiliation, and gender of the adherents at Brocton Colony in the late 1860s.[45] American members came from across the country, but most hailed from the South. Among the predominant Protestants were no Catholics, a few Shakers, one Quaker, and the Buddhist Japanese. More than half the members were women. Furthermore, most were from upper-class backgrounds, and some were extremely wealthy.

As did many utopian communities, the Brotherhood of the New Life required new members to become "completely free of the world" by turning over all their money, property, and worldly possessions to its common fund.[46] Laurence Oliphant and his mother, for example, gave more than $100,000, while Jane Lee Waring contributed as much as $500,000 of her family's fortune. Despite their wealth and upper-class backgrounds, all members worked at menial jobs in the colony. Among the samurai-class Japanese, Mori cooked and helped with laundry and housework, while Nagasawa helped take care of the dairy cattle. The other Japanese worked in the fields, tending the grape vines. In general, Brocton Colony operated on the basis of labor equality.

Harris, however, did not perform much manual labor.[47] He spent most of his time administering the colony, writing, and lapsing into convulsive, hypnotic trances during which he absorbed painful "spheres"—emanations originating from the outside world—and "states"—emanations caused by backsliding members of the Brotherhood of the New Life.[48] Harris dictated all work duties, living arrangements, and punishments, many of which came in the middle of the night. He even separated wives from husbands and children from parents "until [their] affection was no longer selfish."[49] On many Sundays, Harris gave sermons for his adherents, local townspeople, and curiosity seekers.

The colony received more Japanese during the fall of 1867. In late September, Tanimoto Hyoemon and Nomura Ichizuke, both from Satsuma, arrived via San Francisco.[50] According to Oliphant, these two Japanese dreamed of Harris their first night at Brocton even though they had not yet met him.[51] After admitting that their past lives were wicked and sinful, Nomura and Tanimoto were put to work washing clothes, washing dishes, and making beds.[52] A few days later, Oliphant reported that the two "work hard every day with great delight" and had found "the greatest happiness" at the colony.[53]

Three more Japanese from Satsuma joined the Brotherhood of the New Life in November 1867.[54] Enatsu Sosuke, Nire Kaganori, and Sadamoto Yuichi were *ryūgakusei* at Monson Academy in Massachusetts.[55] By the end of 1867, probably no more than twenty Japanese resided in the entire United States.[56] At least thirteen were from Satsuma, and eleven of these resided at Brocton Colony. While the original Japanese adherents knew Harris before they joined his utopian community, there is no evidence to suggest the seven others did. They left Japan to search for new knowledge and perhaps a new worldview, and somewhere along the journey they heard of their brethren in Brocton.

As was typical of Harris's philosophy, the Japanese did not live together in Brocton. Soon after their arrival, Nagasawa was placed in Harris's mansion while Sameshima and Yoshida lived in a house with Oliphant and at least three other members.[57] The five Japanese who arrived in the fall lived together in a house with two other community members, while Mori, Hatakeyama, and Matsumura appear to have lived in a house near Harris's mansion.

Their daily routine was to rise early and attend to the tasks assigned them by Harris. All the Japanese worked in the grape orchards at least part of the time. After a schoolhouse was constructed on the grounds in November 1867, the Japanese spent half the day working and the other half studying English and the Bible. One month after the arrival of the first six Japanese from England, Oliphant wrote that they were "every day hard at work with their countenances beaming with delight. . . . They say they never knew what happiness was before."[58] One and a half years later, a reporter met Nagasawa at Brocton studying his Bible after completing the day's work. The reporter informed his readers that "the tawny Pagan actually seemed to have been born again, physically as well as spiritually. How happy he was! His face shone as though it were reflecting rays from the sun of righteousness."[59] These secondhand accounts likely overestimate the Japanese adherents' spiritual joy and contentment, but there is no clear indication that they had become disillusioned during the first few months of their sojourn at Brocton.

Nevertheless, all of the Japanese except for Nagasawa began to leave in the late spring of 1868. According to Oliphant, they desired to return to Japan "on patriotic grounds" to assist in the overthrow of the *bakufu*.[60] One of Harris's most devoted adherents later claimed they "did not leave from any disaffection" with the Brotherhood of the New Life.[61] However, a growing disbelief in the utopian community apparently did contribute to the departure of some Japanese. So, too, did a personal quarrel and the desire for better education opportunities.

Mori and Sameshima left suddenly on June 8, 1868. They wrote their remaining comrades that they left "simply to discharge our duty to our country."[62] They explained, "We still feel, yea more and more, inexpressibly grateful towards the Lord one Heavenly Father, for He is through his beloved servant T.L. Harris working so infinitely and so mercifully for the salvation of all the inhabitants on the globe."[63] They knew some Japanese at Brocton "felt somehow badly towards the teachings" and wanted to emphasize that their departure did not indicate a loss of faith.[64] The Japanese at Brocton Colony were not aware of everything going on in their home country, but occasional letters from home and newspapers kept them abreast of major developments. For Sameshima, Mori, and five others, support for their domain probably provided their principal motivation for leaving the colony.

In addition, their departure was prompted in part by an internal quarrel. After one of Harris's sermons, the Japanese agreed to a group confessional to cleanse their consciences by revealing their personal faults; such group confessionals (or mutual criticisms) were common in utopian communities. Mori and Yoshida got into a bitter personal argument that "broke out fiercely."[65] According to one version, the quarrel was over the hypothetical question of supporting Japan or the United States in a war between the two countries.[66] Mori and Sameshima tried to make peace in their departure letter by confessing they had gone "beyond the limit of our dignity" and asked their countrymen to "freely or generously pardon us."[67] In a letter written three years later that revealed he was still a believer in Harris and still upset with Yoshida and others, Mori fumed that "in the minds of those deserted Japs" the Brotherhood of the New Life was nothing more than "many strange superstitions."[68]

For Yoshida, Matsumura, and Hatakeyama, another reason for departure was the lack of educational opportunities at Brocton. They had studied languages and Western technology in Nagasaki and London, so Brocton's hastily constructed schoolhouse was hardly the place to advance their secular education. Matsumura left Brocton shortly before Sameshima and Mori, studied for a couple of months at Monson Academy, then attended Rutgers College. Yoshida and Hatakeyama, who left Brocton shortly after Sameshima and Mori, went straight to Rutgers. William Griffis later credited Rutgers with saving the three from "the hands of some socialist fanatics"—in other words, from the Brotherhood of the New Life.[69] By midsummer, seventeen-year-old Nagasawa was the only remaining Satsuma samurai at Brocton Colony.[70]

The new Meiji government, dominated by officials from Satsuma and Choshu, sent Mori back to the United States in early 1871 as Japan's first chargé d'affaires in Washington. He brought along Arai Osui, a defeated samurai whom he had befriended in Japan. Arai was from the northern domain of Sendai and had fought against the Satsuma and Choshu armies. With the *bakufu*'s defeat, Arai had become a disillusioned, frustrated samurai and had turned to Christianity. Arai met Mori just before the latter left for his diplomatic assignment and pleaded to be taken to the United States to study Christianity. Mori readily agreed, paid Arai's passage and expenses, and brought him to Brocton in early 1871. Arai immediately became one of the most devoted adherents of the Brotherhood of the New Life.[71]

Fountaingrove

Harris decided to move the Brotherhood of the New Life's colony to California in 1875, primarily to take advantage of the superb climate for grape cultivation.[72] In February 1875, the advance team of Harris, Nagasawa, Arai, and two others arrived in San Francisco to find suitable land. Japan's consul general in San Francisco, Takagi Saburo, helped them select an area just outside of Santa Rosa.[73] Harris purchased 400 acres immediately and added nearly 1,600 more acres within a few years, thereby encompassing most of the small valley to the north of town. He chose Fountaingrove as the name for the new colony.

Fountaingrove included a vineyard, an orchard, a dairy farm, a horse stable, a botanical garden, a printing press, and a Victorian-style mansion.[74] Of the approximately twenty residents, Nagasawa and Arai were the only Japanese. Nagasawa was in charge of Fountaingrove's most important worldly and scientific business, the vineyard operations. By now, Nagasawa had become Harris's "right hand man" and was "looked up to and respected, in the highest possible degree, by all the brothers and sisters."[75] In time, Nagasawa became known around Santa Rosa as the "samurai of the vines," the "grape king," the "Prince," and the "Baron" of Fountaingrove.[76] Arai was kept busy running the printing press that churned out Harris's many publications.

Despite some setbacks, including Oliphant's break with Harris and departure for Palestine to form his own utopian colony, Fountaingrove evolved into a harmonious colony and a profitable business enterprise. Fountaingrove wines were popular in both the United States and England. Harris cultivated good public relations by allowing curiosity seekers and picnickers on the grounds. Furthermore, Fountaingrove's huge economic contribution to the small community of Santa Rosa endeared Harris to many of the townspeople and local newspapers.

The harmony was shattered in 1891 when Harris was stridently attacked in Margaret Oliphant's widely read biography of her brother, who had died in Palestine three years earlier. She portrayed Harris as "a mercenary schemer and false prophet, a diabolical agency for evil."[77] She depicted her brother, not surprisingly, as "the martyr who had given up everything."[78] This prompted the editor of the *San Francisco Chronicle* to hire Alzire Chevaillier, a professional muckraker, to infiltrate Fountaingrove.

Chevaillier and her mother stayed at Fountaingrove for nearly six months before "escaping" and exposing Harris as "the greatest imposter of the age," whose "weird and sensuous teachings" made him the prophet of a sexually promiscuous "den of infamy."[79] Alluding to polygamy, she represented the Brotherhood of the New Life as "worse than Mormonism."[80] Chevaillier's lurid exposés were widely reprinted in American and British newspapers. She also gave lectures on Harris's "Spiritual Harem" for a fifty-cent admission fee.[81]

Chevaillier reported that Nagasawa "lords it over the one servant given over to his tender care" and "fervently believes that the sun rises and sets in

Harris."[82] Meanwhile, poor Arai had to work day and night in the printing shop and was supposedly "the most abject slave of the whole colony," who stayed with the utopian community "by his blind, simple faith."[83] Chevaillier asked Arai how he endured his hard life at Fountaingrove and, according to her, he cryptically replied, "I am only a guest on this planet."[84] She also claimed the two Japanese joined the Brotherhood of the New Life because of an "Edenic bath system"—presumably a *sentō,* or traditional Japanese communal bath in which men and women bathed together.[85]

Although she was at Fountaingrove for nearly six months, Chevaillier's stories in the *San Francisco Chronicle* were based completely on hearsay and innuendo.[86] She presented no real evidence that adherents of the Brotherhood of the New Life were sexually promiscuous or that the sixty-eight-year-old Harris was coercing women into his bed. Prominent citizens of San Francisco and Santa Rosa came to Harris's defense with testimonials in local newspapers.[87] Yet, Harris was flustered by the scandals and decided it was time to return to New York. Before departing, he married his longtime assistant and companion, Jane Lee Waring, now sixty-five years old, and placed Nagasawa in charge of Fountaingrove.[88]

Harris sold Fountaingrove for $40,000 to five members of the Brotherhood of the New Life, with the provision that the last survivor would inherit all of the property. That turned out to be Nagasawa.[89] Fountaingrove became less utopian and more commercial under Nagasawa's direction, though Nagasawa's devotion to Harris remained steadfast. He became a good friend and business associate of George Shima, generally considered the most successful Japanese immigrant farmer in America.[90] Nagasawa and Harris made plans to establish a huge colony of Japanese immigrants in a forty-mile-long by ten-mile-wide area on the west coast of Mexico in the late 1890s.[91] They failed to attract the necessary funds, however, so the plan never materialized. Shortly afterward, Arai apparently committed some unknown "indiscretions."[92] Harris gave Arai his "Divine Forgiveness," but the Sendai native decided to return to Japan after spending nearly thirty years with the Brotherhood of the New Life in America.[93] According to Gaye LeBaron and Ivan Hall, Arai spent the rest of his life as an independent Christian missionary in Japan.[94] By 1900, thousands of Japanese were immigrating to the United States, especially to California, but Nagasawa was the sole remaining Japanese member of the Brotherhood of the New Life.

His closest friend seems to have been Edwin Markham. Born in Oregon City, Oregon, Markham grew up in northern California and started his career as a schoolteacher and education official in El Dorado County. He later moved on to New York and became a nationally known poet.[95] Markham believed that Harris was "the most advanced man since Sakyamuni [Buddha]" and had been a frequent visitor at Fountaingrove.[96] In their later years, Markham and Nagasawa corresponded regularly, reminiscing about the good old days at the colony, and complaining about the severe economic effects of Prohibition on Fountaingrove's main industry. For example, Nagasawa wrote to Markham in 1921: "What changes since that time [1875]. At one time there were over twenty people lived on this place. Now I am the only one of that group; as you know most of them have passed away. . . . I have gone through many trials and tribulations; at times I had become almost in despair in continuing to carry on the duty assigned for me by our Beloved Father."[97] Fortunately, Nagasawa had apparently managed to avoid growing prejudice toward Japanese and Japanese Americans. Although a citizen of Japan, he had become the legal owner of Fountaingrove before California's Alien Land Law of 1913 and was not directly affected by it. In the 1920s, he told Robert Park of Stanford University that he was well aware of racial prejudice against Japanese "in other parts of California," but he lived "on the best of terms with his neighbors" in Santa Rosa.[98] Nagasawa died at Fountaingrove in 1932, sixty-five years after coming to the United States.

Former Utopians

Several Brotherhood of the New Life colonists—Matsumura Junzo, Hatakeyama Yoshinari, and Yoshida Kiyonari—went on to Rutgers College and careers in the military and government. Sameshima Naonobu returned to Japan with Mori Arinori in 1868 and initially held a position as an interpreter in the Meiji government. He quickly rose through the ranks and was made chargé d'affaires in London while Mori held the same post in the United States. He later served as Japan's minister to France before reaching the position of vice minister in the Foreign Ministry.

Although Mori's career in Japan's Foreign Ministry and Education Ministry is well known, some of his specific contributions and ideas during the "civilization and enlightenment" period of the 1870s can be traced to his experience at the Christian utopian community.

In "Life and Resources in America"—a Tocquevillean description and analysis of American society, circa 1870, and meant for a Japanese audience—Mori included some revealing observations about religion.[99] He believed that the Bible carried "a tremendous power of freedom and justice, guided by a combined force of Wisdom and Goodness."[100] Since Mori was an official in a government that still legally prohibited its citizens from converting to Christianity, his praise of the Bible is stunning.

Mori Arinori. (Lanman and Mori, *Japanese in America*)

In another revealing passage, Mori wrote that Americans were "entirely free to choose any kind of religion. . . . They all believe in one eternal and incomprehensible Diety, and in the immortality of the soul."[101] Freedom to choose one's religion and the incomprehensibility of God, which implied the necessity of a prophet to lead believers, likely came more from his utopian religious experience than from mainstream Christianity.

As were some *ryūgakusei,* Mori was unimpressed with hypocrisy and American claims of Christian superiority. He opined that "a very large proportion of the American people are known by the name of Christians, and yet a great many things are said and done by them, which do not accord with the principles of their own Bible. . . . It would be a very wonderful thing, should the time ever arrive, when the so-called Christians, who profess the faith, but do not live up to it, shall cease to boast of the superiority of their religion."[102] Mori's praise of Christianity's practical virtues and criticism of the hypocrisy of some of its adherents was more in the vein of a secular analysis than Niijima's testimony of strong personal, puritanical faith.

More important than Mori's analysis of American Christianity, however, was his influential role in Japan's repeal of anti-Christian edicts dating back to the early seventeenth century. In his privately published but widely distributed essay "Religious Freedom in Japan: A Memorial and Draft of Charter," Mori argued that "in all the enlightened nations of the earth, the liberty of conscience, especially in matters of religious faith, is sacredly regarded as not only an inherent right of man, but also as a fundamental element to advance all human interests."[103] A couple of years later, he wrote that "religious matters should be left to the individual preference of the people."[104]

However, Mori clearly favored Christianity, and strongly implied in "Religious Freedom in Japan" that it would be in Japan's national interests to adopt Christianity: "The society which receives the addition of a new knowledge, and a power of the character of the Christian morality and faith, will necessarily better its condition by becoming both wiser and stronger. This is no mere assertion. It is fact, demonstrated by the history of the nations of the earth, among which none have so grandly advanced to the head of civilization as those whose religion has been Christianity."[105] This statement reveals Mori's nationalism and that his exposure to industrialized Great Britain and America had convinced him, at least temporarily, of the widespread Western assumption that only Christian nations were civilized. The Japanese government, of course, was not about to adopt Christianity as its national religion no matter how desperately it wanted to enhance its reputation. But, clearly influenced by Mori's essay, Japanese officials did decide to remove the edicts against Christianity in 1873, four months after its publication.[106]

Mori's influence did not stop with religion. With Fukuzawa Yukichi, he cofounded *Meirokusha*—a group of elite Japanese who advocated Japan's adoption of Western liberalism during the "civilization and enlightenment" era of the 1870s.[107] Mori also proposed the elimination of the Japanese language in favor of English because the latter was "the language of commerce, science, and art."[108] This radical proposal was never adopted, but English quickly became a mandatory subject in Japanese schools, including the Commercial Training School (later Hitosubashi University) founded by Mori and Fukuzawa.[109] While not exclusively due to his connection with the Brotherhood of the New Life, his promotion of liberalism was clearly the result of his overseas experiences and faith in Western progress.

His continued faith in the Brotherhood of the New Life, however, is a mystery. As soon as he arrived in America as Japan's chargé d'affaires in early 1871, he journeyed to Brocton to take Arai to the colony. He stayed with Arai, Nomura, and Nagasawa for five days and discussed with Harris the possibility of taking two members of the colony to Washington as housekeepers.[110] After a Sunday service by Harris, Nagasawa recorded in his diary that Mori "seemed extremely affected by the sermon."[111] Yet, there is no evidence that Mori ever visited Brocton again during his three years as Japan's diplomatic representative in Washington. Nor is there any evidence that he kept in touch with Nagasawa and Arai when the utopian colony moved to California. Unfortunately no letters between Mori and his brother between July 1866 and June 1868—the very time Mori and his brethren from Satsuma became interested in Harris and resided at Brocton—survive. Ivan Parker Hall believes that Mori or family members destroyed these letters because of anti-Christian edicts or "to cover up an embarrassing incident out of his youthful past."[112] It is possible, as Hall suggests, that Charles Lanman and other Americans in Washington convinced Mori that he should not be associated with the fringe Brotherhood of the New Life because he needed to project the image of a proper, responsible diplomat.[113] This explanation is not totally satisfying, however, since nineteenth-century America was full of communal, religious utopias and no stigma would be attached to membership. Mori was unusual because he was a *Japanese* participant in a utopian community in the United States, not because he was simply a participant in such group. The evidence—or rather the lack of evidence—suggests that Mori distanced himself from Harris and the Brotherhood of the New Life sometime after 1871, but his reason for doing so remains unknown.

After his duties as a diplomat in the United States, England, and China, Mori's liberalism of the 1870s gave way to the more conservative, nationalist atmosphere of 1880s. In the Education Ministry, he pushed for centralized control of the school system. He demanded that schools, teachers, and students become more physically and mentally disciplined servants of the nation and the emperor. However, he objected to the heavy infusion of Confucian ideology with Shinto worship promoted by other government officials. On February 11, 1889, the same day the Meiji Constitution was promulgated by the emperor, Mori was assassinated by a former samurai who cited Mori's disrespect to the Shinto gods on a recent trip to the Grand Shrines at Ise.

The Brotherhood of the New Life and the Japanese

According to the anthropologist Clifford Geertz, "Religious concepts spread beyond their specifically metaphysical contexts to provide a framework of general ideas in terms of which a wide range of experience—intellectual, emotional, moral—can be given meaningful form."[114] Although Thomas Lake Harris had become Kanaye Nagasawa's and Arai Osui's benefactor, teacher, and father and had provided them with the framework of a new worldview and a spiritual refuge in an expanding, industrial, and international world of uncertainty, it is difficult to ascertain Harris's effect on the other Japanese members of the Brotherhood of the New Life. Mori Arinori, Matsumura Junzo, Yoshida Kiyonari, Sameshima Naonobu, and Hatakeyama Yoshinari had returned to Japan by the early 1870s and eventually held important positions in the Meiji government. As young, well-educated samurai from Satsuma, they were already in line to obtain positions in the central government after the overthrow of the *bakufu* in 1868. Further, their experience with the Christian utopian community was only one phase of their overseas experience. Their years of study and travel in Europe and the United States were likely more important to their impact on Japan's modernization than was their time with Harris. Nevertheless, their participation in the Brotherhood of the New Life contributed to their search for Western skills and values that, indirectly or perhaps directly, contributed to the work of modernizing Japan in the second half of the nineteenth century.

FIVE

The *Gannenmono*, Eugene Van Reed, and the Emergence of Japan-Hawaii-U.S. Relations

At about the same time that Mori Arinori and Sameshima Naonobu returned to Japan, a group of 148 Japanese departed for the Kingdom of Hawaii, where they would work as laborers on sugar cane plantations for four dollars per month. Because 1868 was the first year of the Meiji era, this group became known as the *Gannenmono* (literally, "first year people"). Evidence indicates that they were the first organized group of laborers to leave Japan since the early seventeenth century.

In 1935, Ishii Sentaro, the last surviving member of the *Gannenmono*, told an interviewer that he joined the group because working for four dollars per month was a "splendid offer," though he did not know what sugar cane was or where Hawaii was located. Fighting between the *bakufu* and anti-*bakufu* forces in the Kanto region also impelled him to leave. Despite the grinding, back-breaking work in the hot sun, he nostalgically recalled that "the plantation treated us very nicely." When the initial three-year contracts for the *Gannenmono* expired in mid-1871, Ishii and the majority of this group of laborers chose to remain in Hawaii rather than return to Japan.[1]

Many scholars view the *Gannenmono* as the vanguard of exploited Japanese immigrant laborers in Hawaii and North America. Eugene Van Reed, the man at the center of the *Gannenmono* controversy, has generally been depicted as a scheming, deceptive American merchant who kidnapped Japanese off the streets of Yokohama and sold them into semislavery to work on Hawaiian sugar cane plantations run by tyrannical, whip-wielding whites. Furthermore, the resulting diplomatic controversy among the governments of Japan, the United States, and Hawaii has often been cited as the only explanation for the Japanese government's subsequent prohibition of labor emigration.[2]

Although the *Gannenmono* did begin Japanese labor immigration to the West, their hardships and the chicanery of Eugene Van Reed have been exaggerated, especially in the context of their lives in Japan.[3] Scant attention has been paid to the dire economic and physical situation of many Japanese in 1868. Furthermore, a close examination of the effort to create a labor force reveals that these Japanese immigrants and Eugene Van Reed ushered in the three-way relationship among Japan, the United States, and Hawaii.

Hawaii, the American Frontier

Even though the U.S. government did not formally annex the Hawaiian Islands until shortly after the Spanish-American War at the close of the nineteenth-century, Americans had exercised a commanding influence in the islands since the mid-1840s through its sailors, planters, merchants, and missionaries. Ships and sailors from New England had dominated Pacific whaling from the beginning of the nineteenth century. Because of its geographic proximity to the American mainland and to North Pacific whaling areas, Hawaii became the natural base for these operations. New England ships plying the China trade also stopped for supplies in Hawaii. To use but one statistic as an example, between 1845 and 1854, 4,402 ships from the United States stopped in Hawaii while only 405 ships from all other countries combined put in during the same period of time.[4]

After the 1850s, whaling declined in the Pacific Ocean, primarily because cheaper kerosene oil replaced whale oil as a fuel. Yet, Americans managed to retain their dominance of Hawaii's economy because they had begun establishing sugar cane plantations as early as the 1830s. California and the West Coast's growing population in the second half of the nineteenth century, thanks to the Gold Rush, provided Hawaii with its largest market for sugar and served as a major market for Hawaii's other agricultural products. American merchants in Honolulu and San Francisco dominated Hawaiian trade.

In addition, American Protestant missionaries, most of whom were sent by the American Board of Commissions for Foreign Missions, vastly outnumbered their British Anglican and French Catholic spiritual rivals. And when Hawaii's first legislature convened in 1845, four of the five members of King Kamehameha III's cabinet were Americans. American influence and presence in Hawaii was so pervasive by the 1840s that one scholar claimed that "commercially and spiritually the Hawaiian Islands were as much a part of the American frontier as were Oregon and California."[5]

Japan's connection to Hawaii was not nearly this strong or influential, but it came earlier. Shipwrecked Japanese sailors had drifted to Hawaii long before any European or American had set foot in the islands.[6] Just four years after *bakufu* officials reluctantly signed the Kanagawa Treaty with Commodore Perry in 1854, they appointed a commercial agent in San Francisco to buy and ship goods from Hawaii and the United States to Japan. This agent, Charles Wolcott Brooks, also operated a trading firm that funded Hawaiian sugar cane plantations.[7] And when the U.S. Navy ship *Powhattan* stopped at Honolulu carrying the shogun's ambassadors on their way to Washington, D.C., in 1860, Japan and Hawaii began discussing a treaty.

Japan and Hawaii finally agreed to the Treaty of Amity and Commerce in 1871. Signing the treaty on behalf of the Hawaiian Kingdom was the American minister to Japan, who had been temporarily appointed as Hawaii's minister to Japan.[8] Eugene Van Reed had been appointed years earlier as Hawaii's diplomatic representative to Japan by King Kamehameha V, but Japan's Foreign Ministry refused to accept his signature on the treaty because of "his discourteous action towards this Japanese government."[9]

Eugene Van Reed: Adventurer, Merchant, Diplomat

The Gold Rush brought James Van Reed and his sixteen-year-old son, Eugene, to San Francisco in early 1851. Success as a gold dust broker allowed James to bring his wife and three daughters from Reading, Pennsylvania, within a couple of years. He later became a prominent real estate agent and developer in the Bay Area.[10]

Eugene's interest in Japan began in the early 1850s when he met Joseph Heco (then known as Hikozo) in San Francisco.[11] Van Reed learned some Japanese from Heco, and the two had a portrait taken together in 1858 just prior to Heco's return to Japan.[12] Van Reed caught up with Heco in Hawaii, and the two arrived in Japan together in early 1859.

Van Reed's motivations for going to Japan are not fully known, though his friendship with Heco was certainly a major factor. He had also obtained a position with Augustine Heard and Company, an American trading firm with business in China and Japan. Van Reed's sister Margaret later wrote that he was "urged by the spirit of adventure."[13] Since his own father had journeyed to California during the early, adventurous years of the Gold Rush, perhaps Eugene was equally inspired to see exotic Japan, newly opened to the West.

Both Van Reed and Heco obtained positions at the U.S. Consulate in Kanagawa, but Van Reed quit his position after six months to devote his full attention to Augustine Heard and Company. During this era of political uncertainty, intrigue, assassinations, and war, Van Reed ran a thriving business in arms and munitions with the shogun's *bakufu* officials as well as with samurai from the anti-*bakufu* domains of Choshu and Satsuma.[14] In 1865 or 1866 he left Augustine Heard and Company and established his own trading company in Kanagawa. He published a Japanese-English phrase book and later a newspaper called the *Moshiogusa.*[15] In 1870, he established the Van Riido Kaisho rice exchange in Tokyo soon after the city was opened to foreigners.[16] Van Reed's business activities gained the attention—though not always the admiration—of many people during the fourteen years he lived in Japan. One admirer was American Minister Charles De Long, who told Secretary of State William Seward in a letter that "Mr. Van Reed is one of our most respectable citizens, a merchant here in good standing."[17]

To Japanese officials, however, "a merchant in good standing" could hardly be considered respectable because in the Confucian hierarchy, merchants—especially foreign ones—resided at the bottom. Political control of Japanese society depended on maintaining this hierarchy. Anti-*bakufu* forces, the imperial court, and sometimes even *bakufu* supporters berated the *bakufu* for allowing foreign merchants to gain money by "defrauding our nation."[18] Japanese officials complained to American diplomats that exports were driving up the price of many goods, causing hardship for those living near the open ports.[19] Some American diplomats agreed that foreign merchants were damaging the Japanese economy. One American minister in the early 1860s wrote to Washington that "the presence of merchants from abroad . . . is a danger felt and acknowledged."[20] To most Japanese officials and some Americans, foreign merchants such as Van Reed were disrupting both the political and the economic system.

Van Reed irritated Japanese officials in other ways as well. In early 1860 he traveled to Edo, then off-limits to foreigners except members of diplomatic legations. He had obtained a passport for Edo by lying to Japanese officials in Yokohama that he had important business with American Minister Townsend Harris.[21] His real purpose in going to Edo was business and sightseeing. Such travel was a violation of the 1858 treaty between Japan and the United States, and Japanese officials wasted no time in complaining to Harris, who in turn complained to Secretary of State Lewis Cass.[22] Van Reed evidently paid little attention; he was caught by the governor of Yokohama later that same year making another unauthorized trip to Edo.[23]

In addition to selling weapons to all sides during this tumultuous era, Van Reed occasionally interfered in internal Japanese political affairs. In December 1868, for example, he traveled to Sendai Bay and met with *bakufu* Admiral Enomoto Takeaki and some "rebel" *daimyō* from the Tohoku region still opposed to the new imperial government. Van Reed had no authority to negotiate, nor did he even have permission to travel to Sendai. Nevertheless, he offered to mediate between Enomoto and the emperor. He also offered Enomoto political asylum in Hawaii.[24] Enomoto decided to stick to his original plan of seizing Hakodate. Needless to say, the Japanese government was not pleased with Van Reed's meddling in such an important internal matter.

Van Reed's last major problem with Japanese officials occurred after he opened his business in Tokyo soon after the city was opened to foreigners. The Van Riido Kaisho was an exchange house at which oils, silks, teas, and primarily rice were bought on sample and deliverable in the future. Van Reed had 105 Japanese brokers who received a share of the profits in return for their labor.[25] After operating for a few months, the government ordered Van Reed's brokers "to refrain from transacting any business there under pain of immediate imprisonment."[26] Japanese officials told De Long that they were shutting down Van Reed's business because it was "a species of gambling."[27] De Long vigorously denied the charges and argued that Van Reed had a right to operate such a business in Japan. Nevertheless, Secretary of State Hamilton Fish sided with the Japanese government, and the Van Riido Kaisho never reopened.[28]

Not content with being a foreign merchant and a self-appointed arbitrator of Japanese political affairs, Van Reed also became a part-time diplomat. He had visited Hawaii briefly only twice before and once after he became that country's diplomatic representative in Japan. Furthermore, his correspondence with Hawaii's officials does not indicate that he received a salary or other form of compensation.[29] Perhaps he wanted to expand the relationship between the two countries so that he could personally profit from the increased trade that would result. Because he was already an expatriate American businessman in a foreign land, perhaps the "spirit of adventure" led him to try his hand at diplomacy. In any event, after his father and others sent recommendation letters to Hawaii's foreign minister, Van Reed was appointed consul general of the Hawaiian Kingdom to Japan in April 1865.[30] The Hawaiian foreign minister immediately put Van Reed to work negotiating a Japan-Hawaii treaty.

A Treaty for Expanding Trade, Expanding Economic Development, and Expanding the Population

The negotiation and conclusion of a treaty was the most important issue between the governments of Japan and Hawaii in the 1860s and early 1870s. Hawaiian officials actively sought two major items in treaty negotiations. First, they wanted increased trade with Japan that only a formal treaty could deliver. In particular, they wanted sugar put on the duty-free list of imported items in Japan. Second, they wanted laborers, preferably immigrants who would chose to make Hawaii their permanent home.

These laborers would help restore Hawaii's sliding economic base following the decline of the whaling industry and the rise of plantation sugar cane production. This labor-intensive enterprise relied upon a constant source of workers, but the number of native Hawaiians—the immediate source of labor—had plummeted. When Captain James Cook visited the islands in 1778 there were approximately 250,000 native Hawaiians; by the 1860s the introduction of European and American diseases had decreased that number to just over 60,000.[31] Further, most native Hawaiians lived off subsistence agriculture and had little desire to work in an expanding capitalist economy for the benefit of foreigners. Beginning in the 1850s planters recruited Chinese laborers and hired them on five-year contracts, but most Chinese either returned home or set up their own businesses in Honolulu after fulfilling their obligations.[32] In addition to recruiting more Chinese, planters looked to Portugal, to the South Pacific islands, and to Japan to fill their need for laborers and immigrants.

Before appointing Van Reed as Hawaii's consul general in Japan, Foreign Minister Robert Wyllie wrote to Joseph Heco, asking him if there were "agricultural labourors with their wives and families" in Japan who would be willing to immigrate to Hawaii.[33] According to Hawaii's Bureau of Immigration, "Japanese were more like the natives of these islands than any others . . . [and] there was not the slightest doubt that they would most readily amalgamate."[34] Clearly, Hawaiian officials hoped that a treaty between Hawaii and Japan would at once develop the economy and repopulate the islands.

The American minister in Edo and the American consul general in Kanagawa assisted Van Reed in the negotiations. After some delays, a treaty containing both trade and emigration provisions was about to be signed in the fall of 1867. Suddenly, two *bakufu* officials notified Van Reed that the shogun's government refused to accept his signature on the treaty as Hawaii's diplomatic representative. "During your long residence in Japan," they explained, "you have been engaged in trade as a merchant here."[35] The rejection of Van Reed's diplomatic credentials was quite unexpected. In addition to his commission as Hawaii's consul general, he had presented the Japanese government with a special "Letter of Credence" from King Kamehameha V that specifically empowered him to negotiate a treaty with Japan.[36] Furthermore, his authority had been formally recognized in a letter to him from the *bakufu*'s top foreign affairs officials.[37] Nevertheless, Van Reed's authority to sign the treaty was rejected and the Japan-Hawaii treaty was shelved.

It is difficult to believe that the shogun's foreign affairs officials suddenly rejected Van Reed's diplomatic credentials because he was a merchant. He had been living in Japan for eight years and his occupation was hardly a secret. More likely, the shogun wanted to cancel the treaty because of increasing turmoil between the *bakufu* and the anti-*bakufu* coalition fighting to "restore" all political and military authority to the emperor.

The stalled treaty negotiations did not stop discussions on sending Japanese laborers to Hawaii, however. In April 1868, *bakufu* officials finally gave Van Reed permission to send up to 400 laborers to Hawaii on three-year contracts.[38] The two parties agreed to the following conditions for each laborer:

> Four dollars per month in pay; two dollars in cash at the end of each month and the remainder to be paid upon completion of the three-year contract.
>
> Ten dollar advance to be paid before leaving Yokohama.
>
> Free room, board, and medical treatment.
>
> Free passage to and from Hawaii.[39]

Wakatsuki Yasuo has calculated that the most money Japanese farm workers, carpenters, day laborers, or domestic servants could possibly earn in Japan was less than half the amount being offered by Van Reed and Hawaii's Bureau of Immigration.[40]

Van Reed made an agreement with a local Japanese merchant named Kimura Hambei to recruit up to 400 Japanese who would be willing to go to Hawaii for work on sugar cane plantations.[41] He also hired a physician, Dr. David Lee, to select 180 healthy Japanese from among the 400 recruited by Kimura to send "for a trial" to the islands.[42] Lee selected men who were between twenty and thirty-five years old and free from skin diseases. However, he later reported that some of those rejected "were smuggled by their friends on board" the vessel that took them to Hawaii.[43] By the end of April, Van Reed chartered an eight-hundred-ton British vessel, the *Scioto,* to take the Japanese laborers to Hawaii. He paid $3,000 in Mexican dollars to the captain and promised that the Hawaiian government would pay an additional $5,900 in American gold coins after the ship arrived in Honolulu.[44] Van Reed put 180 Japanese, including twenty workers' wives, on board the *Scioto* on May 6. The ship was scheduled to depart at dawn on May 10.[45] Van Reed's plans for sending the Japanese to Hawaii then began to unravel.

On May 9 Captain William Reagan of the *Scioto* informed Van Reed that his ship would not be ready for a few more days.[46] On the same day anti-*bakufu* forces (now calling themselves "imperial forces") marched into the area and took over the administration of Yokohama. Despite Van Reed's acquaintance with Terashima Munenori of Satsuma, the new vice governor of Yokohama, all of his meetings and negotiations had been with *bakufu* officials, the enemies of the new imperial government. Apparently Van Reed did not realize the change of government officials in Yokohama could cause problems. On the very day that imperial forces took over the area, he voluntarily returned 180 passports issued by the *bakufu* to the new governor of Yokohama, Higashikuze Michitomi.[47] For reasons that are unclear, he expected to receive 350 passports in return.[48]

Between May 9 and May 16 Van Reed frantically wrote letters to Higashikuze, Terashima, and other officials trying to get the *bakufu*-issued passports returned to him. He also wanted the new officials to explicitly approve agreements previously made by *bakufu* authorities allowing the Japanese to immigrate to Hawaii. If they did not, he demanded a refund of the money he paid for the charter of the *Scioto* and his expenses in recruiting the laborers. Terashima had two meetings with Van Reed and told him the new Japanese government wanted one of the treaty powers to guarantee the return of the Japanese laborers at the end of the three-year period because Japan and Hawaii had yet to sign a treaty.[49] Van Reed considered this "an insult to Hawaii" and refused.[50] He suggested to the new officials that "a Japanese Consul be sent to Hawaii to look after Japanese interests, should you fear any ill result from their leaving."[51] On the morning of May 16, the *Scioto* was ready to sail. The captain received his departure papers from the British consul and, despite the lack of an agreement between Van Reed and the new government, the *Scioto* was cleared by Japanese customs house officials at Yokohama. Van Reed was unsure of exactly how many Japanese were on board because he ordered the crew to allow anyone who had second thoughts to return ashore.[52]

Still the ship did not sail, even though Van Reed was likely to suffer from its continued presence. The longer the *Scioto* waited, the greater the chances the new government would prevent the ship from sailing altogether. Van Reed was apparently not making any money from this initial enterprise, but he could lose $4,000—about half of which was his own money—if the new officials stopped the ship and refused to refund his money. Nevertheless, he sent three letters to government officials on May 16 warning them that the ship would sail the next morning with the Japanese on board unless they took actions to stop it and refund his money.[53] By 9:00 A.M. on May 17, he had received no reply to his letters and so ordered the ship to depart. After final preparations, the *Scioto* set sail at 2:00 P.M.

The new officials at Yokohama did not return the 180 passports that were issued by *bakufu* officials or explicitly give Van Reed permission to send Japanese laborers to Hawaii. And Van Reed pointedly refused to get one of the treaty powers to guarantee the agreements he made as Hawaii's diplomatic representative. Yet, there is no indication that Japanese officials ever directly ordered him to stop the shipment of Japanese to Hawaii. Nor did they order their own officials at the Yokohama customs house to refuse clearance for the *Scioto*. Robert Van Valkenberg, the American minister to Japan at this time, later told officials at the Japanese Foreign Ministry they could have—and, in his view, should have—easily prevented the *Scioto* from sailing.[54] It is unclear why these officials did not actively stop the shipment of Japanese to Hawaii. The most logical explanation is that the administration of the area was in a state of confusion and transition due to the change in government and could not attend to the relatively small matter of one ship with Japanese laborers bound for Hawaii. One week after the *Scioto* sailed, however, officials addressed a long letter of complaint to Van Valkenberg. Higashikuze told him they would have allowed the Japanese to go to Hawaii, since they "had already been granted such permits by the late government." But Van Reed was "unreasonable in his discussion of this matter" and demanded that they give permission for the ship to sail or refund the money he had spent. According to these officials, the *Scioto* then "suddenly sailed . . . before the matter had been settled."[55]

The events were not in dispute, but the central issue remained contentious. Van Reed believed that permission granted by the previous government of the *bakufu* remained valid after the new imperial government took over the administration of the country. The new officials maintained that they had to sanction the permission granted by the previous government, which they had not done.

Van Valkenberg responded to Higashikuze's complaint by reminding him that while Van Reed was an American citizen, he acted in this matter as Hawaii's consul general to Japan. In addition, the *Scioto* was a British vessel, which the Americans obviously held no authority over. But Van Valkenberg clearly sympathized with the new Japanese government. He described the shipment of Japanese laborers as "nefarious traffic." Because the shipment of Chinese contract laborers to the United States had been made illegal by an act of Congress, he would see to it that shipment of Japanese contract laborers would likewise be outlawed. On his own authority, he immediately issued the following public notice: "I, Robert B. Van Valkenberg—Minister Resident of the United States in Japan do hereby decree the following regulation, which shall have the force of law in the Courts of the United States in Japan. 'The Act of Congress to prohibit the Coolie trade etc. approved February 19, 1862—and which was framed with regard to China, is hereby made applicable to Japan.'" Higashikuze and the Japanese government were undoubtedly pleased.[56]

Van Reed, however, believed Van Valkenberg had no right to interfere and he castigated the decree as "preposterous and ridiculous."[57] Secretary of State William Seward agreed with "the spirit" of Van Valkenberg's action, but ordered him to rescind the decree because it "was without foundation in law, and is, therefore, invalid and ineffectual."[58]

A few months after the first complaint, Higashikuze told Van Valkenberg, "We want to call our people back and have Mr. Van Reed punished."[59] As the government was still new and inexperienced at diplomacy with Western countries, Higashikuze also asked the American minister, "What is the proper way to do this?"[60] Van Valkenberg advised him to prosecute Van Reed in the U.S. Consular Court in Japan. If he was found guilty, the Japanese government could then punish and deport him.[61] Van Valkenberg twice advised the Japanese government to prosecute Van Reed, but, for reasons that are unclear, the officials declined.

Aloha

Meanwhile, the *Scioto* was on its way to Hawaii with 141 Japanese men, 6 women, and 1 child on board. Sakuma Yonekichi kept a diary of the voyage, but primarily wrote brief descriptions of the weather—it rained often—and the direction the ship was headed (south, then east).[62] According to another Japanese on board, few knew where Hawaii was located, but most thought it to be in China or India.[63] There was plenty of food for the voyage: five hundred bags of brown rice, twenty bags of white rice, plus large supplies of *miso* and *shōyu*.[64] The ship could have held over 300 passengers—

perhaps Van Reed's reason for wanting extra passports—so there was plenty of room for the Japanese laborers. Accompanying the Japanese were Dr. Lee and D. A. Baum, who had been hired by Van Reed to attend to any medical needs and explain to Hawaiian officials the hectic and confused circumstances leading up to the *Scioto*'s departure.

Although the voyage to Hawaii was mostly uneventful it was marred by some discord and death. A few of the Japanese were *rōnin* and got into a fight with a Chinese cook, who pulled a knife to defend himself. Makino Tomisaburo, whom Van Reed had placed in charge of the Japanese group, intervened before anyone was seriously hurt.[65] A man named Wakichi died after twenty days at sea. According to Dr. Lee, the man died from an "unknown cause" after a brief illness.[66] The *Scioto* arrived in Honolulu on June 19, 1868, after a thirty-four-day voyage. King Kamehameha V greeted the arriving vessel and sent a barrel of salted fish to the Japanese.[67]

In meetings on June 22 and 29, 1868, the Board of Immigration decided the contract price of each Japanese laborer to be $70 and to uphold the contract terms agreed upon by Van Reed and the former *bakufu* government. They agreed with Van Reed, Lee, and Baum that the problems and confusion leading up to the departure of the *Scioto* was due to Captain Reagan's failure to sail from Yokohama on May 10 as promised, but reluctantly paid him the full $5,900 as agreed in the charter arrangement.[68] The board sold the work contracts to twenty-two planters. Thirteen planters took only one or two Japanese, while Samuel Wilder took the most, thirty-six. Two Japanese went to work at Queen's Hospital in Honolulu.[69] Makino was granted an annual salary of $150, plus room and board. He was not assigned any physical labor, but was to be the liaison between the Japanese, the planters, and the Board of Immigration.[70]

The *Hawaiian Gazette* soon published an article informing planters about their new laborers and instructing them in how to manage them. According to the article, Japanese lacked "physical stamina," "fortitude in sickness," and "courage in distress" because they were vegetarians. The *Gazette* recommended that planters "be firm, but not blustering nor tyrannical" in handling their Japanese laborers. "They are not the ceaseless workers the Chinese are. . . . They must be taught how to do their task and they will be found willing to learn and will intelligently perform it. They have lived a life irregular and precarious, never prompt, never hurried, and it will require patience to train them to the promptness of civilization." In addition to these racially patronizing assumptions, the *Gazette* also informed its readers that the Japanese did display "self-reliance and self-respect."[71]

As a result of such attitudes and despite efforts by the Board of Immigration to minimize potential difficulties, problems between Japanese laborers and planters soon surfaced. For reasons unknown, one Japanese man committed suicide soon after arriving at the Makee Plantation.[72] Most Japanese were sick during their first few days of work and required medical care.[73] One Japanese man at Kalaea Plantation did not recover and died. Expressing no sympathy, the owner demanded a full refund from the Board of Immigration because the man had done no work before he died.[74] A man working as a domestic servant at another plantation was sent to the hospital, where his lungs were found to be diseased. Expressing little sympathy for his suffering worker, the owner demanded his seventy dollars, plus hospital expenses, from the board.[75] Then Samuel Wilder notified the board that his Japanese workers wanted their full four dollars in cash at the end of each month rather than the two dollars per month in cash and two dollars per month paid upon completion of the contract, as they previously had agreed.[76]

The board refused to refund any money, maintaining that all planters had taken the same chance when purchasing contracts for the Japanese laborers.[77] The board also passed a resolution advising planters to pay the Japanese "the full amount of their wages due them at the end of each month, if the laborers themselves should so desire."[78] Wilder was very upset at this action because he then had to pay $144 in cash per month instead of $72.

These early problems were exacerbated by a lack of mutual understanding. None of the planters, government officials, and members of the Board of Immigration understood the Japanese language and only Makino understood English to any extent. Even though the contracts had been written in both languages, some of the Japanese immigrants were undoubtedly illiterate and likely did not fully understand the terms of their contracts. Because his English was barely adequate, the board decided to pay for Makino to study English at a school in Honolulu.[79] Whether it was the board's compromise over pay, increased mutual understanding, or the Japanese resigning to their fate, problems between planters and Japanese laborers subsided after a few months.

The Labor Question, Economic Expansion, and Political Controversy

The introduction of Japanese laborers created diplomatic problems between Edward McCook, the American minister in Hawaii, and Hawaii's government. McCook told Acting Foreign Minister Stephen Phillips that hiring or forcing Asian workers to perform low-paying work—commonly called the coolie trade—was "so repulsive that it meets with the reprobation of the civilized world."[80] Phillips responded by reminding McCook that Hawaii's constitution forbade "involuntary servitude."[81] Phillips went on to explain that "these laborers are not 'coolies' in any sense in which that term can be offensively used. They came here voluntarily."[82] Moreover, Phillips continued, the Hawaiian government had "superintended all these transactions, and have carefully protected the Japanese against imposition, and . . . every right of personal liberty has been scrupulously guarded."[83] Phillips concluded his explanation by emphasizing the potential economic benefits to the United States. As the "excessive population of Oriental countries" helped populate the islands, natural resources would be developed, the islands' commerce would increase, and Hawaii would "directly contribute to the material growth" of the United States.[84]

McCook was not convinced. Less than two weeks after receiving Phillips's explanation, he published an 1867 congressional resolution condemning the "traffic in laborers . . . as inhuman and immoral" in the local newspapers.[85] He was immediately supported by the native Hawaiian newspaper, *Ke-Kuokoa*. "The Japanese recently imported seem to labor under . . . ignorance as to the nature of their contracts," the editors observed, and announced their support for McCook's efforts "to rid these islands of a system so utterly at variance with the spirit of the age."[86]

Hawaii's Masters and Servants Act of 1850 permitted labor contracts for up to five years. It also contained punishments—including serving time at hard labor—for workers who ran away or refused to complete their contracts.[87] Planters could be fined up to one hundred dollars for cruelty toward laborers. Contracts with Chinese were normally for five years, with Polynesians and native Hawaiians for one year, and with the *Gannenmono* for three years. Planters, holding obvious advantages in this contract labor system, sometimes committed abuses. Whipping laborers was not unheard of on some plantations, but it was not a widespread practice.[88] In his exhaustive study of the Hawaiian Kingdom, Ralph Kuykendall concluded that Hawaii's contract labor system, "with all its faults, was mild compared with that of some other countries."[89]

During the American Civil War some in Hawaii compared the contract labor system to slavery. New England missionaries argued that there was perhaps a difference in degree, but not in kind. Planters and government officials—some of whom were the children of missionaries—countered that contract labor was vital to the economic development of the islands.[90] By the fall of 1868, the expansion of the sugar industry, a possible treaty with the U.S. government allowing Hawaiian sugar to enter the country duty-free, the impending expiration of contracts with Chinese laborers who arrived in

1865, and the arrival of the *Gannenmono* from Japan reignited the debate over contract labor.[91]

The Board of Immigration and the planters were not counting on Japanese alone to emigrate to Hawaii as laborers. In their two September 1868 meetings, the board discussed the possibility of bringing hundreds of men, women, and children from the Polynesian and Malaysian islands.[92] They hoped that England and Holland, the two European powers holding nominal control over these areas, would allow the "voluntary emigration" of native peoples from these islands.[93]

At the same time Van Reed had been unsuccessfully trying to get the new imperial government to send its own envoys to Hawaii to investigate the treatment of the Japanese workers.[94] He also made a grandiose offer to become "a Prisoner of State to the Mikado" as a guarantee of the good intentions of Hawaii's government and good treatment of the Japanese by planters in Hawaii.[95] Japanese officials spurned his suggestions, claiming they were too expensive, especially since their own civil war was still in progress.[96] Frustrated, Van Reed arranged and paid for Shiroyama Seiichi, a young samurai from Satsuma, to travel to Hawaii and investigate the treatment of the *Gannenmono* laborers.[97] However, Shiroyama never reached Hawaii. He returned to Japan from San Francisco after hearing about the ill treatment of the Japanese in Hawaii from Charles Brooks, Japan's consul general in San Francisco.[98]

Shiroyama was accompanied by two companions who continued on to Hawaii. They spent one week in the islands and returned to Japan with two letters charging planters with nonfulfillment of the contracts and with beating Japanese laborers.[99] Van Reed believed the authors were forced to write these letters "owing to fear of personal violence" from the Japanese government.[100] Because the Japanese laborers had left Yokohama without the permission of the new imperial government, Van Reed's explanation was certainly plausible. Further, the Japanese government issued another series of demands to American officials for Van Reed's punishment.[101] In an about-face from his previous position, Van Valkenberg told the Japanese Foreign Ministry that he believed Van Reed had broken no American law.[102]

The Japanese government did not pursue the matter of the *Gannenmono* again until the fall of 1869. Van Valkenberg's change of position may have delayed this action, as did further events in Japan. With the defeat of Aizu in late 1868 and the surrender of *bakufu* Admiral Enomoto in Hakodate in mid-1869, the new imperial government could finally concentrate on establishing itself as the legitimate government and organize its foreign relations.

In the fall of 1869, Van Valkenberg was replaced by Charles De Long, a friend of Van Reed. At the same time the Japanese government finally appointed a special envoy, Ueno Keisuke, to journey to Hawaii and "settle all matters" between Japan and Hawaii.[103] Accompanying Ueno was Miwa Hochi, an acquaintance of Van Reed who translated the draft of the Japan-Hawaii treaty in 1867.[104]

Ueno and Miwa arrived in Honolulu in late December 1869 and were immediately greeted by King Kamehameha V. Ueno presented two proposals for settling the *Gannenmono* controversy to Charles Harris, now Hawaii's foreign minister. The first proposal was for all Japanese to be brought to Honolulu and returned to Japan at the expense of the Japanese government.[105] The second proposal was for the return of the sick, the disabled, and those who were "mechanics"—meaning skilled in a particular craft—and "unadapted by education or habits for the service at which they are now employed."[106] Ueno estimated this number of persons to be forty. Those who were not in the above categories were to serve out the remaining one and a half years of their contracts and then return to Japan at the expense of Hawaii's government. In addition, Ueno told the foreign minister that Japan "will be pleased to entertain treaty relations" with Hawaii as soon as the *Gannenmono* controversy was resolved.[107] After some negotiation, the Hawaiian government accepted the second proposal, provided those Japanese who completed their contracts could remain in Hawaii if they desired to do so.[108] Ueno reluctantly agreed to this stipulation.[109]

Ueno and Miwa presented a list of names, with previous occupations, of the forty Japanese to be returned to Japan.[110] Among the forty were six listed as sick or disabled. There were also four women and two children, one of whom was born in the islands—the first known birth of a child by Japanese parents in Hawaii.[111] All the other returnees were *chōnin*—city people—with occupations such as cook, tailor, vegetable merchant, potter, and barber. The repatriation list was apparently written by Makino and clearly states that it was "prepared before the arrival of the Embassy."[112] Because the returnees were chosen by occupation, it is impossible to determine how many personally chose to go home. According to Van Reed, he later sent five of these returnees back to Hawaii after they begged him "on their knees" to return them to the islands.[113]

After the agreement was reached, Ueno toured some of the sugar cane plantations on Oahu. He found that abuses had taken place at Waialua Plantation, where sixteen Japanese worked for Warren Chamberlain. The Japanese had been forced to pay for their own medical expenses and food while they were sick and unable to work.[114] Moreover, they complained to Ueno that "the overseer whips them everyday."[115] Harris feebly responded that he always paid "personal attention" to any complaints by the Japanese, but Makino's lack of diligence had kept him from discovering the abuses at Waialua Plantation.[116]

Despite the mistreatment he uncovered, Ueno wrote Harris, "We have everywhere found our countrymen well cared for, and kindly treated by their employers."[117] Henry Pierce, who succeeded McCook as American minister to Hawaii, accompanied Ueno on his tour of plantations. He reported that the Japanese envoy "expressed to me satisfaction at the result of his investigation and examination of plantation life and experience of his countrymen at these islands," and an "amiable conclusion" was reached concerning the *Gannenmono*.[118] De Long reported that the foreign minister and the vice foreign minister of Japan "both assured me that they were quite satisfied" with the result of their envoys' mission to Hawaii.[119] Most importantly for Hawaii, Ueno and Miwa's visit and resolution of the *Gannenmono* dispute included an agreement to conclude the delayed Japan-Hawaii treaty.

The controversy, however, was not quite over. On April 4, 1870, a letter by "Riosuke and 38 other Japanese" appeared in the *Japan Gazette* of Yokohama that contained complaints about miserable treatment by plantation owners, imprisonment of those who complained, and a reduction in wages from four dollars to three dollars per month. According to the authors, "We had almost determined to die, when we received certain information of the arrival of the Imperial Ambassadors."[120] The letter is suspicious, especially because it was supplied to the newspaper by a Japanese official known to resent Van Reed.[121] While the authenticity of the letter is questionable, it probably did represent the views of some Japanese who returned from Hawaii in 1870.

Expanding the Frontier of Immigration

Only twelve *Gannenmono* chose to return to Japan when their contracts expired in May 1871.[122] Of the ninety-four who remained in Hawaii, some eventually returned to Japan, some made their way to the mainland of the United States, and some remained in Hawaii for the rest of their lives. A list prepared by Makino in May 1871 indicates that thirty-seven wished to remain in Hawaii while thirty-six wished to go to the mainland, with the remaining Japanese either undecided or wanting to return to Japan.[123] Unfortunately, it is impossible to know what eventually became of all but a few *Gannenmono*.

In the fall of 1871, Makino Tomisaburo went to San Francisco to join other *Gannenmono* who had already arrived there.[124] Before departing Hawaii, he apologized to the Hawaiian Foreign Office for the "trifling matters" that he and others caused.[125] Harris paid for Makino's passage, plus a gratuity of one hundred dollars, while Pierce gave him fifty dollars.[126] It is not known if he ever returned to Japan.

Sakuma Yonekichi, who kept the diary during the voyage of the *Scioto,* stayed on at the Lihue Plantation on Kauai. In 1917, he told an interviewer, "My entire family is grateful to my master for his generosity."[127] Sakuma was retired, receiving a twenty-five-dollar-per-month pension, and living in a "comfortable home" built by the planter. The planter was also paying for the education of Sakuma's children, including putting the oldest son through college.[128]

By 1922, there were four *Gannenmono* still living in Hawaii: Sakuma, Yoshida Katsusaboru, Aoki Matsu, and Ishii Sentaro. Thirteen years later, Ishii turned 102 years old and was the last known living *Gannenmono.* Unlike most of the *Gannenmono,* who were either farmers or *chonin,* Ishii was a samurai. Originally from the southern domain of Hizen, he was in Edo in April 1868 when he heard he could make four dollars per month working on sugar cane fields in Hawaii. He also feared for his safety because the *bakufu* and imperial forces were fighting in the Edo and Yokohama areas. After arriving in Hawaii, Ishii was sent with fourteen others to work at the Ulupalakua Plantation on Maui. Because he had never been a farmer, the work was difficult for him at first. He especially disliked being "ordered about by the *lunas* [overseers], but I got used to it."[129] "In fact," he told the interviewer, "the plantation treated us very nicely. We worked at $4 a month for three years. After the third year, we were paid $9 a month."[130] There were many Chinese and native Hawaiian laborers at Ulupalakua, and Ishii learned to speak Hawaiian because it was the common language among the native Hawaiians, Chinese, Japanese, and whites on the plantation. In the early 1880s, he went to work at the Kipahulu Plantation on Maui. When twenty Japanese from the first group of government contract laborers arrived in 1885 at Kipahulu, Ishii was promoted to *luna.* He became a Catholic, married a native Hawaiian woman, and had six children.[131] Believing that he had disgraced the *daimyō* of Hizen by leaving the country in 1868, Ishii never returned to Japan.

A Treaty, a Conclusion, and a Beginning

In August 1871, the Treaty of Amity and Commerce between the Hawaiian Islands and Japan was concluded.[132] After the Japanese Foreign Ministry refused to accept Van Reed's signature on the treaty as Hawaii's diplomatic representative, Charles De Long, the American minister to Japan, was tem-

The four surviving *Gannenmono* in 1922: Sakuma Yonekichi, Yoshida Katsusaboru, Aoki Matsu, and Ishii Sentaro. (Okahata, *A History of Japanese in Hawaii*)

porarily appointed as Hawaii's minister to Japan by King Kamehameha V and signed the treaty on Hawaii's behalf.[133] In spite of the controversy over the *Gannenmono,* Article 5 of the treaty stated,

> The Japanese Government will place no restriction whatever upon the employment by Hawaiian subjects of Japanese in any lawful capacity.
>
> Japanese in the employ of foreigners may obtain Government passports to go abroad, on application to the Governor of any open port.[134]

With the resolution of the *Gannenmono* controversy and the inclusion of Article 5 in the long-delayed Japan-Hawaii treaty, the Hawaiian government had seemingly gained a source of immigrant laborers. In fact, the Japanese government did not permit groups of Japanese laborers to go to Hawaii or to the mainland of the United States until the mid-1880s.

Because Japan's informal ban on labor emigration came on the heels of the *Gannenmono* controversy, scholars have assumed the ban resulted from this "misadventure."[135] Obviously the Japanese government did not want a repeat of the controversy, especially since the time-consuming issue distracted attention from more important foreign affairs, such as relations with Korea and revision of the unequal treaties with Western powers. But there were other reasons for the prohibition of labor emigration, each of which was at least as important as the *Gannenmono* controversy.

One was that the Japanese government was well aware of the tens of thousands of Chinese in the Pacific and in the Americas who were widely regarded as nothing more than cheap laborers. Japanese officials were shocked at the conditions aboard the *Maria Luz,* a Peruvian ship crowded with Chinese laborers that arrived in Yokohama for emergency repairs in the summer of 1872. These officials believed that China was paid little respect by the major Western powers not only because of its political and military weakness but also because of the large numbers of Chinese working overseas. Japanese officials thus did not want their people working overseas at a time when they were trying to promote and expand the country's international presence.

Second, the new government instituted colonization projects within its own boundaries. The most important of these was in Hokkaido. The Kaitakushi (Hokkaido Colonization Bureau) was established in 1869 to encourage Japanese to immigrate to Hokkaido, develop the island's resources, and solidify Japan's claim of sovereignty over the island. The Japanese government did not want Japanese in search of work to go overseas; it wanted them to go to Hokkaido.

Finally, relations between Japan and the United States cooled so considerably in the aftermath of the Iwakura mission of 1871–72 that De Long told Secretary of State Hamilton Fish that a "reactionary sentiment" directed at Americans was influencing the Japanese government.[136] Japanese officials were upset that the United States, followed by European nations, refused to renegotiate the unequal treaties of the 1850s. Other evidence of the strained relationship soon surfaced: Mori Arinori was recalled from his diplomatic post in Washington; Charles Brooks was dismissed from his post as Japan's consul general in San Francisco; an increasing number of government-sponsored students were sent to Europe—especially Germany—rather than to the United States; and American advisors working with the Japanese government were kept on an increasingly short leash by Japanese officials.

Rather than interpret the *Gannenmono* episode as the only cause behind the Japanese ban on labor emigration, it should be interpreted as one cause among several and occurring during a period of strained relations between the United States and Japan. Nevertheless, the *Gannenmono* episode represents the emergence and expansion of the three-way relationship among Japan, the United States, and Hawaii. Furthermore, the *Gannenmono* represent the vanguard of immigration to Hawaii, which made a substantial economic, cultural, and political contribution to the islands.

SIX

From Aizu to Gold Hill

In June 1869, Honolulu's *Pacific Commercial Advertiser* reprinted a news article from San Francisco about Japanese settlers who planned to establish an agricultural colony in northern California. At the time, Hawaii's predominantly European-American government leaders and planters were trying to attract Japanese to the islands, so the newspaper expressed annoyance that the Japanese had chosen California over Hawaii:

> And yet these islands are needing population much more than that country. . . . There are thousands of acres of government lands on each of the islands . . . which might be given to actual settlers, or perhaps leased at nominal rental . . . to immigrants who will settle on and cultivate them.
>
> The Japanese referred to intend to cultivate the tea plant, grow mulberry trees, and engage in the silk business; and where, let us ask, is there a country in the world that offers finer inducements for this branch of industry than Hawaii?[1]

Led by a German resident of Japan, the Japanese established an agricultural settlement in Coloma, California. The Wakamatsu Colony—named after their home city—lasted for only two years before it failed.

Because little was known of the colony's existence until relatively recently and no colonist's letters or memoirs have been found, one Japanese American writer has compared the Wakamatsu Colony to the Lost Colony of Roanoke.[2] The California state government and the Japanese American Citizens League has recognized the Wakamatsu colonists as the first Japanese immigrants in the United States.[3] Scholars may question the identification of the Wakamatsu colonists as the first Japanese immigrants in the United States. The castaways Nakahama Manjiro and Joseph Heco each lived in America for many years in the 1840s and 1850s. Niijima Jo and other *ryūgakusei,* such as those at Rutgers College, had been in America for years by the time the Wakamatsu colonists arrived in 1869. Samurai-students from Satsuma arrived at the Brotherhood of the New Life Christian utopian community in New York nearly two years earlier, and for all we know, planned to stay there for the rest of their lives—as one did. Furthermore, many of these Japanese who arrived in the United States before the Wakamatsu colonists and resided in the country for one or more years displayed a willingness to accommodate to and participate in American life. Exploring the question of who, exactly, were the first Japanese immigrants in the United States may be an interesting and useful exercise, but perhaps not of great historical importance. The Wakamatsu colonists are, however, historically important for three reasons. First, they established the largest Japanese enclave in the United States before the beginning of systematic Japanese immigration in the mid-1880s. Second, they were the first group of Japanese intending to permanently settle in the country. Finally, although they did not directly influence the process of emigration from Japan, they were the vanguard of Issei (first-generation Japanese immigrants) to the United States.

These colonists sought to improve their economic situation by establishing an agricultural settlement in the United States, but they were pushed from Japan for primarily political reasons.[4] Wakamatsu, the castle town of Aizu domain, was controlled by Matsudaira Katamori, a prominent supporter of the shogun and an opponent of the anti-*bakufu* movement. The Wakamatsu colonists were thus on the losing side of the Meiji Restoration and left their country as refugees in search of a new life.

Matsudaira Katamori, Aizu, and Civil War

Matsudaira Katamori (1835–93) was one of a small number of *kamon daimyō,* all of whom carried the Matsudaira name but were only indirectly related to the Tokugawa family and thus were not in line for the shogun's position.[5] In 1862, with Kyoto fast becoming the headquarters for the anti-*bakufu* movement, the shogun appointed twenty-six-year-old Matsudaira as *shugoshoku* (defender) of the imperial capital. According to Conrad Totman in his detailed study *The Collapse of the Tokugawa Bakufu, 1862–1868,* Matsudaira was chosen because *bakufu* officials believed *fudai daimyōs* "lacked the manpower necessary to counter the influence of great *daimyō* and *rōnin* in Kyoto" and because of Aizu domain's "tradition of stern warrior deportment and loyal service to Edo."[6] In this hazardous position, Matsudaira carefully navigated between the disparate anti-*bakufu* forces, who demanded Japan's return to the national seclusion policy and the expulsion of all foreigners, and the *bakufu* government, which contended that increased, regulated contact and trade with the West was regrettable but inevitable. In a message to the *bakufu* in late 1862, Matsudaira criticized the shogun's government for treating foreigners "with consideration," which had led to "a truly grievious state of affairs."[7] Yet, he also disparaged the idea of returning to national seclusion because Japan would then "have no means of understanding foreign conditions and adopting their ways where they are good."[8] By this Matsudaira meant that Westerners "built great ships and guns," which he believed would help strengthen Japan's own military forces.[9] Such views may appear contradictory, but they demonstrate Matsudaira's belief in Sakuma's "Eastern ethics, Western science" philosophy. Furthermore, as Harold Bolitho writes of Matsudaira during this period, he "managed to tread a very distinct path which, while leaving him on reasonably good terms with both *Bakufu* and Court, also helped him avoid anything like a total commitment to either of them." In keeping with this vague, middle-of-the-road policy promoted by a handful of *daimyō* and court nobles, Matsudaira identified himself as an advocate of "Court-*Bakufu* harmony."[10]

Relations between Matsudaira and the samurai of Satsuma, Choshu, and other anti-*bakufu* proponents in Kyoto were anything but harmonious. Political intrigue, assassinations, and sporadic fighting typified the fractious relationship throughout the 1860s. Satsuma officials challenged Aizu by trying to have their own *daimyō,* Shimazu Hisamitsu, replace Matsudaira as defender of Kyoto immediately after the Aizu *daimyō* took up his post.[11] Increased lobbying and influence at the imperial court upset Matsudaira and Aizu officials.[12] Samurai from Choshu, generally considered more radical and belligerent than those from Satsuma, were quick to defy *bakufu* policies and constantly antagonized the Aizu *daimyō* and his samurai in Kyoto. In 1864, Matsudaira wanted to battle Choshu samurai encamped just outside the imperial city, but the shogun demurred.[13] The following year, Matsudaira helped lead the first *bakufu* campaign against Choshu domain, which ended when Choshu officials pledged their allegiance to the shogun.[14] In 1866, he became furious with the *bakufu* for calling off the second campaign against Choshu.[15] In essence, while Matsudaira promoted the vague, fence-riding policy of Court-*Bakufu* harmony, his military policy was staunchly oriented against Satsuma and Choshu.

Soon after Tokugawa Yoshinobu resigned his post as shogun in late 1867, the imperial court dismissed Matsudaira and his Aizu samurai from guarding the palace in Kyoto. They were replaced by Satsuma and Choshu samurai, who had gained control of the imperial court and the fifteen-year-old emperor, Meiji (then known as Mutsuhito).[16] In late January 1868, the forces of Aizu and Kuwana (the domain of Matsudaira's brother, Sadaaki), along with *bakufu* samurai from other Tokugawa domains were defeated in fierce battles with Satsuma, Choshu, and other newly designated "imperial forces" at Toba and Fushimi outside Kyoto. These military encounters marked the end of 268 years of Tokugawa *bakufu* control of Japan and the beginning of the Meiji era. They also represented the beginning of a civil conflict, known as the Boshin War, that raged throughout most of 1868.

The imperial forces marched to Edo and took control of nearby Yokohama and the central government. The new government, consisting primarily of samurai from Satsuma and Choshu, issued an imperial proclamation declaring that Matsudaira and those in the Aizu domain were "traitors" fighting in the "rebellion."[17] The shogun, Tokugawa Yoshinobu, relinquished power to the emperor and quietly returned to his home domain of Mito. Matsudaira and his samurai returned to Aizu in northern Japan and prepared for war.[18]

Matsudaira refused to capitulate because the new imperial forces had yet to prove that they actually controlled Japan. At the time Japan had over 250 quasi-autonomous domains, and it would have been an enormous burden to centralize and control such an unwieldy conglomeration of mini-states. Moreover, he and some other northern *daimyō* considered the "imperial restoration" little more than a coup that might not succeed if decisively challenged. As Bolitho writes, "it was by no means a foregone conclusion that he would be defeated."[19] In 1868, no one knew that the Satsuma-Choshu coup would ultimately succeed and the result would be the Meiji Restoration.

Matsudaira may not have realized that among his supporters were Americans living in Japan. A U.S. Navy doctor stationed in Yokohama gleefully wrote in his diary on May 26, 1868, that "Aidzu has flogged the troops of Satsuma in every engagement. From all accounts the cause of Aidzu is not a bad one. We are all anxious to see him win the day."[20] The next day he wrote,

"Everyone is an Aidzu man now."[21] Matsudaira probably received such unsolicited support because American officials presumed he was fighting on behalf of the shogun, whom they credited with "observing the treaties, and of strengthening the friendly relations with other countries, especially the United States."[22] The American consul general in Yokohama wrote to *bakufu* Foreign Minister Ogasawara Iki in early February 1868 that the United States was one of the "well wishers of the Tycoon's cause."[23] Although Robert Van Valkenberg, the American minister to Japan, maintained formal neutrality during Japan's civil war, his messages to the State Department throughout 1868 clearly indicated his support for Matsudaira and Shogun Yoshinobu.[24] He even allowed the shogun and some of his *bakufu* officials safe haven aboard the USS *Iroquois* after the battles at Toba and Fushimi.[25] In comparison with the constant anti-foreign rhetoric of the anti-*bakufu* forces and the danger posed by anti-foreign *rōnin,* the shogun and Matsudaira appeared supportive of American interests.

After battling other northern domains in the summer of 1868, the imperial forces marched into Aizu in September. The single most famous, tragic, and romanticized event in Aizu's long history took place during this war when twenty teenaged boys of the *Byakkotai* (White Tiger Brigade) committed mass suicide because they mistakenly thought Tsuruga Castle in Wakamatsu—Matsudaira's headquarters—was burning down.[26] Yamakawa Sutematsu, then a young girl whose father was an Aizu samurai, later described life inside Tsuruga Castle during the war: "During the last thirty days of the seige, [*sic*] our foe drew his lines so closely about us that our warriors, who up to that time had been guarding the mountain passes nearby, were obliged to take refuge in the castle. . . . We were surrounded on every side."[27] An estimated thirty thousand troops besieged Tsuruga Castle. Inside were three thousand samurai and two thousand dependents. The imperial armies plundered and burned much of Wakamatsu. They then sealed off the entrances to the castle and began a massive bombardment. Yamakawa's older sister was wounded and died an agonizing death. Out of food, with many of his samurai dead or dying, Matsudaira realized the futility of further resistance and surrendered on November 5, 1868.[28] Satsuma and Choshu, Bolitho maintains, "gambled and won, earning for themselves positions of national eminence and responsibility."[29] Matsudaira and Aizu gambled and lost, earning the opprobrium of being stubborn opponents of the new imperial order.

Satsuma and Choshu had condemned Matsudaira to death before the battles of Toba and Fushimi but, surprisingly, he was spared. He and Tokugawa Yoshinobu were formally pardoned in a decree issued the following year.[30] Charles De Long, who replaced Van Valkenberg as the U.S. minister to Japan, believed that the new government, well aware of its precarious control over Japan, feared that their deaths by execution or ritual suicide would have the "inevitable consequences" of elevating them to martyrdom and acting as a unifying symbol to *daimyōs* still incensed at their defeat.[31] After a brief period of imprisonment, Matsudaira became a Shinto priest and eventually served for many years as the chief priest at Toshogu Shrine in Nikko, the mausoleum of Tokugawa Ieyasu, the founder of the Tokugawa shogunate.

The people of Aizu faced a bitter winter in 1868–69. The wartime destruction led to impending starvation and *yonaoshi* (world rectification) uprisings.[32] The new imperial government took direct charge of the domain's affairs and, according to Marius Jansen, "no other domain was treated as harshly" as Aizu in the aftermath of the civil war.[33] Disillusioned, destitute, and branded as traitors, thousands of Aizu's people migrated to northern Tohoku and Hokkaido in search of food, refuge, and a new life in post-Tokugawa Japan.[34] The destruction of Aizu, resulting from the political transformation from Tokugawa to Meiji, also pushed a handful of these refugees to seek a new life in a place they may have heard of but certainly knew almost nothing about: the California frontier.

Gold, Silk, Tea, and the Wakamatsu Colony

Twenty years before the Meiji Restoration in Japan, James Marshall discovered gold in a northern California valley that the local Nisenan Indians called Kolo-ma. At first the discovery was kept secret, but as news leaked out it launched the Gold Rush that rapidly transformed California into the mining, agricultural, commercial, and shipping leader of the western United States. People came from across the country and around the world seeking their fortune. President Millard Fillmore and Commodore Perry even tried unsuccessfully to induce the *bakufu* into trade relations with the United States by informing them of the gold and silver in California.[35] Many of the "forty-niners" who rushed to California in search of gold were pushed by a combination of legal, economic, and family problems. Many who came overland from the eastern United States did not make it past the Plains, the Rocky Mountains, the deserts, or the Sierra Nevada. Some died along the way from the cholera. Many Chinese who joined the Gold Rush ended up working as exploited laborers in mining camps, on railroads, and on farms. Some individual gold rushers found their fortunes, but most did not. Old graveyards in California's frontier mining towns are a sad testament to the many who failed to find the precious metal. Although substantial quantities of gold were still being mined using mechanized, capital-intensive methods, the state's economy had turned toward agriculture by the 1860s. Settlers discovered that the massive Central Valley and the surrounding foothills were places more conducive to growing fruits and vegetables than by striking it rich digging the earth for gold. While the Gold Rush gave California its image as the land of opportunity, it was agriculture that turned that image into reality for many immigrants seeking a new start in life.

John Henry Schnell and his brother Edward were from Baden-Württemburg, Germany, and they sought their fame, fortune, and a new start in life in Japan. John Henry worked part-time for the German legation while Edward did the same for the Dutch legation.[36] They collected lacquerware for export to Europe and sold maps in Japan—important items in an era when very few Japanese had any conception of the world's geography.[37] However, the Schnells' primary business—as with many Western foreigners then living in Japan—was importing and selling weapons and munitions. One of the Schnell brothers' best customers was Matsudaira of Aizu.[38]

John Henry had a house in Wakamatsu and married a samurai-class Japanese woman from the area. Matsudaira gave him the honorary name Hiramatsu, using the same two *kanji* characters as in Matsudaira's own name.[39] Schnell trained Matsudaira's samurai in the use of Western firearms and was in charge of a unit of Aizu samurai during the Boshin War.[40] Since the new government in Japan was well aware of Schnell's direct support of their main enemy, his future prospects in the country were limited. With Matsudaira's support, Schnell devised a plan to establish a colony of Aizu settlers in California that would produce tea and silk. Such a venture would be profitable for Aizu, which had lost most of its land to the central government as a result of the civil war.

The production of silk and tea had been established in the traditional Japanese economy long before the *bakumatsu* era, and by the nineteenth century raw silk and tea were Japan's most important export products.[41] From the opening of Yokohama as a foreign trade port in 1859 until the mid-1860s, Japanese tea exports were shipped in roughly equal quantities to England, continental Europe, and the United States.[42] By 1866, the United States had become the largest market in the world for Japanese tea.[43] For most of the next twenty-five years, the United States purchased between 80 and 90 percent of Japan's tea exports.[44] From 1868 to the early 1880s, tea accounted for close to 25 percent of Japan's total export trade.[45] Silkworm egg sheets, which would produce silkworm cocoons, and raw silk were even more crucial than tea for Japan's export trade. As Lillian Li notes, "Japan's silk export trade had profound significance for its general economic development."[46] Moreover, Aizu had been a major silk producing area since the mid-Tokugawa era.[47]

Beginning in the 1850s, a parasitic epidemic attacked silk cocoons in Europe, devastating the continent's silk industry and resulting in a windfall for China and Japan. In addition to providing a vital source of income for many rural households, from 1868 to 1882 silk products accounted for a whopping 48 percent of Japan's total export trade.[48] According to one estimate, the silk export trade "financed no less than 40% of Japan's entire imports of foreign machinery and raw materials" from 1870 to 1930.[49] In other words, the silk and tea trades went a long way toward paying the bills for Japan's industrialization.

Californians also sought to take advantage of Europe's predicament by competing with Japan in breeding silkworm cocoons. In 1868, a San Francisco newspaper claimed that "California cocoons were decidedly superior to the Japanese," while two years later the *Overland Monthly* opined that "most foreign orders will . . . hereafter be filled in California" rather than in Japan.[50]

Pushed from Japan as refugees in search of safe haven and pulled to California by the prospect of establishing an agricultural colony, John Henry Schnell, his wife, Jou, and six Japanese left Yokohama on the PMSS *China* and arrived in San Francisco on May 20, 1869.[51] Because the presence of Japanese in America was still quite a rarity, the arrival of the colonists attracted press attention. San Francisco's *Alta Daily News* of May 27, 1869, fascinated its readers with a story of political intrigue, agricultural development, and racial comparison:

> Arrival of Japanese Immigrants
> Three Japanese Families—Thirty More Coming Soon—Probability That The Defeated Prince Will Follow—Japan No Home For Them Since The Civil War
>
> A Prussian gentlemen, Herr Schnell by name, who for ten years lived in the northern part of Japan, has landed in San Francisco with three Japanese families. These three families form the advance guard of a group of forty families now on its way to this port. Eighty more families are to follow, making a total of 120 families and four hundred persons coming to California to establish a permanent colony here.
>
> Most of them are silk producers, while some are cultivators of tea. They have brought with them 50,000 three-year old *kuwa* trees, which . . . are used in the production of high-quality silk. . . . Besides these, 500 three-year old, five-feet saplings of the wax tree and six million tea seeds are coming later. . . .
>
> These Japanese, far from being serfs, are free people. Should the prince of Aizu come, many more immigrants and their families are due to follow. . . .

> The whole Japanese party is dignity incarnate. By their nature they are a people who will put up with no insult or deception; that must always be borne in mind. It is dangerous to treat Japanese in the same fashion as Chinese. With their industry and highly developed skills, they have come with their families to help develop our resources.[52]

Jou also caught the attention of the press. She had "refined delicacy, very pretty forms and features, and a very winning address."[53] Moreover, she was credited with being "healthy, frugal, industrious and very affectionate."[54] These male editors had met Jou Schnell only once and certainly could not directly communicate with her because of the language barrier. Nevertheless, they extravagantly endowed her with all of the idealized, domestic virtues of a married American woman.

Unfortunately for Schnell and the Japanese colonists, Matsudaira never came to join his subjects in California after he was pardoned by the Japanese government. Without him, the Wakamatsu Colony could not attract the large numbers anticipated by Schnell and newspaper editors. In the fall of 1869, sixteen more Japanese from Aizu arrived, and a few more (probably less than ten) arrived during the summer or fall of 1870.[55] According to census records taken in July 1870, there were twenty-two Japanese with Schnell in the Gold Hill district of Coloma: fourteen men, six women, and two children.[56] Jou Schnell gave birth to one child during the colony's existence. This child, Mary, was two months old at the time of the July 1870 census, and may have been the first child born in the United States to a Japanese parent.[57] Even though the members of the Wakamatsu Colony never numbered more than thirty-five, this was the largest group of Japanese in the United States to that time.[58]

After their arrival in San Francisco, Schnell and the Japanese traveled to Placerville, where he purchased by promissory note 640 acres of land with a house in Gold Hill, Coloma, from a businessman who owned substantial tracts of land in El Dorado County.[59] Placerville, colorfully known as "Hangtown" during the heady days of the Gold Rush, was the seat of El Dorado County, and the Gold Hill district lay between Placerville and Coloma. The Wakamatsu Colony's land had been managed by Francis Veerkamp, a German immigrant who came to El Dorado County in the early 1850s and whose ranch bordered the property.[60] The colony was three miles from where gold was first discovered in 1848, and James Marshall lived nearby. So did Edwin Markham, Kanaya Nagasawa's close friend who at the time was still a young schoolteacher. There were plenty of miners in the Gold Hill area—many of whom were Chinese—but the area was dominated by farmers.

Unfortunately, contemporaneous accounts of the colony (primarily from northern California newspapers) do not tell us much about the management, distribution of labor, or daily operation of the Wakamatsu Colony during its relatively brief existence. These accounts do, however, reveal the progress of the colony's agricultural endeavors. After recovering from their long journey, the Japanese colonists planted tea seedlings and mulberry trees that had been grafted and shipped from Japan.[61] The colony's high hopes were buoyed by the initial success of their agricultural plans. Six weeks after the tea seedlings were planted, they were "all up to a finger's height."[62] At the California State Agricultural Fair in Sacramento three months later, Schnell displayed "very large and fine cocoons *morus alba japonica* tea plants, and oil plants."[63] Editors from the *Placerville Mountain Democrat* inspected the Japanese colony at Gold Hill and pronounced the tea plants in "vigorous health."[64] The mulberry trees were "perfectly healthy in appearance," while oil plants had "found their element in both soil and climate."[65] Silkworms raised at the colony were "much larger and of a brighter color than the ordinary silkworm," the editors exclaimed.[66] One year after their arrival, Schnell and two unnamed Japanese colonists put on "a fine display of Japanese plants, grown from imported shrubs and seeds" at the Horticultural Fair in San Francisco.[67] Hearing of the initial success of the colony, Eugene Van Reed sent an agricultural expert from Yokohama to determine which plants could be sent from Japan to California for profit.[68]

Despite strong anti-Chinese prejudice in the West—a racial prejudice that manifested itself from the start of the Gold Rush—the Japanese colonists from Aizu were welcomed in California. "The neighbors like these people, and give them hearty welcome," reported one San Francisco newspaper.[69] The editors of the *Placerville Mountain Democrat* informed their readers, "We can see no particular objection to the presence of any people in our midst who are willing to contribute the result of their learning, experience and skill in increasing the variety of our useful productions."[70] Moreover, they applauded the Japanese colonists for "adopt[ing] the habits and customs of the American people."[71] California boosters, such as newspaper editors and business entreprenuers, seemed to have welcomed the Japanese colonists primarily because they planned to contribute to the state's economic development, but likely their few numbers added warmth to this welcome because the colonists did not present a political or social challenge to the white, Protestant, ethnic hierarchy of this era.

The Japanese were, however, subjected to at least one overt discriminatory act. The proprietor of a dry goods store in Placerville placed a large advertisement in the newspaper announcing that he was selling his wares at cost because "THE JAPS HAVE COME AND I AM GOING TO LEAVE." He declared that he had "no desire to live in a community where Pagans probably will have the ascendency."[72] There is plenty of evidence in local newspapers and government records of anti-Chinese sentiment in El Dorado County and throughout California during this era, but this advertisement is the only evidence of overt racial discrimination against the Japanese.

What California boosters did instead was use the Japanese colonists as a "model minority" to deprecate the far more numerous Chinese.[73] The Japanese, proclaimed the patronizing editors of the *Placerville Mountain Democrat,* were "intelligent and industrious—of entirely a different character of people from the Chinese who come to this country."[74] They had a desire "to assimilate . . . with American ideas and customs," while Chinese were supposedly "tenacious of all their pagan rites and ideas."[75] A San Francisco editor bluntly complained that Chinese "circumscribe the opportunities for employment by white men," and so praised the Japanese because they would "not enter into competition" with white labor with their plans for tea and silk production.[76]

Failure, Dispersal, and Historical Memory

Despite its initial success, the Wakamatsu Colony soon encountered problems that led to its failure. Its demise resulted from two common causes of failure on the California frontier: a lack of water and a lack of money. Henry Veerkamp, son of Francis Veerkamp and neighbor of the Wakamatsu Colony, recalled later that the imported plants and seedlings died due to a lack of moisture.[77] Schnell and the colonists had apparently not realized that northern California's dry climate was so unlike Japan's humid one. A local miner also caused problems by diverting valuable water from a nearby stream.[78]

This aridity meant the Japanese colonists could not produce much tea or many silkworm cocoons for market. Schnell sold some of the colony's agricultural products at the September 1869 State Agricultural Fair in Sacramento and again at the June 1870 Horticultural Fair in San Francisco, but that appears to have been the extent of the colony's market sales. Combined with some possible financial mismanagement, the colony was unable to make payment on the promissory note for the land. As a result of two court judgments, most the colony's land reverted to its original owner by the spring of 1871.[79] Promising to return, Schnell took his wife and two children and left the colony by June 1871. Because he owed money either to the Japanese colonists or to the Veerkamps, Schnell left behind a large silk banner and two *tantō* daggers with the Matsudaira family crest emblazoned on them.[80] He never returned to Gold Hill, and nothing was ever heard from him again.[81]

With the demise of the colony, the Japanese dispersed to nearby areas. Some went to San Francisco and sought the help of Charles Brooks, Japan's consul general.[82] Existing records of the Fukuinkai (Gospel Society) indicate that two or three people from the disbanded Wakamatsu Colony were among this organization's first members.[83] A few are believed to have made their way back to Japan and to Aizu by way of Pacific Mail steamships departing from San Francisco. If so, their return was apparently kept quiet because they were still considered enemies of the Meiji government.[84]

The fates of only three Wakamatsu colonists are known in any detail. Masumizu Kuninosuke was a twenty-year-old carpenter when he arrived at Gold Hill with the second group from Aizu in the fall of 1869. After the breakup of the colony, he worked as a miner and farmer in Coloma. In 1877, he married Carrie Wilson, a woman of black and American Indian heritage.[85] They had three children who survived infancy and lived near James Marshall's cabin on a hillside overlooking the American River.[86] According to their granddaughter, the family had a hard time making a living in Coloma.[87] The family moved to Sacramento sometime after 1880, where Masumizu continued to work as a farmer and a miner, in addition to stints as a cook, a barber, and a fisherman. His grandson recalled that Masumizu was "quite a fisherman. I used to go to the river to fish with him."[88] He had one major weakness, however. "He was a gambler. And my grandmother didn't like it," his granddaughter Juanita Wong told an interviewer.[89] Masumizu seemed to be something of a loner, and around 1910 he left his family in Sacramento and drifted north to Colusa, where he died in 1915 at the age of sixty-six.[90]

According to his grandson George Elebeck, Masumizu was not subjected to racial discrimination during his lifetime, perhaps because he did not look Japanese. "You couldn't very well tell my grandfather was Japanese until you looked close at him or talked to him. He looked more like an Indian," Elebeck recalled.[91] However, after the attack on Pearl Harbor in December 1941, eighty-five-year-old Carrie Masumizu, her children, and her grandchildren—who considered themselves African American—were all interrogated by the FBI to determine if they were "enemy aliens" because Masumizu, dead for more than twenty-six years, was Japanese.[92]

Sakurai Matsunosuke, believed to have been a former samurai, and a young girl named Okei went to live with the Veerkamp family after the breakup of the colony. The 1880 manuscript census of El Dorado County shows Sakurai living with two other Japanese men in Coloma, one of whom may have also been a member of the ill-fated colony.[93] Sakurai worked as a farmhand for the Veerkamps until his death in 1901 in Coloma. According to Inez Veerkamp, her grandfather offered several times to assist Sakurai (whom they called "Matsu") in returning to Japan, but he always refused.[94]

Okei arrived in the summer or fall of 1870 with the third group of colonists and served as a nursemaid to Jou Schnell and her two children. Henry Veerkamp later recalled that "Okei-san was a nice girl, and when she wore a Japanese kimono she was really beautiful. She couldn't speak English very much, but was bright, and soon learnt needlework and cooking from my mother, who was very fond of her."[95] Okei died at the age of nineteen during the summer of 1871 after running a high fever for a few days, possibly caused by malaria.[96] When the memory of the Japanese colonists was revived by interested citizens and local history organizations in northern California and Aizu-Wakamatsu in the 1960s, Okei's youth, short life, and tragic death in a strange land became symbolic of the life and death of the Wakamatsu Colony itself.[97]

Looking to the Wakamatsu colonists, the California State government and the Japanese American Citizens League designated 1969 as the centennial year of Japanese immigration to the United States. Governor Ronald Reagan and Japanese Consul General Shima Seiichi came to Coloma on June 7, 1969, and dedicated a state historical plaque at the former site of the Wakamatsu Colony.[98] One sponsor of the centennial year and dedication ceremony was the Bank of Tokyo of California, whose chairman was Matsudaira Ichiro, the grandson of Matsudaira Katamori.[99] The Lost Colony of Wakamatsu had become a bridge of history and memory between California and Japan, El Dorado County and Aizu domain.

Immigrants

Despite their failure to establish a successful agricultural colony, these Japanese immigrants suggest the significant contribution Issei would make to the economy of California. For example, by 1918 over 10 percent of all farm products in California were produced by Japanese immigrant farmers.[100] Moreover, some of these later immigrant farmers adopted the agricultural colony as an institution for maintaining cultural connections and developing the Japanese American economic frontier.[101]

The Wakamatsu colonists were also the vanguard of Japanese refugees in the United States. Beginning in the late 1870s, Katayama Sen, Sugawara Tsutau, Takano Fusataro, Kotoku Shusui, and others seeking political refuge fled to the United States.[102] Unlike the Wakamatsu colonists, these exiles were overtly political—many were socialists or anarchists. Yet, they were fleeing from the increasingly conservative, nationalistic Japanese government dominated by officials from Satsuma and Choshu, many of whom had been the same samurai who defeated Matsudaira and Aizu in 1868.

While the colonists from Aizu had minimal direct influence on the course of relations between the United States and Japan, their departure from Japan as refugees, their intention to settle permanently in the United States, and their establishment of an agricultural colony would soon be imitated by thousands of Japanese immigrants.

EPILOGUE

Japan and the United States, 1880–1924

In 1850, Japan and the United States knew virtually nothing of one another. Between 1850 and 1880 most Americans viewed Japanese as eager students of Westernization and members of a hard-working "model minority." Yet, at the end of the Issei era of immigration in 1924, this once-positive (albeit paternalistic) image of Japanese had been transformed into a negative one: a new "yellow peril" with the business savvy, technological skills, and ambition that some Americans believed represented an economic, political, and racial threat to their country. What had happened to generate such hostility and change the generally positive image Americans had once held of Japan and Japanese immigrants?

Before Commodore Matthew Perry initiated diplomatic relations with Japan in 1853–54, Americans informally met individual Japanese, most of whom were castaway sailors picked up by American whaling and trading ships in the Pacific. One such castaway, Joseph Heco, remained in America throughout most of the 1850s. Like most *ryūgakusei* and other Japanese who followed him to America during the frontier era of U.S.-Japan relations, Heco's successful adaptation to American society was dependent upon assistance from willing benefactors as well as his own ambition and determination. Although he had connections to American and Japanese officials and worked for relatively brief periods of time for both governments, he did not develop a nationalist desire to assist with the modernization of Japan, as Japanese officials may have hoped, nor did he demonstrate a desire to be a bridge between his two countries, as his benefactors in the United States hoped. After returning to Japan, he spent the majority of his life as a private businessman and entrepreneur. His interests in the West ultimately proved to be more personal than patriotic.

Unlike Joseph Heco, early *ryūgakusei,* including Niijima Jo and the Satsuma Six, were influenced by a strong sense of nationalism. They journeyed to the West specifically because of their faith that Westernization would provide the skills and values necessary to modernize Japan into a strong nation-state that could remain independent in the midst of nineteenth-century colonization. As ambitious, young, middle- and lower-class samurai, they had been influenced by the "Eastern ethics, Western science" and "rich nation, strong army" philosophies of the *bakumatsu* era and perhaps by the call for "civilization and enlightenment" in the early Meiji Era. Most initially sought to strengthen Japan materially and militarily without compromising their country's cultural traditions and beliefs. Their success at adapting to American society was dependent upon the opportunities available to them as samurai, their own ambition, and American benefactors interested in spreading Western ideas in Japan. Some of these Japanese also adopted the Western assumption that Christianity was an integral component of Western progress. How many early Japanese residents of America went beyond this secular belief is unknown, but a number of early *ryūgakusei* clearly crossed the barrier between "Eastern ethics, Western science" and not only adopted a Christian worldview but also embraced Christianity as their personal faith. Assisted by benefactors and missionary societies such as the American Board of Commissioners for Foreign Missions, some Japanese returned home to preach the gospel in an attempt to, in their view, spiritually modernize Japan. Others joined the Christian, spiritualist community of the Brotherhood of the New Life and gained a new worldview and a spiritual refuge in an expanding, industrial, and international world of uncertainty.

To many Americans, these Japanese seemed like eager students of Westernization and thus were generally welcomed. The *Gannenmono* who journeyed to Hawaii in 1868, however, had a different reception. They were clearly motivated by the same reason most people migrate: the opportunity to better their economic situation. Yet, they became unwitting participants in a diplomatic triangle among Japan, the Kingdom of Hawaii, and the United

States. Moreover, they were part of the capitalist search for labor in the Pacific during the second half of the nineteenth century. As such, they began to be seen as a group of immigrants—who could be generically praised or condemned—instead of as individuals.

The Japanese who arrived in Coloma, California, in 1869 left their country because of an uncertain future in their home domain of Aizu. Unlike all other early Japanese residents of the United States that we know of, they were refugees. They were viewed by Americans as members of a hard-working "model minority" and were contrasted to the much-despised Chinese. Yet, they were also victims of some of the first overt acts of racism against Japanese in the United States. The agricultural goods they brought with them from Japan and their construction of a silk and tea farm indicated that they planned to remain in America for a long time, perhaps permanently. While they were the single largest group of Japanese residents in America during the frontier era of U.S.-Japan relations, like the *Gannenmono,* they were more representative of the Japanese farmers and laborers who began to emigrate to America and Hawaii in the late 1880s.

The frontier era of U.S.-Japan relations was generally amicable. Although some early Japan residents were subjected to overt acts of racism, the evidence does not indicate that racial discrimination against Japanese by Americans was the norm, as it certainly was for the Chinese in America during the same period. Unfortunately, the relationship between the two countries and the treatment of Japanese in the United States would begin to worsen by the turn of the century and would not recover for many decades.

A Changing World and a Changing Relationship

By 1880, Japan's modernization policies seemed to be working. Japan's position in the international community was much higher that it had been just thirty years earlier, and the standard of living for a modest number of Japanese, particularly in the areas of health and education, had improved. However, these policies had also resulted in severe economic problems, including spiraling inflation and a hemorrhaging government deficit. To counter these crises, the government drastically cut spending and raised taxes in 1881. On a national level, these actions worked: currency values stabilized and government spending was significantly reduced.[1]

Yet, these actions also resulted in a depression and deflation that wiped out many small business owners and farmers. Rice, the primary crop, dropped in value by 50 percent from 1881 to 1884.[2] From 1883 to 1890, over 350,000 farmers were charged with delinquent taxes. From 1884 to 1886, more than

10 percent of all rice paddy land was forfeited in lieu of taxes. Furthermore, workers' wages fell between 30 and 40 percent from 1882 to 1885.[3] The severe government policies halted inflation and government spending but intensified the personal economic hardships for millions of Japanese.[4]

Joining former samurai who had been calling for more representation in the Satsuma- and Choshu-dominated government since the mid-1870s, various critics of the government's heavy-handed policies formed into a coalition that became known as the People's Rights Movement. These critics demanded tax reduction, a representative assembly, and a constitution with democratic rights. The government's moderate response was the proclamation of the Meiji Constitution in 1889, the establishment of a parliament (the Diet) one year later, and the gradual expansion of male suffrage. The government also reacted by clamping down on its critics with what the historian Carol Gluck calls "the double approach of legal suppression and ideological suasion" of security laws and the creation of a spirit of militant nationalism through state-sponsored Shinto worship of the divine emperor.[5] And in a move designed to create a safety valve for those facing economic hardship, the Japanese government began allowing laborers to migrate overseas in the mid-1880s.

The new regulations led to the Issei era of immigration from 1885 to 1924. During these turbulent years, the United States was facing social, political, and economic difficulties. Reconstruction had utterly failed, and racism against African Americans continued almost unabated. Although disputes with Native Americans had essentially ceased with the massacre at Wounded Knee in 1890, new policies concerning them remained contentious. Robber barons, industrialization, and the growing ranks of the urban poor contributed to the economic confusion of the country. Movements for workers' rights and suffrage for women threw the social order into chaos. And then turmoil in Europe broke out into world war, with a resulting peace agreement that was fragile at best.

Prodded by organized labor in the western states, the U.S. government began to restrict immigration with the Chinese Exclusion Act of 1882. As the number of Japanese immigrants increased by the turn of the century, so too did anti-Japanese racism and even violence. For racist Americans, the equation of Japanese with Chinese was easy to make. Like Chinese, who had begun working in the United States primarily as laborers, most Issei Japanese came as laborers. Also like Chinese, Japanese did not remain as laborers for long. Many started their own farms and opened businesses and thus quickly began competing with their white counterparts. "Far from refusing to participate in American life," writes the historian Patricia Limerick, "many

Japanese were acculturating too successfully, in the judgement of their white competitors."[6] In the minds of many Americans, the Japanese soon presented as large a perceived economic threat as the Chinese had. Moreover, to ignorant Americans, Japanese and Chinese appeared physically identical.

In the upheaval of this period, Japan's adoption of the Western path to modernization was viewed as too successful by many Americans and Europeans. With military victory over China in 1895 and especially its victory over Russia in 1905, Japan had become an imperial power, complete with its own colonial territories. According to Jean-Pierre Lehmann, many Europeans interpreted Japan's defeat of Russia as "the fall of the first bastion on the periphery of European civilization, [and thus] the haunting specter of the yellow peril had definitely begun its inexorable march to the center of Western civilization."[7]

To maintain good diplomatic relations but limit Japanese immigration, the American and Japanese governments adopted informal "Gentlemen's Agreements" in 1907 and 1908. Nevertheless, California and other western states began passing laws designed to forbid land ownership by Japanese immigrants. In 1922, the U.S. Supreme Court conclusively ruled in *Takao Ozawa v. United States* that persons of Japanese ancestry born in Japan were not eligible for naturalized American citizenship because they were not black—blacks were granted citizenship in 1870—and not "white persons" as defined by naturalization acts passed by Congress since 1790.[8]

Two years later, Congress passed and President Calvin Coolidge signed the Immigration Act of 1924—with a provision frequently called the Oriental Exclusion Act—which forbid Japanese immigration to the United States. Hanihara Masanao, the Japanese ambassador in Washington, resigned in protest; so too did Cyrus Woods, the American ambassador in Tokyo. The date on which the act became effective, July 1, 1924, became known in Japan and in the Japanese American community as National Humiliation Day (*Kokujokubi*) because it humiliated a strong, modern, and proud Japan. In part as a result of this act, relations between Japan and the United States were severely strained for many years, and Japanese would not be allowed to immigrate to the United States again until the 1950s.

By the 1920s, then, the increase in the number of Japanese immigrants, the hard work and success of many Japanese farmers and business owners, and the success of Japan as a nation-state—at least in the view of Americans and Europeans who evaluated national success in terms of Western modernization—had transformed the American image of Japanese from generally positive to negative and racist.[9] This image transformation not only led Congress and the president to halt Japanese immigration but also instigated a long period of severely strained relations between the two countries. Americans who had once thought of their country as the altruistic instructor bringing Japan out of its shell of seclusion and into the modern world now saw its former pupil as a major world power—and America's most serious threat in the Pacific.

NOTES

Introduction

1. See Nordyke and Matsumoto, "The Japanese in Hawaii," 165; and Ichihashi, *Japanese in the United States*, 31–32.

2. U.S. Bureau of Foreign and Domestic Commerce, *Statistical Abstract*, 5.

3. U.S. Bureau of the Census, *Historical Statistics, Colonial Times to 1970*, part 1, 108.

4. Ibid.

5. Japanese Government, *Nihon Teikoku Tokei Nenkan*, 2:723.

6. U.S. Bureau of the Census, *Historical Statistics, Colonial Times to 1970*, part 1, 99.

7. Ibid., 98; Japanese Government, *Nihon Teikoku Tokei Nenkan*, 2:723; Wilcox and Ferenczi, *International Migration*, 374.

8. U.S. Department of the Interior, *Ninth Census*, 8; U.S. Census Office, *Statistics of the Population*, 3:378–79.

9. A copy of this agreement can be found in appendix C of Conroy, *The Japanese Frontier*, 148–49. See also U.S. Department of State, *Foreign Relations of the United States*, 1885–86, 1:474–75.

10. U.S. Bureau of Foreign and Domestic Commerce, *Statistical Abstract*, 5. These figures do not include Hawaii.

11. Japanese Foreign Ministry, *Kokaijin Meisaikan*, reel 59; Japanese Foreign Ministry, *Kokaijin Meisaibo*, reel 59.

12. G. Chang, "Asian Americans," 113. See also Ian Tyrrell's discussion of transnational history in "American Exceptionalism."

13. See Silberman, *Ministers of Modernization*, and the discussion of samurai subdivisions in Beasley, *Meiji Restoration*, 24–31.

14. Confucius, *The Analects,* 74. According to the legendary *Kojiki* (Record of Ancient Matters), Confucianism was first introduced to Japan in the third century C.E. by an emissary from Korea who presented Japanese Emperor Ojin with a copy of *The Analects.* There is no doubt, however, that Prince Shotoku and the imperial family were well-acquainted with Confucianism by 600 C.E.

15. Walthall, *Social Protest and Popular Culture,* 3.

16. Asao, *Sakoku;* Toby, *State and Diplomacy.*

17. Toby, *State and Diplomacy,* 158.

18. Sakai, "Satsuma Ryukyu Trade."

19. Walker, "Reappraising the Sakoku Paradigm."

20. Ellison, "Christianity and the Daimyo."

21. For example, see Hayashi Razan, "The Confucian Way," in Tsunoda, De Bary, and Keene, *Sources of Japanese Tradition,* 1:347–48. Hayashi and his descendants were official scholars to the Tokugawa shoguns. They emphasized the rationalist and humanist approach of the twelfth-century Chinese philosopher Chu Hsi. Chu Hsi's philosophy, and the Confucian ideology of the Hayashi family and the Tokugawa *bakufu,* is sometimes called neo-Confucianism. See Nosco, *Confucianism and Tokugawa Culture,* especially chapters 1–3; and Ooms, *Tokugawa Ideology.*

22. Ellison, *Deus Destroyed,* 3.

23. Pacheco, "The Europeans in Japan," 80.

24. Kaga no kami, Hotta Hotta Masamori, et al., to Sakakibara Hida no kami and Sengoku Yamato no kami, "Edict of 1635 Ordering the Closing of Japan," in Lu, *Sources of Japanese History,* 216–17.

25. Ibid.

26. For more detailed descriptions and analyses of this episode, see "Shimabara no ran," in Asao, *Sakoku,* 279–325; and "The Japanese Messiah," in Ivan Morris, *The Nobility of Failure,* 143–79.

27. "Completion of Exclusion, 1639," in Lu, *Sources of Japanese History,* 218.

28. "Memorandum" attached to "Completion of Exclusion, 1639," in Lu, *Sources of Japanese History.*

29. "The Fate of the Embassy from Macao, by Antonio Cardim," in Cooper, *They Came to Japan,* 401–2.

30. "Proclamation Board No. 3, 3rd Month of the 4th Year of Keio [Apr.–May 1868]," in U.S. Department of State, *Foreign Relations of the United States,* 1868–69, 749.

31. "A Decree of the Mikado's Court," June 8, 1868, in U.S. Department of State, *Foreign Relations of the United States,* 1868–69, 771.

32. Yoshiya Abe, "From Prohibition to Toleration," 132.

33. Asao, *Sakoku,* 307–8; Goodman, *Japan,* 14–15.

34. Goodman, *Japan,* 16–17. For an overview of this era of Dutch overseas history, see Israel, *Dutch Primacy.*

35. Sakamaki, *Japan and the United States,* 122.

36. Quoted in Wakabayashi, *Anti-Foreignism and Western Learning,* 60. Chinese, Korean, Ryukuan, and Dutch vessels were exempted from this expulsion edict.

37. Sakamaki, *Japan and the United States,* 12–19. See also Osada, "Life of Takano Nagahide."

38. Aizawa Seishisai, *Shinron* (1825), quoted in Wakabayashi, *Anti-Foreignism and Western Learning,* 169.

39. Goodman, *Japan,* 228.

40. Ibid., 231.

41. Totman, *Early Modern Japan,* 541.

42. Kennedy, *Rise and Fall,* 149–50.

43. Sakuma Shozan, "Kaibosaku," in Rei, *Nihon no Meicho,* 123. See also Kimata Ohira's biography, *Sakuma Shozan,* 62–68.

44. Sakuma, "Kaibosaku," 123.

45. R. Chang, *From Prejudice to Tolerance,* 146.

46. Sakuma Shozan, "Seikenroku," in Rei, *Nihon no Meicho,* 91–110. An abbreviated English translation is included in Tsunoda, De Bary, and Keene, *Sources of Japanese Tradition,* 1:101–9.

47. Sakuma, "Seikenroku," 95.

48. Ibid., 96.

49. Ibid., 100.

50. Ibid., 102.

51. Potter, *The Impending Crisis,* 17.

52. Japanese Foreign Ministry, *Nihon Gaiko Bunsho,* 15:127–58, and U.S. Department of State, *Foreign Relations of the United States,* 1879–80, 1:643–49, contain documents on Grant's visit to Japan. Grant and his wife, Julia, stayed in Japan from June 20 to September 3, 1879, the last stop on their world tour.

53. Edward Livingston to Edmund Roberts, Jan. 27, 1832, in U.S. Department of State, *Diplomatic Instructions, Special Missions,* vol. 1, reel 152.

54. Ibid.

55. John Forsyth to Edmund Roberts, Mar. 20, 1835, in U.S. Department of State, *Diplomatic Instructions, Special Missions,* vol. 1, reel 152.

56. "Extract of Sailing Instructions to Commodore James Biddle, May 22, 1845," and James Biddle to George Bancroft, July 31, 1846, both in U.S. Senate, *Senate Documents,* 64.

57. "Translation from the Japanese Explanatory Edict," in U.S. Senate, *Senate Documents,* 68. This edict implies, and Biddle states, that it originated from the emperor, but it almost certainly came from the *bakufu* in Edo. The edict given to Biddle was in Dutch and Chinese.

58. "Extract of Sailing Instructions" and Biddle to Bancroft, both in U.S. Senate, *Senate Documents,* 64–65.

59. Daniel Webster to John Aulick, June 10, 1851, in U.S. Department of State, *Diplomatic Instructions, Special Missions,* vol. 1, reel 152; John Kennedy to Matthew Perry, Nov. 13, 1852, in U.S. Department of State, *Correspondence,* 2–4. The most

valuable primary sources of the Perry mission are *Correspondence Relative to the Naval Expedition to Japan,* which consists of orders and messages by Perry and government officials, and the lengthy official report written by Francis L. Hawks, *Narrative of the Expedition of an American Squadron to the China Seas and Japan.*

60. In addition to the steam frigates *Mississippi* and *Susquehanna,* the sloops *Plymouth* and *Saratoga* and a supply ship composed Perry's fleet on the first visit to Japan in July 1853.

61. Hawks, *Narrative of the Expedition,* 269.

62. Ibid., 273; "Notes Referring to Events which Transpired Pending the Preliminary Negotiations of Commodore M. C. Perry with the Authorities of Japan in July 1853," in U.S. Department of State, *Correspondence,* 46–47. These notes were written by Perry and dated July 30, 1853.

63. Millard Fillmore, President of the United States of America, to His Imperial Majesty, the Emperor of Japan, Nov. 13, 1852, in U.S. Department of State, *Correspondence,* 9–11. The same document can be found in U.S. Department of State, *Diplomatic Instructions, Special Missions,* vol. 1, reel 152, and in Hawks, *Narrative of the Expedition,* 256–57. Fillmore was no longer the president by the time this letter was presented to the Japanese in July 1853.

64. Fillmore to the emperor, 10.

65. Tokugawa Nariaki to Bakufu, Aug. 14, 1853, in Japanese Foreign Ministry, *Bakumatsu Gaikoku Kankei Bunsho,* 1:509–22.

66. Ibid., 1:514–15.

67. Shimazu Nariakira to Bakufu, Sept. 2, 1853, in ibid., 1:636–38.

68. Ibid., 1:638.

69. Matsudaira Yoshinaga to Bakufu, Sept. 9, 1853, in ibid., 2:57–58.

70. Ii Naosuke to Bakufu, Oct. 1, 1853, in ibid., 2:256–57.

71. Ibid., 2:257.

72. Ibid., 2:258–59.

73. Treaty of Peace and Amity between the United States of America and the Empire of Japan, Mar. 30, 1854, in Japanese Foreign Ministry, *Kyujoyaku isan* 1–5. The same document can be found in Hawks, *Narrative of the Expedition,* and in U.S. Department of State, *Correspondence.* The treaty was signed in Kanagawa by Hayashi Noboru, Ido Satohiro, Udono Choei, and Perry and is commonly known as the Kanagawa Treaty.

74. Treaty of Peace and Amity, in *Kyujoyaku isan,* 9–12. Harris was elevated to the post of minister to Japan in 1861. His secretary, Henry Heusken, a Dutch-born American citizen who was fluent in Dutch and English and rapidly learned to speak and read Japanese, was crucial to Harris's diplomatic success.

Chapter 1: Joseph Heco, a Castaway in America

1. *Daily Alta California,* Mar. 5, 1851.

2. For more information on these early castaways, see Sakamaki, *Japan and the United States;* Plummer, *Shogun's Reluctant Ambassadors;* Kohl, "Strangers in a

Strange Land"; Grace P. Morris, "Wreck of a Japanese Junk"; and Arakawa, *Ikoku Hyoryu Monogatari.*

3. Brooks, *Japanese Wrecks.* See also the list of shipwrecks compiled by Plummer in the appendix of *The Shogun's Reluctant Ambassadors.*

4. Unless otherwise noted, the rest of this section is based on the following sources: Hisakazu Kaneko, *Manjiro;* Warriner, *Voyager to Destiny;* Bernard, *Life and Times of John Manjiro;* and Plummer, *Shogun's Reluctant Ambassadors.* These works are primarily dependent upon Nakahama, *Nakahama Manjiro Hyoryuki* and *Nakahama Manjiro Den.* Toichiro Nakahama was the son of Nakahama Manjiro.

5. Very little is known about Denzo and Goemon after their return to Nakanohama.

6. The record is unclear on this point. Some later sources suggest he had a leading role in advising the *bakufu* during these crucial negotiations. However, official and contemporaneous sources do not mention Manjiro at all.

7. Original copies of *Hyoryuki,* published in two small volumes in Edo in 1863, are extremely rare. Fortunately, I was able to locate one in the Bancroft Library at the University of California at Berkeley. *Hyoryuki* was reprinted in full in the relatively more accessible *Ikoku Hyoryu Kidanshu,* compiled by Ishii Kendo. Working from the 1863 original, Tosh Motofuji translated it into English in 1955. I have used the Motofuji translation and Ishii edition of *Hyoryuki* because they are relatively more accessible to scholars than the original. I carefully compared the original *Hyoryuki* with the Ishii edition and found the latter to be virtually identical, except that Ishii changed the chapter headings and some punctuation. Motofuji's work is an accurate translation of the original, though he included Ishii's chapter headings and placed all of Heco's drawings at the back of the book instead of leaving them where they appeared in the original.

8. Heco, *Narrative of a Japanese.*

9. Goodwin, *Autobiography,* 23, 16.

10. Hikozo, *Hyoryuki,* xi (Motofuji trans.), 527 (Ishii ed.).

11. Ibid.

12. Heco, *Narrative of a Japanese,* 1:231, 278, 2:1–2; Francis Hall, *Japan through American Eyes,* 306.

13. Francis Hall, *Japan through American Eyes,* 306.

14. Heco, *Narrative of a Japanese,* 1:278.

15. James Murdoch, "Introduction," in Heco, *Narrative of a Japanese,* 1:i.

16. In *Humanity above Nation,* Halloran, Sakai, and Shinoda state that Heco gave the notebooks to Murdoch (34).

17. For example, documents in U.S. Department of State, *Despatches;* U.S. Department of State, *Diplomatic Instructions, Japan;* Francis Hall's 1859–66 diary in *Japan through American Eyes;* Beverly Sanders's personal papers cited in Saul, "Beverly C. Sanders"; John Brooke's personal papers cited in Brooke, *John M. Brooke;* personal papers cited in Hine, *Edward Kern;* personal papers cited in Altman, "Eugene Van Reed"; Jonas's study of newspapers in Japan, "Foreign

Influence"; Brooks's *Japanese Wrecks;* Muragaki's *Kokkai Nikki;* sources cited in Chikamori's biography, *Josefu Hiko;* and contemporaneous newspaper articles from Hawaii, San Francisco, and Washington, D.C., verify the major facts of Heco's experiences in the 1850s and 1860s.

18. Hikozo, *Hyoryuki,* 1 (Motofuji trans.); Heco, *Narrative of a Japanese,* 1:1.

19. Heco, *Narrative of a Japanese,* 1:3.

20. Ibid., 1:33.

21. Ibid., 1:33–34.

22. Ibid., 1:14–15.

23. Ibid., 1:26–27.

24. Ibid., 1:27, 33.

25. Ibid., 1:32.

26. Ibid., 1:36–37.

27. Hikozo, *Hyoryuki,* 2, 4, 5, 7 (Motofuji trans.).

28. Heco, *Narrative of a Japanese,* 1:37.

29. Brooks, *Japanese Wrecks,* 7–8. For a description of Japanese ship construction during the Tokugawa era, see Plummer, *Shogun's Reluctant Ambassadors,* 33–36.

30. Hikozo, *Hyoryuki,* 13 (Motofuji trans.).

31. Hikozo, *Hyoryuki,* 13 (Motofuji trans.).

32. Heco, *Narrative of a Japanese,* 1:61.

33. Ibid., 1:63.

34. While spoken Japanese and Chinese are completely different languages, written Japanese uses many Chinese-based ideographic characters known as *kanji.*

35. Hikozo, *Hyoryuki,* 13–14 (Motofuji trans.), 537–38 (Ishii ed.).

36. Ibid., 66–67 (Motofuji trans.).

37. Ibid., 66.

38. Ibid., 67–68.

39. Ibid., 70–71.

40. Ibid., 72–73. This phrase can also be translated as "Ignorance is bliss."

41. Ibid., 74.

42. Ibid., 77.

43. Ibid., 79.

44. Ibid., 80.

45. Ibid., 81.

46. Lotchin, *San Francisco,* 100. See also Paul, *Far West,* 66–91.

47. Heco, *Narrative of a Japanese,* 1:100, 108; Plummer, *Shogun's Reluctant Ambassadors,* 224. The U.S. government intended to return the Japanese from the *Eiriki Maru* with an American expedition to Japan, which turned out to be Commodore Perry's 1853–54 expedition. Because of delays in starting the expedition, however, most of Heco's shipmates managed to return to their homeland before Perry arrived in Japan in June 1853. See Hawks, *Narrative of the Expedition,* 396–98, 557–58; and Williams, *Journal,* 122.

48. Heco, *Narrative of a Japanese,* 1:121.

49. Ibid., 1:105.
50. Saul, "Beverly C. Sanders," 156.
51. Ibid., 156–57; Soule, Gihon, and Nisbet, *Annals*, 738.
52. Saul, "Beverly C. Sanders," 157.
53. Ibid., 157, 159.
54. *Daily Alta California*, July 31, 1853.
55. Saul, "Beverly C. Sanders," 159; Hikozo, *Hyoryuki*, 41 (Motofuji trans.).
56. Beverly Sanders to Joseph Heco, July 2, 1858, in Heco, *Narrative of a Japanese*, 1:162. Sanders had one son, but Heco mentions him only once (Saul, "Beverly C. Sanders," 170; Hikozo, *Hyoryuki*, 42 [Motofuji trans.]).
57. *Washington, D.C., Evening Star*, Nov. 3, 1857. Sanders's letter to Gwin is dated September 3, 1857.
58. *Daily Alta California*, Mar. 5, 1851.
59. Heco, *Narrative of a Japanese*, 1:134.
60. Saul, "Beverly C. Sanders," 157.
61. Heco, *Narrative of a Japanese*, 1:144.
62. Hikozo, *Hyoryuki*, 54 (Motofuji trans.).
63. Ibid.; Heco, *Narrative of a Japanese*, 1:144.
64. Saul, "Beverly C. Sanders," 167.
65. Heco, *Narrative of a Japanese*, 1:148; *Washington, D.C. Evening Star*, Nov. 3, 1857.
66. Hikozo, *Hyoryuki*, 56 (Motofuji trans.).
67. Heco, *Narrative of a Japanese*, 1:148.
68. Hikozo, *Hyoryuki*, 30–31, 81–91 (Motofuji trans.). He made these drawings when he returned to America in late 1861 and early 1862.
69. Ibid., 46.
70. Heco, *Narrative of a Japanese*, 1:138.
71. Ibid., 1:138.
72. Hikozo, *Hyoryuki*, 47 (Motofuji trans.). This was in August 1853.
73. Heco, *Narrative of a Japanese*, 1:139.
74. See Schivelbusch, *Railway Journey*, especially chap. four.
75. The term *kokujin* appears in *Hyoryuki* (see Ishii ed., 544).
76. In the sixteenth and early seventeenth centuries, the Portuguese, Spanish, and British brought a few black servants with them to Japan, while the staff of the Dutch East India Company at Deshima during the Tokugawa era usually included a few black African slaves.
77. Hikozo, *Hyoryuki*, 22 (Motofuji trans.), 544 (Ishii ed.).
78. Ibid.
79. Heco, *Narrative of a Japanese*, 1:90–91.
80. Hikozo, *Hyoryuki*, 73 (Motofuji trans.).
81. Ibid., 75–76.
82. Ibid., 76.
83. Heco, *Narrative of a Japanese*, 1:145.

84. Sanders's obituary in the *New York Times,* Dec. 27, 1883, noted his military service in the Confederacy.

85. Gwin was a native of Mississippi, where he still owned a large plantation with slaves at the start of the Civil War. After being jailed on suspicion of treason, Gwin fled to France for the duration of the war.

86. *Honolulu Friend,* July 1, 1862. This newspaper was both pro-North and pro-abolition.

87. U.S. Bureau of Foreign and Domestic Commerce, *Statistical Abstract,* 5; Loosely, *Foreign Born Population,* 6–10.

88. Heco, *Narrative of a Japanese,* 1:115.

89. In *Humanity above Nation,* Halloran, Sakai, and Shinoda verify Heco's baptism by citing the church registry for October 30, 1854 (23). Chikamori includes a photocopy of Heco's Certificate of Baptism from the same church, also dated October 30, 1854 (*Josefu Hiko* 17).

90. Heco, *Narrative of a Japanese,* 1:147.

91. Hikozo, *Hyoryuki,* 72 (Motofuji trans.).

92. Ibid.

93. Ibid., 78.

94. Heco, *Narrative of a Japanese,* 2:144. Complaints by foreign diplomats and responses by the Japanese government concerning this crackdown can be found in Japanese Foreign Ministry, *Nihon Gaiko Bunsho,* 5:462–71, 495–600; and U.S. Department of State, *Foreign Relations of the United States,* 1870–71, 453–85.

95. Heco, *Narrative of a Japanese,* 1:139; Hikozo, *Hyoryuki,* 50 (Motofuji trans.).

96. Shigeki Oka, "Kaikoku Isshi: Amerika Hikozo Jijoden," pt. 2, p. 2, Shigeki Oka Papers, Japanese American Research Project Collection.

97. Hikozo, *Hyoryuki,* 51 (Motofuji trans.).

98. Ibid.; Saul, "Beverly C. Sanders," 159.

99. Heco, *Narrative of a Japanese,* 1:140–41. There is a slightly briefer, but similar description of this encounter in Hikozo, *Hyoryuki,* 50–51 (Motofuji trans.).

100. Heco, *Narrative of a Japanese,* 1:142.

101. Ibid., 1:151; Hikozo, *Hyoryuki,* 56–57 (Motofuji trans.).

102. *Washington, D.C., Evening Star,* Feb. 16, 1858.

103. Ibid.

104. Heco, *Narrative of a Japanese,* 1:152. A similar description appears in Hikozo, *Hyoryuki,* 57 (Motofuji trans.).

105. Heco, *Narrative of a Japanese,* 1:280–81.

106. Ibid., 1:290.

107. Ibid., 1:299.

108. Ibid., 1:299–302.

109. However, *Hyoryuki* includes a section entitled "Additional Notes to a Castaway's Account" on topical subjects that were written as a result of Heco's 1861–62 sojourn in the United States. See Hikozo, *Hyoryuki,* 64–89 (Motofuji trans.), 574–95 (Ishii ed.).

110. Sandburg, *Abraham Lincoln,* 1:376–77.

111. Heco, *Narrative of a Japanese,* 1:300–302.

112. Ibid., 1:158; Brooke, *John M. Brooke,* 162; John Bingham to Hamilton Fish, Sept. 8, 1875, in U.S. Department of State, *Despatches,* reel 30, which includes a copy of Heco's naturalization papers.

113. Heco was granted citizenship under the rules of the May 26, 1824, Naturalization Act (a revision of the 1790 Naturalization Act), which can be found in U.S. Congress, *Statutes,* 69.

114. Hamilton Fish to John Bingham, July 2, 1875, in U.S. Department of State, *Diplomatic Instructions, Japan,* vol. 2, reel 105.

115. Bingham to Fish, Sept. 8, 1875.

116. For example, California enacted an anti-Chinese foreign miners' tax in 1852 and Oregon enacted a law requiring Chinese merchants and miners to pay a four-dollar monthly fee in 1858. See Hing, *Making and Remaking Asian America,* appendix C, 201–31.

117. U.S. Bureau of the Census, *Chinese and Japanese,* 10–11.

118. *Takao Ozawa v. United States,* 260 U.S. 178 (1922).

119. Bingham to Fish, Sept. 8, 1875. Heco's citizenship papers are dated June 30, 1858.

120. *Washington, D.C., Evening Star,* Nov. 3, 1857.

121. Heco, *Narrative of a Japanese,* 1:201; C. O. Shepard to Charles De Long, Jan. 6, 1873, in U.S. Department of State, *Despatches,* reel 22, includes Heco on a registry list of Americans in the Kanagawa-Yokohama area. Upon Heco's death in 1897, he was buried in the foreign section of Aoyama Cemetary in Tokyo.

122. Brooke, *John M. Brooke,* 162.

123. Heco, *Narrative of a Japanese,* 1:162–64, includes a farewell letter from Sanders to Heco.

124. Ibid., 1:172, 212. Hine, *Edward Kern,* and Brooke, *John M. Brooke,* contain independent descriptions of Heco and the *Fenimore Cooper*'s journey from San Francisco to Hawaii. Heco was sick most of the time.

125. Heco, *Narrative of a Japanese,* 1:184; Margaret Van Reed Biddle, "Eugene Miller Van Reed: An Opening Wedge of Japan," 5, ca. 1907, box 19.1, group 1, Griffis Collection.

126. Heco, *Narrative of a Japanese,* 1:159.

127. Biddle, "Eugene Miller Van Reed," 5. Many letters contained in the Marumoto Papers attest to Van Reed's Japanese language ability.

128. Heco, *Narrative of a Japanese,* 1:212. This photograph is reproduced in Jonas, "Foreign Influence," 53, and Chikamori, *Josefu Hiko,* 48.

129. Heco, *Narrative of a Japanese,* 1:340–43.

130. In addition to Heco's descriptions in his memoirs, Francis Hall documents such activities in *Japan through American Eyes.*

131. Heco, *Narrative of a Japanese,* 1:218–20.

132. Francis Hall, *Japan through American Eyes,* 306.

133. Heco, *Narrative of a Japanese,* 2:80–81. This appears to be a reference to A. L. Portman.

134. Ibid., 1:309–10.

135. Ibid., 2:16.

136. Jonas, "Foreign Influence," 50–53. Chikamori's *Josefu Hiko* is especially devoted to this aspect of Heco's life.

137. Heco, *Narrative of a Japanese,* 2:163.

138. Halloran, Sakai, and Shinoda, *Humanity above Nation,* 34.

139. Heco, *Narrative of a Japanese,* 2:90, 134.

140. Ibid., 2:94.

141. Altman, "Eugene Van Reed," 11.

142. Heco, *Narrative of a Japanese,* 2:236.

143. Ibid., 2:243–44.

Chapter 2: *Ryūgakusei,* Rutgers, and the American Experience

1. Ferris, "How the Japanese Came to New Brunswick," 30.

2. Ibid.

3. Harootunian, *Toward Restoration,* 355.

4. Samuels, *Rich Nation, Strong Army,* 35.

5. Inoweye Kawatsi, Matsudaira Suwo, and Matsudaira Nin to Robert Van Valkenberg, Nov. 6, 1866, and Robert Van Valkenberg to William Seward, Nov. 10, 1866, both in U.S. Department of State, *Foreign Relations of the United States,* 1865–66, pt. 2, p. 227.

6. Umegaki, *After the Restoration,* 79; Beasley, *Meiji Restoration,* 208.

7. Ishizuki, *Kindai Nihon,* 49–85. See also Bandera, "Case Study," 6–7.

8. Ishizuki, *Kindai Nihon,* 141, 445–54; Conte, "Overseas Study," 9. See also Japanese National Commission for UNESCO, *The Role of Education,* 118.

9. Ishizuki, *Kindai Nihon,* 141; Conte, "Overseas Study," 21.

10. Ishizuki, *Kindai Nihon,* 141; Conte, "Overseas Study," 21. Forty-nine went to England, thirty-two to France, thirty-three to the United States, and thirty-nine to other countries.

11. Japanese Government, *Nihon Teikoku Tokei Nenkan,* 1:81–83, 2:723. See also Conte, "Overseas Study," 27; and Ishizuki, *Kindai Nihon,* 204. After the United States, the two destinations with the largest percentage of students were "other," with 22 percent, and England, with 20 percent.

12. Ishizuki, *Kindai Nihon,* 204.

13. Japanese Government, *Nihon Teikoku Tokei Nenkan,* 1:81–83, 2:723; Conte, "Overseas Study," 27; Ishizuki, *Kindai Nihon,* 204; Schwantes, *Japanese and Americans,* 199; and Japanese National Commission for UNESCO, *Development of a Modern System of Education,* 17.

14. Tsunoda, De Bary, and Keene, *Sources of Japanese Tradition,* 2:136–37.

15. Fukuzawa Yukichi, "Gakumon no Susume," in *Fukuzawa Yukichi on Education,* 66–67.

16. Harootunian, *Toward Restoration,* 147.

17. Beasley, *Japan Encounters the Barbarian,* 1.

18. Harootunian, *Toward Restoration,* 349.

19. By the mid-1870s, the Meiji government began sending more government-sponsored students to Germany and England than to the United States. Including privately and domain-sponsored students, however, significantly more *ryūgakusei* journeyed to the United States than to any other country. See Conte, "Overseas Study," 36–38; and Ishizuki, *Kindai Nihon,* 204–5.

20. Kemble, *Hundred Years,* 12–13.

21. Minakawa, *Christian Teaching,* 52–59.

22. Conte, "Overseas Study," 92–93; Schwantes, *Japanese and Americans,* 195. Most missionaries and other Americans in Japan were Protestant. *Heathen* was commonly used by Protestants in the nineteenth century to describe non-Christians.

23. See Iriye, *Across the Pacific,* 45–50.

24. Conte, "Overseas Study," 33–34; Aruga, "Japanese Scholarship," 39.

25. For example, C. O. Shepard to Charles De Long, Jan. 6, 1873, in U.S. Department of State, *Despatches,* reel 22, includes a registry list of 278 Americans (not including wives and children) living in Kanagawa/Yokohama. This group was far larger than any other group of Westerners living in the area.

26. William Griffis, "Rutgers and the Orient," 8, 1925, box 12.7, group 1, Griffis Collection.

27. This figure is based upon my examination of the 1870s volumes of *The Scarlet Letter* (the Rutgers annual yearbook); the *Rutgers College Targum* (the student newspaper); Griffis, *Rutgers Graduates in Japan,* 21–27; and Ishizuki, *Kindai Nihon,* 445–85. William Demarest estimates that there were "perhaps forty" Japanese at Rutgers in the 1860s and 1870s (*History of Rutgers College,* 440).

28. Griffis, *Rutgers Graduates in Japan,* 21.

29. Ibid., 25.

30. Bandera, "Case Study," 55–65; Griffis, *Rutgers Graduates in Japan,* 21–26; Ishizuki, *Kindai Nihon,* 445–85.

31. U.S. Department of the Interior, *Ninth Census,* 8, 50, 203.

32. Griffis, *Rutgers Graduates in Japan,* 21.

33. Demarest, *History of Rutgers College,* 412.

34. The student enrollment estimate is based upon an examination of *Scarlet Letter* volumes from the 1870s.

35. Schwantes, *Japanese and Americans,* 154.

36. Griffis, *Rutgers Graduates in Japan,* 22, 25.

37. Griffis, *Mikado's Empire,* 8.

38. Demarest, *History of Rutgers College,* 444; Tadashi Kaneko, "Contributions of David Murray," 303.

39. David Murray to Mori Arinori, Mar. 7, 1872, in Mori, *Education in Japan,* 102.

40. Ibid., 100.

41. Mori Arinori to David Murray, n.d., in Okubu, *Mori Arinori Zenshu,* 3:154.

42. Lanman and Mori, *Japanese in America.* This book is in three parts. Part 1 is by Lanman and concerns the Iwakura mission. Part 2 contains the students' essays. Part 3 is Mori's "Life and Resources in America." Parts 2 and 3 were originally intended for a Japanese audience.

43. Inoue Ryoichi (E. R. Enouys), "The Practical Americans," in Lanman and Mori, *Japanese in America,* 81–82. Inoue was briefly a student at Rutgers, then he went to Harvard University to study law. See Ishizuki, *Kindai Nihon,* 446.

44. Inoue, "The Practical Americans," 83.

45. Ibid., 84.

46. Hicomaro Yashida, "Oriental Civilization," in Lanman and Mori, *Japanese in America,* 101.

47. Takasu, "My First Impressions of Foreigners," folder 5, box 20.1, group 1, Griffis Collection.

48. Ibid.

49. Ibid.

50. Takato Shioji, "Co-Education of Boys and Girls," in Lanman and Mori, *Japanese in America,* 94. Takato attended Columbia Law School in the early 1870s and died in New York without returning to Japan. See Ishizuki, *Kindai Nihon,* 470.

51. Takato, "Co-Education of Boys and Girls," 95.

52. Mori, "Life and Resources in America," 329.

53. Japanese National Commission for UNESCO, *Development of a Modern System of Education,* 15–17.

54. Japanese Foreign Ministry, *Nihon Gaiko Bunsho,* vol. 7, pt. 1, pp. 89–90. See also Rose, *Tsuda Umeko;* and Kuno, *Unexpected Destinations.*

55. Lanman and Mori, *Japanese in America,* 77.

56. Takato, "Co-Education of Boys and Girls," 93.

57. Kanda Naibu, "Christmas," in Lanman and Mori, *Japanese in America,* 164; Griffis, *Rutgers Graduates in Japan,* 25.

58. Lanman and Mori, *Japanese in America,* 153.

59. Inoue, "The Practical Americans," 83.

60. Toyama Masakazu, "Expedition to a Romish Church," in Lanman and Mori, *Japanese in America,* 139. Toyama was working for Mori in Washington, D.C., at the time he wrote his essays. When he returned to Japan, he became a professor at Tokyo Kaiseigakko. Many years later, he was appointed president of Tokyo Imperial University (the former Tokyo Kaiseigakko).

61. Toyama Masakazu, "Raid on the Missionaries," in Lanman and Mori, *Japanese in America,* 158.

62. Toyama Masakazu, "The Chinese Ambassador in France," in Lanman and Mori, *Japanese in America,* 88.

63. Silberman, *Ministers of Modernization,* 108–17.

64. Robert Van Valkenberg to Date Chuinguong, July 19, 1869, and Date Chuinguong to Japanese Students, July 8, 1869, both in U.S. Department of State, *Despatches,* reel 12. The U.S. government permitted twelve Japanese to enroll at the Naval Academy from 1869 to 1906, four of whom graduated from the regular course of study. See Ellicott, "Japanese Students."

65. Griffis, *Rutgers Graduates in Japan,* 23; Ellicott, "Japanese Students," 303.

66. Hatakeyama Yoshinari to William Griffis, July 18, 1872, Hatakeyama folder, Griffis Collection; Griffis, *Rutgers Graduates in Japan,* 22; Murray, "Hatakeyama Yoshinari," 108–13.

67. Japanese Foreign Ministry, *Nihon Gaiko Bunsho,* 15:127–58; U.S. Department of State, *Foreign Relations of the United States,* 1879–80, 1:643–49. For a narrative of Grant's visit to Japan, see McCabe, *Tour around the World,* 720–85.

68. Griffis, *Rutgers Graduates in Japan,* 23.

69. *Scarlet Letter,* 1873, 37; *Scarlet Letter,* 1874, 33.

70. *Scarlet Letter,* 1874, 46, 50.

71. Ibid., 54. Hattori is not listed as a player, however.

72. Bandera, "Case Study," 64–65.

73. Ibid.; Demarest, *History of Rutgers College,* 441–42.

74. Ferris, "How the Japanese Came to New Brunswick," 30.

75. Ibid.

76. Sentaro Ise to Mrs. Van Arsedale, Aug. 25, 1869, and Numagawa to Mrs. Van Arsedale, Sept. 18, 1869, both in folder A, Maria Van Arsedale Papers.

77. Griffis, *Rutgers Graduates in Japan,* 22; Ishizuki, *Kindai Nihon,* 453.

78. Date Chuinguong to Japanese Students, July 8, 1869, in U.S. Department of State, *Despatches,* reel 12; Ishizuki, *Kindai Nihon,* 84.

79. Sentaro Ise to Mrs. Van Arsedale, Jan. 15, 1870, in folder A, Maria Van Arsedale Papers.

80. Griffis, *Rutgers Graduates in Japan,* 22; Ellicott, "Japanese Students," 303. Ishizuki erroneously indicates that Yokoi graduated from the Naval Academy (*Kindai Nihon,* 454).

81. Sawa Nobuyuki and Terashima Munenori to Charles De Long, Jan. 28, 1870, in U.S. Department of State, *Foreign Relations of the United States,* 1870–71, 474.

82. William Griffis, "Japanese Students Educated Abroad: Their Influence and Record," ca. 1887, box 8.1, group 1, Griffis Collection.

83. For example, Hatakeyama became a Christian while Ogimi Motoichiro and Kimura Kumage became missionaries. See Murray, "Hatakeyama Yoshinari of Japan," 111; and Griffis, *Rutgers Graduates in Japan,* 22, 24.

84. The Matsudaira brothers were from Kuwana domain, whose *daimyō* before the Meiji Restoration was Matsudaira Sadaaki, the younger brother of Matsudaira Katamori of Aizu. However, I have been unable to confirm that Sadaaki was their father.

85. Ruth J. Simmons, "Matsudaira Brothers, Memo to the Files," "Class of '79,

Scientific Section," and "New City Engineer of Bradford and His Record of Enterprise," *Philadelphia Times,* Mar. 20, 1884, all in Matsudaira brothers file, Griffis Collection.

86. "Curious Scientific Instrument," *New York Times,* Feb. 18, 1880; "A Japanese Inventor," *New York Daily Tribune,* Feb. 29, 1880.

87. *Philadelphia Times,* Mar. 20, 1884; "Our New City Engineer—Something about Bradford's Japanese Official," undated newspaper article from Bradford, Pennsylvania, Matsudaira brothers file, Griffis Collection. These articles state that Matsudaira was "elected" to the post but he was actually appointed by the Bradford City Council.

88. Obituary notice of Tado Atsz Matsudaira, *Denver Republican,* Nov. 6, 1888; Joe Grant Masaoka, "Surveyed Wild West in Roaring '80s," *San Francisco Pacific Citizen,* Apr. 16, 1968.

89. Griffis, "Japanese Students Educated Abroad."

90. William Griffis, "Progress in Japan," in *Mikado's Empire.*

Chapter 3: Niijima Jo, Japanese Puritan

1. Hardy, *Life and Letters of Neesima,* 1; Niijima Jo to Fukushi, Aug. 9, 1864, in *Niijima Jo Zenshu,* 6:3.

2. Hardy, *Life and Letters of Neesima,* 2; Watanabe, *Niijima Jo,* 49.

3. Much of this correspondence, plus letters written to Niijima from these benefactors, were collected in *Life and Letters of Joseph Hardy Neesima,* edited by Arthur Hardy, soon after Niijima's death in 1890. Most of these letters, plus other writings, are included in volumes 6 and 7 of *Niijima Jo Zenshu* (The Complete Works of Niijima Jo), collected and edited by a group of professors and former professors from Doshisha University and published in 1985 and 1995. Other correspondence and documentary materials used in this chapter are from the Joseph Neesima Papers at Amherst College.

4. Scheiner, *Christian Converts;* Watanabe, *Niijima Jo.*

5. Cary, "Uchimura," 441.

6. Hardy, *Life and Letters of Neesima,* 2–3; Niijima, "Hakodate Kiko," 867–69.

7. Hardy, *Life and Letters of Neesima,* 3–12. Niijima's written statement was given to Hardy on October 11, 1865. In 1885, he revised his original statement (see 12–45). Because the original statement is less coherent and more proximate, I believe it is a more accurate representation of his views in 1865.

8. Ibid., 4–5.

9. Ibid., 6.

10. Kawanishi, "Teachers and Friends," 303–22. See also Cary, "Foreword," 6:vi–vii.

11. Hardy, *Life and Letters of Neesima,* 6.

12. Yamato Kudsi and Tsushima Ando to Secretary of State, May 1861, in U.S. Department of State, *Foreign Relations of the United States,* 1861–62, 795–96.

13. Townsend Harris to Secretary of State, May 8, 1861, in U.S. Department of

State, *Foreign Relations of the United States,* 1861–62, 794–95. An analysis of this economic situation can be found in Howell, "Hard Times in the Kanto."

14. Hardy, *Life and Letters of Neesima,* 6.

15. Ibid., 7, 27–28, 30; Watanabe, *Niijima Jo,* 32–33. Two Japanese translations of *Robinson Crusoe* were available before 1868. See Hirakawa, "Japan's Turn to the West," 477–80.

16. Hardy, *Life and Letters of Neesima,* 30.

17. Hirakawa, "Japan's Turn to the West," 479.

18. Ibid.

19. Hardy, *Life and Letters of Neesima,* 3, 30. The Chinese translation of Bridgeman's book was published in Shanghai in 1862.

20. Ibid., 4.

21. Ibid.

22. Ibid., 7; Watanabe, *Niijima Jo,* 33–34.

23. Hardy, *Life and Letters of Neesima,* 7–8.

24. Davis, *Maker of New Japan,* 39.

25. Niijima Jo to Fukushi, Feb. 23, 1866, in *Niijima Jo Zenshu,* 6:6; Hardy, *Life and Letters of Neesima,* 49.

26. Hardy, *Life and Letters of Neesima,* 8.

27. Neesima to Prudential Committee of the American Board of Commissioners for Foreign Missions, "My Humble Schemes of the Speedy Evangelization of Japan," Dec. 16, 1884, in *Niijima Jo Zenshu,* 7:357.

28. Scheiner, *Christian Converts,* 4–5, 172. Scheiner quotes part of Niijima's 1884 explanation to the ABCFM (24–25), but he mistakenly cites it as occurring in 1874.

29. Scheiner, *Christian Converts,* 24–25.

30. Ibid., 51.

31. Niijima, "Hakodate Kiko," 869; Watanabe, *Niijima Jo,* 37–38.

32. The Hardys had two sons of their own, Alphaeus H. and Arthur.

33. Niijima to Fukushi, Feb., 23, 1866.

34. Ibid.

35. Ephraim Flint to Julius Seeyle, Aug. 31, 1867, in Hardy, *Life and Letters of Neesima,* 68–69. This appears to be a recommendation letter.

36. Ibid., 71.

37. Le Duc, *Piety and Intellect,* 4. See also Cary, "Uchimura," 440–41.

38. Cary, "Uchimura," 440.

39. Le Duc, *Piety and Intellect,* 42.

40. Uchimura, *How I Became a Christian,* 148.

41. His father's letter is discussed in a letter from Niijima Jo to Mrs. Hardy, Apr. 7, 1868, in Hardy, *Life and Letters of Neesima,* 82–83.

42. Hardy, *Life and Letters of Neesima,* 83.

43. Neesima to Mrs. Flint, Dec. 1, 1867, in ibid., 78. Unfortunately, Niijima did not identify the two Japanese he met. According to another source, there were five Japanese at Monson Academy at that time (Nire Kagenori, Enatsu Sosuke,

Tanegashima Keisuke, Yoshihara Shigetoshi, and Sadamoto Yuichi). See Kadota and Jones, *Kanaye Nagasawa,* 94.

44. Neesima to Mrs. Flint, Dec. 1, 1867, in Hardy, *Life and Letters of Neesima,* 79.

45. Ibid.

46. Neesima to John Smart, Mar. 17, 1869, 3, folder 9, box 1, Neesima Papers.

47. Ibid., 5.

48. Ibid., 6.

49. Ibid.

50. Ibid., 8.

51. "1870 Class Day Exercises," folder 3, box 1, Neesima Papers.

52. "Gov. Claflin at Commencement," newspaper article, July 15, 1870, folder 3, box 1, Neesima Papers.

53. "Commencement at Amherst College," newspaper article, July 13, 1870, folder 3, box 1, Neesima Papers.

54. This is according to Arthur S. Hardy, son of Alphaeus Hardy, in Hardy, *Life and Letters of Neesima,* 99. Americans and other Westerners had extraterritorial rights in Japan until the 1890s.

55. Ibid., 100.

56. Watanabe, *Niijima Jo,* 80–81.

57. Neesima to Mrs. Flint, Mar. 21, 1871, in Hardy, *Life and Letters of Neesima,* 102.

58. Neesima to Mrs. Flint, June 7, 1871, in ibid., 103.

59. Neesima to Mrs. Hardy, Sept. 17, 1871, and Neesima to Mr. Hardy, Sept. 27, 1871, both in ibid., 111–12.

60. Tanaka later became Japan's first minister of education.

61. Neesima to Ephraim Flint, Feb. 16, 1872, in Hardy, *Life and Letters of Neesima,* 115.

62. Neesima to the Hardys, Mar. 8, 1872, in ibid., 120.

63. Hardy, *Life and Letters of Neesima,* 121.

64. Ibid., 122.

65. Neesima to Mr. Hardy, Mar. 20, 1872, in ibid., 130.

66. Neesima to the Hardys, Mar. 22, 1872, in ibid., 132; Neesima to Julius Seeyle, Mar. 10, 1873, folder 9, box 1, Neesima Papers. See Watanabe, *Niijima Jo,* 87–91, for a brief description of Niijima's sojourn in Europe with Tanaka.

67. Hardy, *Life and Letters of Neesima,* 167–68.

68. Neesima to the Secretaries of the American Board of Commissioners for Foreign Missions, Apr. 30, 1874, in *Niijima Jo Zenshu,* 6:136.

69. Ibid.

70. Ibid., 137.

71. Ibid.

72. Ibid.

73. "Order of Exercises for the Ordination of Mr. Joseph Neeshima at Mount Vernon Church," Sept. 24, 1874, folder 5, box 1, Neesima Papers.

74. Neesima to Willie Seeyle, Oct. 5, 1874, folder 5, box 1, Neesima Papers.

75. Hardy, *Life and Letters of Neesima,* 168–69; "The American Board, Proceedings of the Fourth and Final Day," *Rutland (Ver.) Herald Weekly,* Oct. 15, 1874.

76. Hardy, *Life and Letters of Neesima,* 169.

77. Neesima to the Hardys, Oct. 25, 1874, in ibid., 174.

78. Ibid.

79. Neesima to Julius Seeyle, Oct. 29, 1874, folder 5, box 1, Neesima Papers. See also Neesima to the Hardys, Oct. 25, 1874, in Hardy, *Life and Letters of Neesima,* 174–76.

80. Neesima to Julius Seeyle, Oct. 29, 1874.

81. Ibid.

82. Neesima to Mrs. Hardy, Aug. 18, 1871, in Hardy, *Life and Letters of Neesima,* 107–8. Harte's poem, "The Heathen Chinee," was first published in *Overland Monthly* 5 (Sept. 1870).

83. Hardy, *Life and Letters of Neesima,* 108.

84. Neesima to Mr. Hardy, Oct. 29, 1874, in ibid., 174–75.

85. Neesima to Elizabeth Seeyle, Oct. 29, 1874, folder 9, box 1, Neesima Papers.

86. Neesima to Mr. Hardy, Oct. 29, 1874, in Hardy, *Life and Letters of Neesima,* 175.

87. Neesima to Julius Seeyle, Oct. 29, 1874.

88. Neesima to Mrs. Hardy, Nov. 21, 1874, in Hardy, *Life and Letters of Neesima,* 176.

89. Ibid.; Neesima to the Hardys, Dec. 22, 1874, in Hardy, *Life and Letters of Neesima,* 190; and Neesima to Julius Seeyle, Jan. 10, 1875, folder 9, box 1, Neesima Papers.

90. Letter from Mr. Neesima, Dec. 22, 1874, and Letter from Mr. Neesima, July 7, 1875, *Missionary Herald* 70 (1875): 73–74, 298–99.

91. Neesima to Julius Seeyle, Mar. 27, 1876, and Neesima to Mrs. Seeyle, Dec. 24, 1876, both in folder 9, box 1, Neesima Papers; Neesima to Mr. Hardy, Sept. 4, 1879, in *Niijima Jo Zenshu,* 6:194–201.

92. Neesima to Julius Seeyle, Sept. 3, 1889, folder 9, box 1, Neesima Papers.

93. Hardy, *Life and Letters of Neesima,* 328–29.

Chapter 4: From Satsuma to Utopia

1. Bright, *Diaries,* 305–6. Bright, a veteran British politician and member of Parliament, had dinner on May 12, 1867, with Laurence Oliphant and five Japanese students from Satsuma, including Sameshima and Yoshida, and recorded this information in his diary that evening.

2. Ishizuki, *Kindai Nihon,* 62–63, for the students, aliases, and ages, see 68; Ivan Parker Hall, *Mori Arinori,* 60–61; Kadota and Jones, *Kanaye Nagasawa,* 39–41.

3. Borus, "Edward Bellamy's Utopia," 1. Originally published in 1888 by Houghton Mifflin, *Looking Backward* sold well over five hundred thousand copies.

4. Walters, *American Reformers,* 41. See also Kesten, *Utopian Episodes,* 23–24.

5. More, *Utopia. Utopia* was first published in 1516.

6. Hine, *California's Utopian Colonies,* 5.

7. Kanter, *Commitment and Community,* 3; Walters, *American Reformers,* 41; Hine, *California's Utopian Colonies,* 5; Kesten, *Utopian Episodes,* 4–5.

8. Kanter, *Commitment and Community,* 116–17; Walters, *American Reformers,* 41.

9. Kanter, *Commitment and Community,* 5.

10. Kesten, *Utopian Episodes,* 5. See also Walters, *American Reformers,* 61.

11. Walters, *American Reformers,* 74.

12. For a detailed explication of these idealized values among utopian communities, see Kanter, *Commitment and Community,* 32–58.

13. This biographical information is based on Slade, "Historical Sketch," 2–4; and Harris, "An Autobiographic Sketch," reel 12, frame 264.

14. Sigstedt, *Swedenborg Epic,* viii.

15. Ibid., 495.

16. Schneider and Lawton, *A Prophet and a Pilgrim,* 22.

17. Slade, "Historical Sketch," 6; William White, *Life of Emanuel Swedenborg,* 80.

18. Harris, "An Autobiographic Sketch," 2.

19. Harris, *Breath of God with Man,* 100.

20. Slade, "Historical Sketch," 7. Nagasawa's 1871 diary reveals that Harris spent a great deal of time alone with Jane Lee Waring, whom he married twenty years later. See Nagasawa, "Diaries."

21. Slade, "Historical Sketch," 7; Hine, *California's Utopian Colonies,* 26.

22. Harris, *Breath of God with Man,* 7.

23. Ibid., 17.

24. Bright, diary entry for May 12, 1867, *Diaries,* 306.

25. Oliphant, *Memoir,* 153–58. This attack is the subject of messages in U.S. Department of State, *Foreign Relations of the United States,* 1860–61, 422–23. The attack on Oliphant occurred six months after the fatal attack on Henry Heusken, secretary and interpreter of the American legation in Edo.

26. Oliphant, *Memoir,* 186; Hayashi, *Mori Arinori,* 91.

27. Kadota and Jones, *Kanaye Nagasawa,* 72; Hayashi, *Mori Arinori,* 75–87. Kanaye Nagasawa had not been taking courses because he was only thirteen years of age in 1865. He lived in Aberdeen, Scotland, and attended secondary school there.

28. Kadota and Jones, *Kanaye Nagasawa,* 83–85; Ivan Parker Hall, *Mori Arinori,* 105.

29. See, for example, Ivan Parker Hall, *Mori Arinori,* 105; Kadota and Jones, *Kanaye Nagasawa,* 83; Hayashi, *Mori Arinori,* 88–89; and Ishizuki, *Kindai Nihon,* 82–83.

30. Cuthbert, *Life and World-Work,* appendix C, xvi.

31. Ibid.

32. Harris, *Breath of God with Man,* 17, 7; Schneider and Lawton, *A Prophet and a Pilgrim,* 175.

33. Lassalle, *Zen Meditation for Christians,* 133. Similar views can be found in Eudsen, *Zen and Christian;* and Dumoulin, *Christianity Meets Buddhism.*

34. Suzuki, *Zen and Japanese Culture,* 45–46.

35. Laurence Oliphant to William Cowper, Sept. 29, 1867, in Hayashi, *Mori Arinori,* 239. Laurence Oliphant regularly corresponded with William and Georgianna Cowper of England during his residence at Brocton Colony.

36. Winchell, "Mystical Experience of Thomas Lake Harris."

37. Ibid., 62.

38. Ibid. The only "Orientals" at the Brotherhood of the New Life were Japanese.

39. Thomas Lake Harris, "Japan: How a Nation May Enter the Divine Path," July 1867, in Ericsom, *Thomas Lake Harris,* reel 8, frame 197.

40. Ibid.

41. Ibid.

42. Slade, "Historical Sketch," 16.

43. Ibid., 15–16; Schneider and Lawton, *A Prophet and a Pilgrim,* 160–62; Kadota and Jones, *Kanaye Nagasawa,* 92.

44. Slade, "Historical Sketch," 11.

45. Schneider and Lawton, *A Prophet and a Pilgrim,* 147–55.

46. Ibid., 162–63.

47. According to Kesten, religious utopias "accepted privilege as part of the divine order" and did not require the leader to perform manual labor (*Utopian Episodes,* 48).

48. Nagasawa's diaries, Oliphant's letters, and many of the documents in Ericsom's *Thomas Lake Harris* contain references to Harris suffering as a result of "states" and "spheres."

49. *New York Sun,* Apr. 30, 1869.

50. Laurence Oliphant to William Cowper, Sept. 29, 1867, in Hayashi, *Mori Arinori,* 238–39.

51. Ibid., 238.

52. Ibid.

53. Laurence Oliphant to Georgianna Cowper, Oct. 6, 1867, in Hayashi, *Mori Arinori,* 235. According to Kadota and Jones, only Nomura actually became a member of the Brotherhood of the New Life (*Kanaye Nagasawa,* 94).

54. Laurence Oliphant to William Cowper, Dec. 1, 1867, in Hayashi, *Mori Arinori,* 226; Kadota and Jones, *Kanaye Nagasawa,* 94.

55. The two Satsuma *ryūgakusei* who remained at Monson Academy and did not join the Brotherhood of the New Life—Tanegashima Keisuke and Yoshihara Shigetoshi—may have been the same two who visited Niijima Jo in Amherst at the end of November. See Neesima to Mrs. Flint, Dec. 1, 1867, in Hardy, *Life and Letters of Neesima,* 78–79.

56. U.S. Bureau of the Census, *Historical Statistics, Colonial Times to 1957,* 59, reveals that sixty-seven Japanese entered the United States in 1867. Most of these were diplomats, businessmen, and a group of jugglers who remained in the country for a short period of time. For the latter, see *Harper's Weekly,* June 15, 1867.

57. Laurence Oliphant to William Cowper, Dec. 1, 1867, in Hayashi, *Mori Arinori,* 226.

58. Laurence Oliphant to William Cowper, Sept. 1867, in Hayashi, *Mori Arinori,* 242.

59. *New York Sun,* Apr. 30, 1869.

60. Laurence Oliphant to Georgianna Cowper, Nov. 6, 1868, in Hayashi, *Mori Arinori,* 206.

61. Cuthbert, *Life and World-Work,* 192.

62. Noda (Sameshima) and Sawai (Mori) to "Our dear Brethren," June 17, 1868, in Ericsom, *Thomas Lake Harris,* reel 13, frame 302.

63. Ibid.

64. Ibid.

65. Georgianna Cowper, "Conversations of Harris," May 16, 1871, to June 1871, in Ericsom, *Thomas Lake Harris,* reel 13, frame 302.

66. Ivan Parker Hall, *Mori Arinori,* 125; Hayashi, *Mori Arinori,* 149.

67. Noda (Sameshima) and Sawai (Mori) to "Our dear Brethren."

68. Mori Arinori to Kanaye Nagasawa, Apr. 8, 1871, in Ericsom, *Thomas Lake Harris,* reel 8, frame 235.

69. Griffis, *Rutgers Graduates in Japan,* 22.

70. Sometime before January 1, 1871, Nomura returned to live at Brocton Colony; he is mentioned throughout Nagasawa's January 1 to April 23, 1871, diaries. Before the Brotherhood of the New Life moved to Santa Rosa, California, in 1875, Nomura left the colony.

71. Information in this paragraph is based on Nagasawa, entries for March and April 1871, "Diaries," 90–100; Thomas Lake Harris to Arai Osui, June 25, 1899, in Ericsom, *Thomas Lake Harris,* reel 14, frame 314; Ishizuki, *Kindai Nihon,* 456; Ivan Parker Hall, *Mori Arinori,* 203–5; and LeBaron, *Japanese Baron,* 15.

72. Kadota and Jones, *Kanaye Nagasawa,* 104.

73. Ibid., 105; Schneider and Lawton, *A Prophet and a Pilgrim,* 276–77. Santa Rosa is sixty miles north of San Francisco.

74. See also the description of Fountaingrove in Hine, *California's Utopian Colonies,* 21.

75. Cuthbert, *Life and World-Work,* 191–92.

76. Kawamura Masahei, "Satsuhan no Kaitakusha Kanaye Nagasawa to Tomas Reki Harisu," 2, folder 2, box 154, Japanese American Research Project Collection; Kadota and Jones, *Kanaye Nagasawa,* 122, 128; LeBaron, *Japanese Baron,* 18–19.

77. Oliphant, *Memoir,* 216.

78. Ibid., 215.

79. "Hypnotic Harris—Miss Chevaillier's Strange Story," *San Francisco Chronicle,*

Dec. 13, 1891. This was the first of many articles by Chevaillier to appear in the *Chronicle* during December 1891 and early 1892.

80. Ibid.

81. "Secrets of the Sonoma Eden," advertisement, *San Francisco Chronicle,* Feb. 16, 1892.

82. "Hypnotic Harris," *San Francisco Chronicle,* Dec. 13, 1891.

83. Ibid.

84. Ibid.

85. "The Chevailliers," *San Francisco Chronicle,* Dec. 27, 1891.

86. Hine, *California's Utopian Colonies,* 31.

87. *Sonoma Democrat,* Feb. 27, 1892; "Testimonials re Thomas Lake Harris," in Ericsom, *Thomas Lake Harris,* reel 8, frame 244.

88. Boddy, *Japanese in America,* 192; Kanaye Nagasawa, interview by Robert Park, July 18, 1924, no. 145, box 26, Survey of Race Relations.

89. Schneider and Lawton, *A Prophet and a Pilgrim,* 488. The estate was valued at $250,000.

90. Kadota and Jones, *Kanaye Nagasawa,* 138. George Shima's Japanese name was Ushijima Kinji.

91. Diary of Jane Waring Harris, May 19, 1897, in Ericsom, *Thomas Lake Harris,* reel 14, frame 313; Schneider and Lawton, *A Prophet and a Pilgrim,* 485.

92. Thomas Lake Harris to Arai Osui, June 25, 1899, in Ericsom, *Thomas Lake Harris,* reel 13, frame 302.

93. Ibid.

94. LeBaron, *Japanese Baron,* 15; Ivan Parker Hall, *Mori Arinori,* 205.

95. Markham is probably most remembered for his poem "The Man with the Hoe." See Markham, *The Man with the Hoe.*

96. Edwin Markham, "General Introduction by the Editor," 1, in Ericsom, *Thomas Lake Harris,* reel 13, frame 320. Markham made an identical comment in *California the Wonderful* (342).

97. Kanaye Nagasawa to Edwin Markham, Mar. 14, 1921, in Ericsom, *Thomas Lake Harris,* reel 13, frame 303.

98. Nagasawa interview.

99. Mori, "Life and Resources in America," 177–406.

100. Ibid., 264.

101. Ibid., 259.

102. Ibid., 290–91.

103. Mori, "Religious Freedom in Japan," 3.

104. Mori, "Religion," 78.

105. Mori, "Religious Freedom in Japan," 7.

106. According to *Japanese Religion,* produced under the auspices of the Japanese Agency for Cultural Affairs, Mori, Nakamura Keiu, and the Iwakura mission—which Mori advised while it was in the United States—were responsible for the repeal of the anti-Christian edicts (83).

107. For a complete translation of the journal in which these elites discussed the political and social issues of the mid-1870s, see Braisted, *Meiroku Zasshi.* Although the Meirokusha Society existed in one form or another until the early twentieth century, the *Meiroku Zasshi* was published only from March 1874 to November 1875.

108. Mori, *Education in Japan,* 56.

109. See Sugiyama and Nishizawa, "Captain of Industry," 151–69.

110. Nagasawa, "Diaries," 92–93. Mori stayed at Brocton from March 11 to March 15, 1871.

111. Ibid., 92.

112. Ivan Parker Hall, *Mori Arinori,* 99–100.

113. Ibid., 203–4.

114. Clifford Geertz, "Religion as a Cultural System," in *The Interpretation of Cultures,* 123.

Chapter 5: The *Gannenmono,* Eugene Van Reed, and the Emergence of Japan-Hawaii-U.S. Relations

1. Y. B. Goto, "Samurai Who Came in 1868 Likes Islands," *Honolulu Star-Bulletin,* Feb. 19, 1935.

2. Versions of this interpretation can be found in Takaki, *Pau Hana;* Takaki, *Strangers;* Chan, *Asian Americans;* Hosokawa, *Nisei;* Yoneda, *Zaibei Nihonjin Rodosha;* and Okahata, *Hawaii Nihonjin Iminshi.*

3. Although there are significant differences, my interpretation of the *Gannenmono* episode resembles those in Marumoto, "First Year Immigrants"; Conroy, *Japanese Frontier;* and Kuykendall, "Earliest Japanese Labor Immigration."

4. Kent, *Hawaii,* 22.

5. Bradley, *American Frontier,* 397. For an official U.S. government retrospective of America's role in Hawaii in the pre-annexation era, see James Blaine to James Comly, Dec. 1, 1881, in U.S. Department of State, *Foreign Relations of the United States,* 1880–81, 635–39.

6. Okahata, *Hawaii Nihonjin Iminshi,* 33–34; Brooks, *Japanese Wrecks.*

7. Townsend Harris to Secretary of State, June 21, 1861, and Kudzi Yamato and Tsusima Ando to Townsend Harris, June 21, 1861, both in U.S. Department of State, *Despatches,* reel 3.

8. Japanese Foreign Ministry, *Nihon Gaiko Bunsho,* vol. 7, pt. 1, pp. 129–33. The highest-ranking American diplomats at this time were ministers. Later, ambassadors ranked first.

9. Sawa Nobuyuki and Terashima Munenori to Charles De Long, Jan. 23, 1871, in U.S. Department of State, *Despatches,* reel 17.

10. Munroe-Fraser, *History of Santa Clara County,* 589; Altman, "Eugene Van Reed," 7.

11. Heco, *Narrative of a Japanese,* 1:159, 172.

12. Altman, "Eugene Van Reed," 7; Heco, *Narrative of a Japanese,* 1:212.

13. Margaret Van Reed Biddle, "Eugene Miller Van Reed: An Opening Wedge of Japan," 7, ca. 1907, box 19.1, group 1, Griffis Collection.

14. Altman, "Eugene Van Reed," 11.

15. Jonas, "Foreign Influence," 57–58.

16. Eugene Van Reed to Governor of Yedo, Jan. 17, 1871, in U.S. Department of State, *Despatches,* reel 18.

17. Charles De Long to Hamilton Fish, Feb. 14, 1871, in U.S. Department of State, *Despatches,* reel 17.

18. The Daimios to the Tycoon, [1863], in U.S. Department of State, *Foreign Relations of the United States,* 1862–63, pt. 2, p. 1022.

19. Kudsi Yamato and Ando Tsusima to Secretary of State, May 1861, in U.S. Department of State, *Foreign Relations of the United States,* 1861–62, 795–97.

20. Robert Pruyn to William Seward, June 16, 1863, in U.S. Department of State, *Foreign Relations of the United States,* 1862–63, pt. 2, p. 1019.

21. Townsend Harris to Lewis Cass, Jan. 12, 1860, in U.S. Department of State, *Despatches,* reel 3.

22. Ibid.

23. Francis Hall, *Japan through American Eyes,* 210.

24. Eugene Van Reed to Stephen Phillips, Dec. 25, 1868, Marumoto Papers.

25. Charles De Long to Hamilton Fish, Feb. 14, 1871, in U.S. Department of State, *Despatches,* reel 17.

26. Eugene Van Reed to Governor of Yedo, Feb. 14, 1871, in U.S. Department of State, *Despatches,* reel 17.

27. De Long to Fish, Feb. 14, 1871.

28. Hamilton Fish to Charles De Long, May 11, 1871, and W. Hunter to Charles De Long, July 1, 1871, both in U.S. Department of State, *Diplomatic Instructions, Japan,* vol. 1, reel 104.

29. The Marumoto Papers contain a nearly complete collection of Van Reed's correspondence with Hawaiian officials over an eight-year period (1864–72). There is no mention in it of a salary or other form of compensation.

30. William Cryder to Robert Wyllie, Mar. 15, 1864, James Van Reed to Robert Wyllie, Jan. 26, 1865, and Robert Wyllie to Eugene Van Reed, Mar. 10, 1865, all in Marumoto Papers. See also a photocopy of "Commission for Eugene M. Van Reed, Esquire from Kamehameha V, King of the Hawaiian Islands" in Altman, "Eugene Van Reed," 10.

31. Schmitt, *Historical Statistics,* 7–9; "Census of the Inhabitants of the Hawaiian Islands," Dec. 27, 1873, in U.S. Department of State, *Foreign Relations of the United States,* 1873–74, 512–13. While Schmitt and most scholars who study the demographics of Hawaii believe the pre-Western contact population to have been between 200,000 and 300,000, David Stannard believes it was between 800,000 and 1,000,000 (*Before the Horror*).

32. Kuykendall, *Hawaiian Kingdom,* 177–78.

33. Robert Wyllie to Joseph Heco, Apr. 15, 1865, Marumoto Papers. Wyllie had met Heco twice in Hawaii. Unfortunately, no response to Wyllie's inquiry can be found, and Heco does mention this matter in his memoirs.

34. Bureau of Immigration Minutes, Mar. 19, 1868, Marumoto Papers. The Bureau of Immigration, sometimes referred to as the Board of Immigration, was a government organization composed of five to seven officials, some of whom were also planters.

35. Edzure Kaga and Ishino Tchikuzen to Eugene Van Reed, Sept. 15, 1867, Marumoto Papers.

36. Letter of Credence from King Kamehameha V and Charles de Varigny, Jan. 21, 1867, Marumoto Papers.

37. Inowye Kawatsi and Matsudaira Soowo to Eugene Van Reed, Apr. 29, 1867, Marumoto Papers.

38. Eugene Van Reed to Charles de Varigny, Apr. 10, 1868, and Eugene Van Reed to Charles de Varigny, Apr. 27, 1868, both in Marumoto Papers.

39. Ibid.

40. Wakatsuki, "Japanese Emigation," 407–8.

41. Hanbey–Van Reed Agreement, Apr. 23, 1868, Marumoto Papers. Another copy of this document can be found in Conroy, *The Japanese Frontier in Hawaii,* 145.

42. Dr. David Lee to Bureau of Immigration, June 19, 1868, Marumoto Papers.

43. Ibid.

44. *Scioto* Charter Party, May 5, 1868, Marumoto Papers. Although the charter agreement is dated May 5, Van Reed's letter to Varigny on April 27, 1868, clearly indicates that he had already made arrangements with Captain William Reagan of the *Scioto.*

45. Eugene Van Reed to Charles de Varigny, May 17, 1868, Marumoto Papers.

46. William Reagan to Eugene Van Reed, May 9, 1868, Marumoto Papers.

47. Eugene Van Reed to Governors of Kanagawa, May 9, 1868, Marumoto Papers.

48. Eugene Van Reed to Governors of Kanagawa, May 10, 1868, Marumoto Papers.

49. Eugene Van Reed to Governors of Kanagawa, May 9, 1868, May 10, 1868; and Eugene Van Reed to Higashikuze Michitomi, May 10, 1868 (two letters), May 11, 1868 (two letters), all in Marumoto Papers.

50. Eugene Van Reed to Terashima Munenori, May 16, 1868, and Eugene Van Reed to Charles de Varigny, June 1, 1868, both in Marumoto Papers.

51. Eugene Van Reed to Higashikuze Michitomi, May 13, 1868, Marumoto Papers.

52. Eugene Van Reed to Charles de Varigny, June 1, 1868, Marumoto Papers.

53. Eugene Van Reed to Terashima Munenori, May 16, 1868, and Eugene Van Reed to Kumegashira, May 16, 1868 (two letters), all in Marumoto Papers.

54. Robert Van Valkenberg to Date Chuinguong and Higashikuze Michitomi, Apr. 26, 1869, in Japanese Foreign Ministry, *Nihon Gaiko Bunsho,* 3:510–13.

55. Higashikuze Michitomi and Hizen Jijin to Robert Van Valkenberg, May 25, 1868, in Japanese Foreign Ministry, *Nihon Gaiko Bunsho,* 1:645–46. The same document can be found in U.S. Department of State, *Foreign Relations of the United States,* 1867–68, pt. 1, 747–48, and U.S. Department of State, *Despatches,* reel 10.

56. This paragraph is based on Robert Van Valkenberg to Hizen Jijin and Higashikuze Michitomi, May 26, 1868, in U.S. Department of State, *Despatches,* reel 10, which includes a copy of the decree. The decree was reprinted in the *Honolulu Pacific Commercial Advertiser* on July 25, 1868.

57. Van Reed to Varigny, June 1, 1868.

58. William Seward to Robert Van Valkenberg, July 15, 1868, in U.S. Department of State, *Foreign Relations of the United States,* pt. 1, 1867–68, 778. I could find no evidence, however, that Van Valkenberg ever publicly rescinded the decree or told Japanese officials that it was invalid.

59. Japanese Foreign Ministry, *Nihon Gaiko Bunsho,* 2:119–20; Higashikuze Michitomi to Robert Van Valkenberg, Sept. 12, 1868, in U.S. Department of State, *Despatches,* reel 11.

60. Michitomi to Van Valkenberg, Sept. 12, 1868.

61. Robert Van Valkenberg to Higashikuze Michitomi, Sept. 17, 1868, in Japanese Foreign Ministry, *Nihon Gaiko Bunsho,* 2:119–20.

62. Okahata, *Hawaii Nihonjin Iminshi,* 45–46. See also Marumoto, "First Year Immigrants," 21–22.

63. Goto, "Samurai Who Came in 1868 Likes Islands."

64. Ibid. *Miso* is bean paste used for making traditional Japanese soup; *shōyu* is soy sauce.

65. The incident is described in Sakuma's diary in Okahata, *Hawaii Nihonjin Iminshi,* 45–46. According to Ishii, these "ruffians" were constantly gambling and fighting during the voyage. See Goto, "Samurai Who Came in 1868 Likes Islands."

66. Okahata, *Hawaii Nihonjin Iminshi,* 46; Dr. David Lee to Board of Immigration, June 19, 1868, Marumoto Papers.

67. Goto, "Samurai Who Came in 1868 Likes Islands."

68. Minutes of the Board of Immigration, June 29, 1868, Marumoto Papers.

69. List of Parties Who Received Japanese Immigrants ex *Scioto,* Marumoto Papers.

70. Board of Immigration Minutes, June 29, 1868, Marumoto Papers.

71. "Hints Concerning the Japanese Immigrants," *Hawaiian Gazette,* July 8, 1868.

72. *Honolulu Pacific Commercial Advertiser,* July 11, 1868.

73. Theodore Davies to Ferdinand Hutcheson, Aug. 4, 1868, Marumoto Papers.

74. Ibid.

75. M. McIrney to Ferdinand Hutcheson, Aug. 3, 1868, Marumoto Papers.

76. Samuel Wilder to Ferdinand Hutchison, Aug. 6, 1868, Marumoto Papers.

77. Minutes of the Board of Immigration, Aug. 6, 1868, Marumoto Papers.

78. Ibid.

79. Minutes of the Board of Immigration, Sept. 3, 1868, and Sablow (Makino Tomisaburo) to Foreign Office of Hawaii, May 23, 1871, both in Marumoto Papers.

80. Edward McCook to Stephen Phillips, July 29, 1868, in U.S. Department of State, *Foreign Relations of the United States,* 1867–68, pt. 2, 343.

81. Stephen Phillips to Edward McCook, Aug. 20, 1868, in U.S. Department of State, *Foreign Relations of the United States,* 1867–68, pt. 2, 344. Phillips is referring to Article 11 of the 1864 Hawaiian Constitution.

82. Ibid., 345.

83. Ibid.

84. Ibid.

85. "Notice to American Citizens and Ship-Owners, Legation of the United States at Honolulu," Aug. 31, 1868, in U.S. Department of State, *Foreign Relations of the United States,* 1867–68, pt. 2, 345. The resolution McCook referred to primarily concerned the traffic in Chinese laborers. See U.S. Congress, *Congressional Globe,* 483.

86. "The Coolie Question," *Ke-Kuokoa,* Sept. 12, 1868.

87. Kuykendall, *Hawaiian Kingdom,* 185. The Masters and Servants Act also applied to ship captains and seamen.

88. Ibid., 186.

89. Ibid.

90. Daws, *Shoal of Time,* 181.

91. Kuykendall, *Hawaiian Kingdom,* 189. For example, see these editorials in the *Honolulu Pacific Commercial Advertiser:* "Bonded Laborers—The Coolie System," Sept. 5, 1868; "The Government and the Coolie Trade," Sept. 12, 1868; and "The Labor Question," Sept. 26, 1868.

92. Minutes of the Board of Immigration, Sept. 3, 1868, Sept. 17, 1868, Marumoto Papers.

93. Ibid.

94. Eugene Van Reed to Charles de Varigny, Sept. 26, 1868, Marumoto Papers.

95. Ibid.

96. Ibid.

97. Eugene Van Reed to Minister of Foreign Affairs, Honolulu, Oct. 27, 1868, Marumoto Papers.

98. Eugene Van Reed to Stephen Phillips, Jan. 25, 1869, Marumoto Papers; Okahata, *Hawaii Nihonjin Iminshi,* 57.

99. Eugene Van Reed to Stephen Phillips, Mar. 13, 1869, Marumoto Papers.

100. Ibid.

101. Japanese Foreign Ministry, *Nihon Gaiko Bunsho,* 3:230–33, 304–5, 364–65, 510–13.

102. Ibid., 3:510–13.

103. "Government of Japan, Their Excellencies the Japanese Commissioners," Oct. 7, 1869, Marumoto Papers.

104. Eugene Van Reed to Stephen Phillips, Oct. 31, 1869, Marumoto Papers.

105. Wooyeno Keisuke to Charles Harris, Dec. 31, 1869, Marumoto Papers.

106. Ibid.

107. Ibid.

108. Charles Harris to Wooyeno Keisuke, Jan. 11, 1870, Marumoto Papers.

109. Keisuke Wooyeno to Charles Harris, Jan. 11, 1870, Marumoto Papers; Japanese Foreign Ministry, *Nihon Gaiko Bunsho,* 5:482–88.

110. Repatriation List, Marumoto Papers.

111. Ibid. Shirokichi, listed as a potter on the repatriation list, and his wife, Nobu, had a son named Junji.

112. Ibid.

113. Eugene Van Reed to Charles Harris, June 21, 1871, Marumoto Papers.

114. Conditions at Waialua, [Jan. 1870], Marumoto Papers.

115. Ibid.

116. Charles Harris to Wooyeno Keisuke, Jan. 19, 1870, Marumoto Papers.

117. Wooyeno Keisuke to Charles Harris, Jan. 19, 1870, Marumoto Papers; Japanese Foreign Ministry, *Nihon Gaiko Bunsho,* 6:253.

118. Henry Pierce to Minister Resident of the United States in Japan, Jan. 28, 1870, in U.S. Department of State, *Despatches,* reel 13.

119. Charles De Long to Hamilton Fish, Apr. 16, 1870, U.S. Department of State, *Despatches,* reel 13.

120. *Japan Gazette,* Apr. 4, 1870.

121. De Long to Fish, Apr. 16, 1870. Van Reed responded in a letter to the *Japan Gazette* on Apr. 7, 1870.

122. Eugene Van Reed to Charles Harris, Sept. 23, 1871, Marumoto Papers; Marumoto, "First Year Immigrants to Hawaii," 33.

123. Conroy, *Japanese Frontier,* 43.

124. Henry Pierce to Gaimusho, May 7, 1872, in Japanese Foreign Ministry, *Nihon Gaiko Bunsho,* vol. 7, pt. 2, p. 570.

125. Sablow (Makino Saburo) to the Foreign Office of Hawaii, May 23, 1871, Marumoto Papers.

126. Charles Harris to Henry Pierce, Oct. 21, 1871, Marumoto Papers.

127. Okahata, *History of Japanese,* 63, 127.

128. Ibid.

129. Goto, "Samurai Who Came in 1868 Likes Islands." See also Goto, *Children of Gannen-mono.*

130. Goto, "Samurai Who Came in 1868 Likes Islands."

131. Ibid. His wife's name was Kahele.

132. "Draft of Treaty between the Kingdom of Hawaii and Japan," Aug. 19, 1871, in Japanese Foreign Ministry, *Nihon Gaiko Bunsho,* vol. 7, pt. 1, pp. 144–49.

133. Japanese Foreign Ministry, *Nihon Gaiko Bunsho,* vol. 7, pt. 1, pp. 129–33. Shortly after the treaty was signed, Van Reed contracted tuberculosis and became increasingly ill. He died in early February 1873 aboard the PMSS *Japan* bound for San Francisco.

134. Ibid., 147–48.

135. Chan, *Asian Americans,* 11. See also Hosokawa, *Nisei,* 35.

136. Charles De Long to Hamilton Fish, Sept. 30, 1872, in U.S. Department of State, *Despatches,* reel 21.

Chapter 6: From Aizu to Gold Hill

1. *Honolulu Pacific Commercial Advertiser,* June 26, 1869.

2. Address by William Hosokawa, Japanese Centennial Commemorative Banquet, Hotel El Dorado, Sacramento, June 7, 1969, Takeda Collection.

3. Executive Department, State of California, "Proclamation by Governor Ronald Reagan," Feb. 3, 1969, California State Archives, Sacramento; Enomoto and Murakami, *Wakamatsu Colony Centennial.* Established in 1930, the Japanese American Citizens League is the largest and most influential national organization devoted to Japanese American interests.

4. *Alta Daily News,* May 27, 1869; *San Francisco Bulletin,* May 27, 1869; *Sacramento Union,* May 28, 1869. See also Daniels, *Politics of Prejudice,* 3.

5. Beasley, *Meiji Restoration,* 110, 434. Another way to delineate the difference is that *sanke daimyō* (from the Tokugawa domains of Mito, Owari, and Kii) were the senior *shimpan* while the *kamon* were the junior *shimpan.* This difference among *shimpan daimyō,* however, was not always clear.

6. Totman, *Collapse of the Tokugawa Bakufu,* 14.

7. Matsudaira Katamori to *Bakufu,* Nov. 8, 1862, in Beasley, *Select Documents,* 225–26.

8. Ibid., 226.

9. Ibid.

10. Bolitho, "Aizu," 9.

11. Totman, *Collapse of the Tokugawa Bakufu,* 45, 59.

12. Ibid., 265.

13. Bolitho, "Aizu," 15.

14. Ibid.

15. Ibid.; Totman, *Collapse of the Tokugawa Bakufu,* 288–89.

16. Yamaguchi, *Kinse Shiriaku,* 98–99.

17. This proclamation by the mikado was issued to foreign legations on February 8, 1868, and can be found in U.S. Department of State, *Foreign Relations of the United States,* 1867–68, pt. 1, 714–15. See also Totman, *Collapse of the Tokugawa Bakufu,* 442.

18. Bolitho, "Aizu," 16.

19. Ibid.

20. Barnes and Barnes, *Naval Surgeon,* 48.

21. Ibid., 49.

22. Robert Van Valkenberg to William Seward, Jan. 16, 1868, in U.S. Department of State, *Foreign Relations of the United States,* 1867–68, pt. 1, p. 619.

23. A. L. Portman to Ogasawara Iki no kami, Feb. 2, 1868, in Japanese Foreign Ministry, *Nihon Gaiko Bunsho,* 1:211.

24. Numerous messages from Van Valkenberg to Secretary of State William H. Seward attest to his support for the shogun and Matsudaira. See U.S. Department of State, *Foreign Relations of the United States,* 1867–69, pts. 1–2, and U.S. Department of State, *Despatches,* reels 8–10.

25. Robert Van Valkenberg to William Seward, Feb. 3, 1868, in U.S. Department of State, *Foreign Relations of the United States,* 1867–68, pt. 1, p. 636. According to this message, the shogun was aboard the *Iroquois* for two hours in Osaka Bay while waiting for his own ship to arrive and take him back to Edo.

26. *Aizu no Rekishi,* 123–24.

27. Dwight, "Marchioness Oyama." Yamakawa later married Oyama Iwao, a major military figure during the Meiji era. Ironically, Oyama had taken part in the siege of Tsuruga Castle as a young Satsuma samurai.

28. Bolitho, "Aizu," 3–4. Aizu lost 2,847 samurai from the beginning of 1868 to Matsudaira's surrender in November. This was more than twice as many samurai as any other domain lost resisting the imperial armies.

29. Bolitho, "Echigo War," 277.

30. "Letter Accompanying Pardon Decree, Signed by Daijokwan," and "Decree," both in U.S. Department of State, *Despatches,* reel 13.

31. Charles De Long to Hamilton Fish, Nov. 26, 1869, in U.S. Department of State, *Despatches,* reel 13.

32. Vlastos, *Peasant Protests,* 142–53.

33. Jansen, "Meiji Restoration," 359. Bolitho makes similar judgments in "Aizu," 3–6.

34. *Aizu no Rekishi,* 127–28. The population of the city of Wakamatsu dropped from seventy thousand before the civil war to around sixteen thousand afterward. Many who left Aizu were forced by the imperial government to move to a newly created, dreary domain on the Shimokita Peninsula in the northernmost corner of Honshu.

35. Millard Fillmore, President of the United States of America, to His Imperial Majesty the Emperor of Japan, Nov. 13, 1852, in Hawks, *Narrative of the Expedition,* 1:256–57.

36. Japanese Foreign Ministry, *Nihon Gaiko Bunsho,* vol. 2, appendix, 42; Charles De Long to Hamilton Fish, July 5, 1873, in U.S. Department of State, *Despatches,* reel 24.

37. De Long to Fish, July 5, 1873. Aizu lacquerware was (and still is) renowned in Japan. The East Asian Library collection at the University of California, Berkeley, includes "A Map of the World in Japanese" by Edward Schnell, dated Feb. 2, 1862, Yokohama. This map is approximately 4 feet in width and 6 feet in length.

38. Yamamoto, *Wakamatsu Koroni,* 26.

39. Taketa, "Wakamatsu Silk."

40. Kurt Meissner, "Hiramatsu—Prussian Samurai of Wakamatsu," *Yomiuri Japan News,* Jan. 24, 1958. This newspaper feature article is a summary of Meissner's earlier article, "General Eduard Schnell." In both articles Meissner confuses the two Schnell brothers. It was John Henry Schell who went to California, not Edward, as Meissner indicates.

41. Howe, *Origins of Japanese Trade Supremacy,* 93; Lockwood, *Economic Development,* 356.

42. Ogura, *Agricultural Development,* 536.

43. Ibid.; Charles O. Shepard to Hamilton Fish, June 20, 1872, in U.S. Department of State, *Despatches,* reel 20. According to this twenty-two-page report on tea cultivation in Japan prepared by the American chargé d'affaires, plus an eleven-page analysis by an American professor of agronomy, as of 1866 the two largest import markets in the world for Japanese tea were San Francisco and New York.

44. Howe, *Origins of Japanese Trade Supremacy,* 99.

45. Ibid., 93.

46. Li, "Silks by Sea," 197. This article is an extension of the comparisions of Chinese and Japanese silk production and trade in *China's Silk Trade.*

47. Li, "Silks by Sea," 205–6.

48. Howe, *Origins of Japanese Trade Supremacy,* 93. See also Li, "Silks by Sea," 195. "Silk products" includes raw silk, silkworm egg sheets, and silk fabrics.

49. Lockwood, *Economic Development,* 94.

50. *Daily Alta California,* Nov. 18, 1868; *Overland Monthly,* May 1870, 453.

51. *Cash Book, 1868–1869,* 67:388, Pacific Mail Steamship Archives; *San Francisco Chronicle,* May 21, 1868.

52. *Alta Daily News,* May 27, 1869. Similar articles can be found in the *San Francisco Bulletin,* May 27, 1868; the *Sacramento Union,* May 28, 1869; and the *Honolulu Pacific Commercial Advertiser,* June 26, 1869.

53. "The Japanese Settlement," *Daily Alta California,* June 16, 1869.

54. Ibid.

55. "Arrival of Japanese," *Placerville Mountain Democrat,* Oct. 30, 1869; Taketa, "Centennial Year," 3–4.

56. Coloma Township, El Dorado County Census, 8–9, in U.S. Bureau of the Census, *Unpublished Manuscript Schedules, 1870.* The names of the Japanese at Coloma as written down by the census taker were Jou Schnell, Nishijawa Taro, Kinjdelyro, Mrs. Kinjdelyro, Daidjiro, Mrs. Daidjiro, Takidado (daughter of the Daidjiros), Tomodjaro, Sinsia, Mrs. Sinsia, Sindyro, Mrs. Sindyro, Tanejero, Kintaro, Juntaro, Tilyjero, Uozezoro, Amarisa (possibly the wife of Uozezoro), Lehild (apparently the daughter of Uozezoro and Amarisa), Mazemuzu (probably Masumizu), Amesabra, and Pakeyce. There is confusion over these names because the Japanese were undoubtedly still having difficulties with English, the census

taker was unfamiliar with Japanese names, and his handwriting is difficult to read. Nevertheless, the place of birth for all of the above is clearly written as "Japan."

57. Coloma Township, El Dorado County Census, U.S. Bureau of the Census, *Unpublished Manuscript Schedules, 1870.*

58. According to the 1870 census, there were fifty-five Japanese living in the United States. Thirty-three were in California; of these, twenty-two were in El Dorado County, all at Gold Hill in Coloma (U.S. Department of the Interior, *Ninth Census,* 8, 15–16, 90–91).

59. Deed from Charles M. Graner to J. Henry Schnell, June 22, 1869, El Dorado County Recorder's Office, Placerville, Calif.; Yamamoto, *Wakamatsu Koroni,* 97–98.

60. *History of El Dorado County,* 266. There is no evidence that Veerkamp and Schnell, both Germans, knew each other before Schnell and the Japanese arrived at Coloma.

61. "The Japanese Colony," *Daily Alta California,* July 30, 1869. The leaves from mulberry trees are used for feeding silkworms.

62. Ibid.

63. Speer, *Oldest and Newest Empire,* 511.

64. "Japanese Colony," *Placerville Mountain Democrat,* Oct. 2, 1869.

65. Ibid.

66. *Placerville Mountain Democrat,* Feb. 26, 1870.

67. *San Francisco Call,* June 16, 1870.

68. "The Japanese Colony," *Daily Alta California,* Oct. 24, 1869.

69. "The Japanese Colony," *Daily Alta California,* July 30, 1869.

70. *Placerville Mountain Democrat,* Oct. 2, 1869.

71. Ibid.

72. Advertisement by B. Meacham for Wolf's Old Stand, *Placerville Mountain Democrat,* Aug. 7, 1869, Aug. 14, 1869.

73. In 1870, El Dorado County had a total population of 10,300. Of this number, nearly 15 percent (1,514) were Chinese. The state population was 560,247, with nearly 8 percent (48,790) Chinese. See U.S. Department of the Interior, *Ninth Census,* vol. 1; and Loosely, *Foreign Born Population.*

The term *model minority,* as specifically applied to desirable, industrious Japanese Americans to contrast them with other American minorities represented as both undesirable and lazy, was first articulated in the 1960s. See Peterson, "Success Story." For explanations and criticisms of the "model minority" thesis, see Chan, *Asian Americans,* 167–71; Takaki, *Strangers,* 474–78; and Daniels, *Asian America,* 317–44.

74. *Placerville Mountain Democrat,* June 12, 1869.

75. Ibid.

76. "The Japanese Immigrants," *San Francisco Chronicle,* June 17, 1869. Other articles with identical comparative views can be found in the *Daily Alta California,* June 16, 1869, and Oct. 24, 1869.

77. Yoshimoto Hachiro, "Okei no haka ni mairu, Okei no tomodachi ga mada ikiteiru," *Nichibei Shimbun,* Sept. 25, 1926.

78. *Placerville Mountain Democrat,* Apr. 2, 1870, Apr. 6 1870, July 16, 1870.

79. Schnell lost a foreclosure notice to Charles Graner on Nov. 22, 1869, and Graner reacquired 160 acres of land on December 31, 1870 (*El Dorado County Sheriff's Office, Register of Sales, 1866–78,* vol. 24, El Dorado County Archives). The recorder noted that Graner was still owed $1,975. Another judgment was brought against Schnell because he was "totally insolvent and unable to pay the amount of the said deficiency or any part thereof." The remainder of the colony's land was apparently lost as a result of this judgment. Francis Veerkamp was appointed as receiver (*Judgment Book E, District Court, El Dorado County,* Feb. 22, 1866, to Dec. 31, 1879, 196–97, El Dorado County Historical Museum, Placerville, Calif.).

80. Inez Veerkamp, interview with author, Placerville, California, Aug. 26, 1991. Veerkamp is the granddaughter of Francis Veerkamp. See also Kawamura, *Kariforunia Kaika Ibun,* 64. As *tantō* daggers were usually worn by samurai class women, they probably belonged to Jou Schnell.

81. *History of El Dorado County,* 112. In 1872–73, Edward Schnell was involved in a legal dispute with the Japanese government over weapons he had sold to the Aizu and Yonezawa domains during the Boshin War. The documentary record of this matter has only one brief mention of his brother, John Henry Schnell, as having "gone to America." See Japanese Foreign Ministry, *Nihon Gaiko Bunsho,* 8:575–80, 9:446–47.

82. *Zaibei Nihonjinmei Jiten,* 5; Heisaburo Fumikura, comp., "Shoki no bu," *Fukuinkai Enkaku Shiryo* (Feb. 1869–Aug. 1885), 1–3, folder 1, box 291, Japanese American Research Project Collection.

83. Heisaburo, "Shoki no bu," 1–3.

84. Masao Takeda, interview by author, Aizu-Wakamatsu, Apr. 3, 1991. Takeda had been the chief librarian of the Aizu-Wakamatsu Public Library.

85. Kuni Massumidzu and Carrie Wilson, marriage license, Dec. 28, 1877, and certificate of marriage, Dec. 31, 1877, El Dorado County Recorder's Office, Placerville, Calif.

86. "What Became of the Pioneer's Children?" *Sacramento Union,* June 6, 1971. This article consists primarily of interviews with Juanita Wong and George Elebeck, grandchildren of Masumizu and Wilson.

87. Ibid.

88. Ibid.

89. Ibid.

90. *Colusa Memorial Society Record* (Jan. 1919–May 1949), 8–10, box 264, Japanese American Research Project Collection; Henry Taketa, "Passing of a Descendant of Wakamatsu Colonist," *Nichibei Times,* Mar. 11, 1983.

91. "First Japanese in U.S. Left Black Kin," *Los Angeles Times,* June 9, 1969.

92. *Sacramento Union,* June 6, 1971.

93. Coloma Township, El Dorado County Census, U.S. Bureau of the Census,

Unpublished Manuscript Schedules, 1880. The names of the other two Japanese with Sakurai are indecipherable, but are clearly marked as being from Japan. Masumizu, his wife, Carrie, and one child are also included in the 1880 Coloma census.

94. Veerkamp interview.

95. Kimura, "Japanese Mayflower," 307. Kimura's interview with Veerkamp had taken place many years earlier. Veerkamp had nearly identical recollections in an article published in *Nichibei Shimbun,* Sept. 26, 1926.

96. *Nichibei Shimbun,* Sept. 26, 1926.

97. For example, the organization in Aizu-Wakamatsu dedicated to preserving the memory of the ill-fated colonists is called the Okei Kenshokai, or Society for Research and Commemoration of Okei. See also Enomoto and Murakami, *Wakamatsu Colony Centennial.*

98. "Wakamatsu Tea and Silk Farm," California State Historical Landmark Number 815, June 7, 1969.

99. Ichiro Matsudaira to James Murakami, May 27, 1969, Takeda Collection.

100. California State Board of Control, *California and the Oriental,* 52, 243. See also Iwata, "Japanese Immigrants."

101. The renowned Japanese American immigrant leader Abiko Kyutaro helped establish three of these colonies (Yamato Colony, Cressey Colony, and Cortez Colony). See Ichioka, *Issei,* 147–53. Valerie Matsumoto's *Farming the Home Place* is a study of the Cortez Colony.

102. Ichioka, *Issei,* 14–16, 102–10; Karl Yoneda, *Zaibei Nihonjin Rodosha,* 68–79; Wakatsuki, "Japanese Emigration," 418–21.

Epilogue

1. Crawcour, "Economic Change," 612.

2. Hane, *Modern Japan,* 99–100.

3. Wakatsuki, "Japanese Emigration," 399–400.

4. For an analysis of this dimension of Japanese history, see Hane, *Peasants, Rebels, and Outcastes,* especially 11–27.

5. Gluck, *Japan's Modern Myths,* 60.

6. Limerick, *Legacy of Conquest,* 272. See also Daniels, *Politics of Prejudice,* 106.

7. Lehmann, *Image of Japan,* 150.

8. Hing, in *Making and Remaking Asian America,* reprints the Ozawa decision delivered by the Supreme Court. For an analysis of this decision, see Ichioka, *Issei,* 210–26.

9. For further analysis of this transformation in relations, see Iriye, *Pacific Estrangement,* chap. 8; and LaFeber, *The Clash,* chap. 3.

BIBLIOGRAPHY

Newspapers and Periodicals

Alta Daily News (San Francisco). 1869.
Daily Alta California (San Francisco). 1851, 1853, 1868–70.
Denver Republican. 1888.
Hawaiian Gazette. 1868.
Honolulu Friend. 1862.
Honolulu Pacific Commercial Advertiser. 1868–69.
Honolulu Star-Bulletin. 1935.
Ke-Kuokoa (Honolulu). 1868.
Los Angeles Times. 1969.
New York Daily Tribune. 1880.
New York Sun. 1869.
New York Times. 1880, 1883.
Nichibei Shimbun (San Francisco). 1926.
Nichibei Times (San Francisco). 1983.
Overland Monthly. 1870.
Philadelphia Times. 1884.
Placerville (Calif.) Mountain Democrat. 1869–70.
Rutgers College Targum (New Brunswick, N.J.). 1870–79.
Rutland (Ver.) Herald Weekly. 1874.
Sacramento Union. 1869, 1971.
San Francisco Bulletin. 1868–69.
San Francisco Call. 1870.
San Francisco Chronicle. 1868–69, 1891–92.
San Francisco Pacific Citizen. 1968.

The Scarlet Letter (Rutgers College yearbook). 1870–79. Department of Special Collections and University Archives, Rutgers University, New Brunswick, N.J.

Sonoma Democrat (Santa Rosa, Calif.). 1892.

Washington, D.C., Evening Star. 1857–58.

Yomiuri Japan News (Tokyo). 1958.

Archival Sources

Brooks, Charles Wolcott. Papers. Phillips Library, Peabody Essex Museum, Salem, Mass.

El Dorado County Archives. Henry Huntington Library, San Marino, Calif.

Griffis, William Elliot. Collection. Special Collections and University Archives, Rutgers University, New Brunswick, N.J.

Japanese American Research Project Collection. Department of Special Collections, University Research Library, University of California at Los Angeles.

Marumoto, Masaji. Papers. Folder 4. Box 115. Japanese American Research Project Collection. Department of Special Collections, University Research Library, University of California at Los Angeles.

Neesima, Joseph [Niijima Jo]. Papers. Archives and Special Collections, Amherst College Library, Amherst, Mass.

Pacific Mail Steamship Archives. Henry Huntington Library, San Marino, Calif.

Survey of Race Relations. Hoover Institution Archives, Stanford University, Palo Alto, Calif.

Takeda, Masao. Collection. Aizu-Wakamatsu Public Library, Aizu-Wakamatsu, Japan.

Taketa, Henry, Collection. Private collection, Sacramento, Calif.

Van Arsedale, Maria. Papers. Special Collections and University Archives, Rutgers University, New Brunswick, N.J.

Government and Secondary Sources

Abe, Masao. *Zen and Western Thought.* Ed. William La Fleur. Honolulu: University of Hawaii Press, 1985.

Abe, Yoshiya. "From Prohibition to Toleration: Japanese Government Views Regarding Christianity, 1854–73." *Japanese Journal of Religious Studies* 5.2–3 (1978).

Aizu no Rekishi. Aizu-Wakamatsu, Japan: Aizu Bukeyashiki, 1989.

Altman, Albert. "Eugene Van Reed, a Reading Man in Japan." *Historical Review of Berks County* 30.1 (1964–65).

Appleby, Joyce, Lynn Hunt, and Margaret Jacob. *Telling the Truth about History.* New York: W. W. Norton, 1994.

Arakawa Hidetoshi. *Ikoku Hyoryu Monogatari.* Tokyo: Shakai Shisosha, 1969.

Aruga, Tadashi. "Japanese Scholarship in the History of U.S.–East Asian Relations." In *Pacific Passage: The Study of American–East Asian Relations on the Eve of the Twenty-First Century.* Ed. Warren I. Cohen. New York: Columbia University Press, 1996.

Asao Naohiro. *Sakoku*. Tokyo: Shogakkan, 1975.

Bandera, Marilyn. "A Case Study in Educational Motivation: *Ryugakusei* and Rutgers College, 1866–1895." Master's thesis, University of Hawaii, 1970.

Barnes, Elinor, and James Barnes, eds. *Naval Surgeon—Revolt in Japan, 1868–1869: The Diary of Samuel Pellman Boyer*. Bloomington: Indiana University Press, 1963.

Barthell, Diane L. *Amana: From Pietist Sect to American Community*. Lincoln: University of Nebraska Press, 1984.

Beasley, W. G. *Japan Encounters the Barbarian: Japanese Travellers in America and Europe*. New Haven: Yale University Press, 1995.

———. *The Meiji Restoration*. Stanford: Stanford University Press, 1972.

———, ed. and trans. *Select Documents on Japanese Foreign Policy, 1853–1868*. London: Oxford University Press, 1955.

Bellamy, Edward. *Looking Backward: 2000–1887*. Ed. Daniel Borus. Boston: St. Martin's Press, 1995.

Bernard, Donald. *The Life and Times of John Manjiro*. New York: McGraw-Hill, 1992.

Bix, Herbert. *Peasant Protest in Japan, 1590–1884*. New Haven: Yale University Press, 1986.

Boddy, Manchester. *Japanese in America*. Los Angeles: Manchester Boddy, 1921.

Bolitho, Harold. "Aizu, 1853–1868." *Proceedings of the British Association for Japanese Studies* 2 (1977).

———. "The Echigo War, 1868." *Monumenta Nipponica* 34.3 (1979).

Borus, Daniel H. "Edward Bellamy's Utopia in His Time and Ours." In *Looking Backward: 2000–1887*, by Edward Bellamy. Ed. Daniel Borus. Boston: St. Martin's Press, 1995.

Boxer, Charles R. *The Christian Century in Japan, 1549–1650*. Berkeley: University of California Press, 1951.

Bradley, Harold Whitman. *The American Frontier in Hawaii: The Pioneers, 1789–1843*. Stanford: Stanford University Press, 1942.

Braisted, William, ed. and trans. *Meiroku Zasshi*. Cambridge, Mass.: Harvard University Press, 1976.

Bright, John. *The Diaries of John Bright*. Ed. R. A. J. Walling. New York: William Morrow, 1931.

Brooke, George M., Jr. *John M. Brooke: Naval Scientist and Educator*. Charlottesville: University Press of Virginia, 1980.

Brooks, Charles Wolcott. *Japanese Wrecks Stranded and Picked Up Adrift in the North Pacific Ocean*. San Francisco: California Academy of Sciences, 1876.

Burks, Ardath, ed. *The Modernizers: Overseas Students, Foreign Employees, and Meiji Japan*. Boulder: Westview Press, 1985.

California State Board of Control. *California and the Oriental*. Sacramento: California State Printing Office, 1920.

Cary, Otis. "Foreword" to *Niijima Jo Zenshu*. Vol. 6. Kyoto: Dohosha, 1985. vi–vii.

———. "Uchimura, Neesima, and Amherst—Recently Discovered Correspondence." *Japan Quarterly* 3.4 (1956).

Chan, Sucheng. "Asian American Historiography." *Pacific Historical Review* 65.3 (1996).

———. *Asian Americans: An Interpretive History.* Boston: Twayne, 1991.

———. *This Bittersweet Soil: The Chinese in California Agriculture, 1860–1910.* Berkeley: University of California Press, 1986.

Chang, Gordon. "Asian Americans and American Foreign Relations." In *Pacific Passage: The Study of American–East Asian Relations on the Eve of the Twenty-First Century.* Ed. Warren I. Cohen. New York: Columbia University Press, 1996.

Chang, Richard T. *From Prejudice to Tolerance: A Study of the Japanese Image of the West, 1826–1864.* Tokyo: Sophia University Press, 1970.

Chikamori Haruyoshi. *Josefu Hiko.* Tokyo: Yoshikawa Kobunkan, 1986.

Cohen, Warren I., ed. *Pacific Passage: The Study of American–East Asian Relations on the Eve of the Twenty-First Century.* New York: Columbia University Press, 1996.

Confucius. *The Analects.* Trans. D. C. Lau. London: Penguin Books, 1979.

Conroy, Hilary. *The Japanese Frontier in Hawaii, 1868–1898.* Berkeley: University of California Press, 1953.

Conroy, Hilary, and T. Scott Miyakawa, eds. *East across the Pacific: Historical and Sociological Studies of Japanese Immigration and Assimilation.* Santa Barbara: ABC-Clio Press, 1973.

Conte, James T. "Overseas Study in the Meiji Period: Japanese Students in America, 1867–1902." Ph.D. diss., Princeton University, 1977.

Cooper, Michael, ed. *The Southern Barbarians: The First Europeans in Japan.* Tokyo: Kodansha, 1971.

———. *They Came to Japan: An Anthology of European Reports on Japan, 1543–1640.* Berkeley: University of California Press, 1965.

Crawcour, E. Sydney. "Economic Change in the Nineteenth Century." In *The Cambridge History of Japan.* Vol. 5, *The Nineteenth Century.* Ed. Marius Jansen. Cambridge: Cambridge University Press, 1989.

Cuthbert, Arthur. *The Life and World-Work of Thomas Lake Harris.* Glasgow, Scotland: C. W. Pearce, 1909.

Curtis, Edith Rolker. *A Season in Utopia: The Story of Brook Farm.* New York: Russell and Russell, 1971.

Daniels, Roger. *Asian America: Chinese and Japanese in the United States since 1850.* Seattle: University of Washington Press, 1988.

———. *The Politics of Prejudice: The Anti-Japanese Movement in California and the Struggle for Japanese Exclusion.* Berkeley: University of California Press, 1962.

Davis, J. D. *A Maker of New Japan—Rev. Joseph Hardy Neesima.* New York: Fleming Revell, 1894.

Daws, Gavan. *Shoal of Time: A History of the Hawaiian Islands.* Honolulu: University of Hawaii Press, 1968.

Demarest, William. *A History of Rutgers College, 1766–1924.* New Brunswick, N.J.: Rutgers College, 1924.

Dumoulin, Heinrich. *Christianity Meets Buddhism.* Trans. John C. Maraldo. LaSalle, Ill.: Open Court, 1974.

Dwight, John. "The Marchioness Oyama." *Twentieth Century Home* (1904).

Ellicott, J. M. "Japanese Students at the United States Naval Academy." *U.S. Naval Proceedings* 73 (1947).

Ellison, George. "Christianity and the Daimyo." In *The Cambridge History of Japan.* Vol. 4, *Early Modern Japan.* Ed. John Whitney Hall and James McClain. Cambridge: Cambridge University Press, 1991.

———. *Deus Destroyed: The Image of Christianity in Early Modern Japan.* Cambridge, Mass.: Harvard University Press, 1973.

Enomoto, Jerry, and James Murakami, eds. *Wakamatsu Colony Centennial.* San Francisco: Japanese American Citizens League, 1969.

Ericsom, Jack T., ed. *Thomas Lake Harris and the Brotherhood of the New Life: A Guide to the Microfilm Collection.* Glen Rock, N.J.: Microfilming Corporation of America, 1974.

Esthus, Raymond. *Theodore Roosevelt and Japan.* Seattle: University of Washington Press, 1967.

Eudsen, John Dykstra. *Zen and Christian: The Journey Between.* New York: Crossroad, 1981.

Fairbank, John King. *The United States and China.* Cambridge, Mass.: Harvard University Press, 1983.

Ferris, John. "How the Japanese Came to New Brunswick." In *The Rutgers Graduates in Japan,* by William Griffis. New Brunswick, N.J.: Rutgers College Alumni Association, 1886.

Fukuzawa Yukichi. *The Autobiography of Yukichi Fukuzawa.* Trans. Eiichi Kiyooka. New York: Columbia University Press, 1966.

Geertz, Clifford. *The Interpretation of Cultures.* New York: Basic Books, 1973.

Gluck, Carol. *Japan's Modern Myths: Ideology in the Late Meiji Period.* Princeton: Princeton University Press, 1985.

Goodman, Grant. *Japan: The Dutch Experience.* London: Athelone Press, 1986.

Goodwin, James. *Autobiography: The Self Made Text.* New York: Twayne, 1993.

Goto, Y. B. *Children of Gannen-mono: The First-Year Men.* Honolulu: Bishop Museum Press, 1968.

Graebner, Norman. *Empire on the Pacific: A Study in American Continental Expansion.* New York: Ronald Press, 1955.

Griffis, William. *The Mikado's Empire.* New York: Harper and Brothers, 1876.

———. *The Rutgers Graduates in Japan.* New Brunswick, N.J.: Rutgers College Alumni Association, 1886.

Hall, Francis. *Japan through American Eyes: The Journal of Francis Hall, Kanagawa, and Yokohama, 1859–1866.* Ed. Fred Notehelfer. Princeton: Princeton University Press, 1992.

Hall, Ivan Parker. *Mori Arinori.* Cambridge, Mass.: Harvard University Press, 1973.

Halloran, Fumiko Mori, Robert Sakai, and Minoru Shinoda. *Humanity above Na-*

tion: The Impact of Manjiro and Heco on America and Japan. Honolulu: Joseph Heco Society of Hawaii and Japanese Cultural Center of Hawaii, 1995.

Hane, Mikiso. *Modern Japan: A Historical Survey.* Boulder: Westview Press, 1986.

———. *Peasants, Rebels, and Outcastes: The Underside of Modern Japan.* New York: Pantheon Books, 1982.

Hardy, Arthur S., ed. *Life and Letters of Joseph Hardy Neesima.* Boston: Houghton, Mifflin, 1891.

Harootunian, H. D. *Toward Restoration: The Growth of Political Consciousness in Tokugawa Japan.* Berkeley: University of California Press, 1970.

Harris, Thomas Lake. "An Autobiographic Sketch." In *Thomas Lake Harris and the Brotherhood of the New Life: Books, Pamphlets, Serials, and Manuscripts.* Ed. Jack T. Ericsom. Glen Rock, N.J.: Microfilming Corporation of America, 1974.

———. *The Breath of God with Man.* New York: Brotherhood of the New Life, 1867.

Hawks, Francis L. *Narrative of the Expedition of an American Squadron to the China Seas and Japan.* New York: D. Appleton, 1857.

Hayashi Takeji. *Mori Arinori.* Tokyo: Chikuma Shobo, 1986.

Heco, Joseph. *The Narrative of a Japanese: What He Has Seen and the People He Has Met in the Course of the Last Forty Years.* Ed. James Murdoch. 2 vols. Yokohama: Yokohama Printing and Publishing, 1892, 1895.

Hietala, Thomas. *Manifest Destiny: Anxious Aggrandisement in Late Jacksonian America.* Ithaca: Cornell University Press, 1985.

Hikozo [Joseph Heco]. *Hyoryuki.* Edo: n.p., [1863].

———. *Hyoryuki.* In *Ikoku Hyoryu Kidanshu.* Comp. Ishii Kendo. Tokyo: Fukunaga Shoten, 1927.

———. *Hyoryuki: Floating on the Pacific Ocean.* Trans. Tosh Motofuji. Los Angeles: Glen Dawson, 1955.

Hine, Robert V. *California's Utopian Colonies.* 2d ed. New Haven: Yale University Press, 1966.

———. *Community on the American Frontier: Separate but Not Alone.* Norman: University of Oklahoma Press, 1980.

———. *Edward Kern and American Expansion.* New Haven: Yale University Press, 1962.

Hing, Bill Ong. *Making and Remaking Asian America through Immigration Policy, 1850–1990.* Stanford: Stanford University Press, 1993.

Hirakawa, Sukehiro. "Japan's Turn to the West." In *The Cambridge History of Japan.* Vol. 5, *The Nineteenth Century.* Ed. Marius Jansen. Cambridge: Cambridge University Press, 1989.

History of El Dorado County, California. Oakland: Paolo Sioli, 1883.

Holliday, J. S. *The World Rushed In: The California Gold Rush Experience.* New York: Simon and Schuster, 1981.

Horsman, Reginald. *Race and Manifest Destiny: The Origins of American Racial Anglo-Saxonism.* Cambridge, Mass.: Harvard University Press, 1981.

Hosokawa, William. *Nisei: The Quiet Americans.* New York: William Morrow, 1969.

Howe, Christopher. *The Origins of Japanese Trade Supremacy: Development and Technology in Asia from 1540 to the Pacific War.* Chicago: University of Chicago Press, 1996.

Howell, David. "Hard Times in the Kanto: Economic Change and Village Life in Late Tokugawa Japan." *Modern Asian Studies* 23.2 (1989).

Hunt, Michael H. *The Making of a Special Relationship: The United States and China to 1914.* New York: Columbia University Press, 1983.

Ichihashi, Yamato. *Japanese in the United States: A Critical Study of the Problems of the Japanese Immigrants and Their Children.* Stanford: Stanford University Press, 1932.

Ichioka, Yuji. *Issei: The World of the First Generation Japanese Immigrants, 1885–1924.* New York: Free Press, 1988.

Iriye, Akira. *Across the Pacific: An Inner History of American–East Asian Relations.* New York: Harcourt, Brace, Jovanovich, 1967.

———. "Japan's Drive to Great-Power Status." In *The Cambridge History of Japan.* Vol. 5, *The Nineteenth Century.* Ed. Marius Jansen. Cambridge: Cambridge University Press, 1989.

———. *Pacific Estrangement: Japanese and American Expansion, 1897–1911.* Cambridge, Mass.: Harvard University Press, 1972.

Ishii Kendo, comp. *Ikoku Hyoryu Kidanshu.* Tokyo: Fukunaga Shoten, 1927.

Ishizuki Minoru. *Kindai Nihon no Kaigai Ryugakushi.* Rev. ed. Tokyo: Chuo Koronsha, 1992.

Israel, Jonathan. *Dutch Primacy in World Trade, 1585–1740.* Oxford: Clarendon Press, 1989.

Iwao, Seichi. "Japanese Foreign Trade in the Sixteenth and Seventeenth Centuries." *Acta Asiatica* 30 (1976).

Iwata, Masakazu. "The Japanese Immigrants in California Agriculture." *Agricultural History* 36.1 (1962).

Jansen, Marius. "The Meiji Restoration." In *The Cambridge History of Japan.* Vol. 5, *The Nineteenth Century.* Ed. Marius Jansen. Cambridge: Cambridge University Press, 1989.

Japanese Agency for Cultural Affairs. *Japanese Religion.* Tokyo: Kodansha International, 1972.

Japanese Foreign Ministry. *Bakumatsu Gaikoku Kankei Bunsho.* Vol. 1. Tokyo: Gaimusho, 1910.

———. *Kokaijin Meisaibo.* 1872–75. Japanese American Research Project Collection. Department of Special Collections, University Research Library, University of California at Los Angeles.

———. *Kokaijin Mesaikan.* 1867–72. Japanese American Research Project Collection. Department of Special Collections, University Research Library, University of California at Los Angeles.

Japanese Government. *Kyujoyaku isan.* Vol. 1. Tokyo: Gaimusho, 1934.

———. *Nihon Gaiko Bunsho.* Vols. 1–15. Tokyo: Gaimusho, 1936–63.

———. *Nihon Teikoku Tokei Nenkan.* Vols. 1–2. Tokyo: Toyo, 1962.

Japanese National Commission for UNESCO, ed. *Development of a Modern System of Education in Japan.* Tokyo: Ministry of Education, 1960.

———, ed. *The Role of Education in the Social and Economic Development of Japan.* Tokyo: Ministry of Education, 1966.

Jonas, F. M. "Foreign Influence on the Early Press of Japan." *Transactions and Proceedings of the Japan Society of London* 32 (1935).

Kadota, Paul Akira, and Terry Earl Jones. *Kanaye Nagasawa: A Biography of a Satsuma Student.* Kagoshima, Japan: Kagoshima Prefectural Junior College, 1990.

Kanai, Madoka. "Fukui, Domain of a Tokugawa Collateral Daimyo: Its Tradition and Transformation." In *The Modernizers: Overseas Students, Foreign Employees, and Meiji Japan.* Ed. Ardath Burks. Boulder: Westview Press, 1985.

Kaneko, Hisakazu. *Manjiro, the Man Who Discovered America.* Boston: Houghton Mifflin, 1956.

Kaneko, Tadashi. "Contributions of David Murray to the Modernization of School Administration in Japan." In *The Modernizers: Overseas Students, Foreign Employees, and Meiji Japan.* Ed. Ardath Burks. Boulder: Westview Press, 1985.

Kanter, Rosabeth Moss. *Commitment and Community: Communes and Utopias in Sociological Perspective.* Cambridge, Mass.: Harvard University Press, 1972.

Kawamura Masahei [Yusen]. *Kariforunia Kaika Ibun.* Tokyo: Sakakibara Bunseido Shuppan, 1932.

Kawanishi Susumu. "Teachers and Friends of Niijima Jo during His Early Years." In *Niijima Jo no Sekai—Eimin Hyakunen no Jiten Kara.* Kyoto: Koyo Shobo, 1990.

Kemble, John Haskell. *A Hundred Years of the Pacific Mail.* Newport News, Va.: Mariner's Museum, 1950.

Kennedy, Paul. *The Rise and Fall of the Great Powers: Economic Change and Military Conflict from 1500 to 2000.* New York: Random House, 1987.

Kent, Noel. *Hawaii: Islands under the Influence.* New York: Monthly Review Press, 1983.

Kesten, Seymour R. *Utopian Episodes: Daily Life in Experimental Colonies Dedicated to Changing the World.* New York: Syracuse University Press, 1993.

Kimura, Ki. "The Japanese Mayflower." *Japan Quarterly* 8.3 (1960).

Kiyooka, Eiichi, and Kazuyoshi Nakayama, eds. and trans. *Fukuzawa Yukichi on Education: Selected Works.* Tokyo: University of Tokyo Press, 1985.

Kohl, Stephen W. "Strangers in a Strange Land: Japanese Castaways and the Opening of Japan." *Pacific Northwest Quarterly* 73.1 (1982).

Kuno, Akiko. *Unexpected Destinations: The Poignant Story of Japan's First Vassar Graduate.* Tokyo: Kodansha International, 1993.

Kuykendall, Ralph S. "The Earliest Japanese Labor Immigration to Hawaii." *University of Hawaii Occasional Papers,* no. 25 (Feb. 1935).

———. *The Hawaiian Kingdom: Twenty Critical Years, 1854–1874.* Honolulu: University of Hawaii Press, 1953.

LaFeber, Walter. *The Clash: A History of U.S.-Japan Relations.* New York: W. W. Norton, 1997.

Lanman, Charles, and Mori Arinori. *The Japanese in America*. London: Longmans, Green, Reader, and Dyer, 1872.

Lassalle, H. M. Enomiya. *Zen Meditation for Christians*. Trans. John C. Maraldo. LaSalle, Ill.: Open Court, 1974.

LeBaron, Gaye. *The Japanese Baron of Fountaingrove*. Santa Rosa, Calif.: Santa Rosa Junior College, 1976.

Le Duc, Thomas. *Piety and Intellect at Amherst College, 1865–1912*. New York: Columbia University Press, 1946.

Lehmann, Jean-Pierre. *The Image of Japan: From Feudal Isolation to World Power, 1850–1905*. London: George Allen and Unwin, 1978.

Li, Lillian M. *China's Silk Trade: Traditional Industry in the Modern World, 1842–1937*. Cambridge, Mass.: Harvard University Council on East Asian Studies, 1981.

———. "Silks by Sea: Trade, Technology, and Enterprise in China and Japan." *Business History Review* 56.2 (1982).

Limerick, Patricia Nelson. *The Legacy of Conquest: The Unbroken Past of the American West*. New York: W. W. Norton, 1987.

Lockwood, William. *The Economic Development of Japan*. Rev. ed. Princeton: Princeton University Press, 1968.

Long, David F. *Sailor Diplomat: A Biography of Commodore James Biddle, 1793–1848*. Boston: Northeastern University Press, 1983.

Loosely, Allyn Campbell. *Foreign Born Population of California, 1848–1920*. San Francisco: R and E Research Associates, 1971.

Lotchin, Roger W. *San Francisco, 1846–1856: From Hamlet to City*. New York: Oxford University Press, 1974.

Lu, David John, ed. *Sources of Japanese History*. New York: McGraw-Hill, 1974.

Markham, Edwin. *California the Wonderful*. New York: Hearst's International Library, 1914.

———. *The Man with the Hoe, and Other Poems*. New York: Doubleday and McClure, 1899.

Marumoto, Masaji. "First Year Immigrants and Eugene Van Reed." In *East across the Pacific: Historical and Sociological Studies of Japanese Immigration and Assimilation*. Ed. Hilary Conroy and T. Scott Miyakawa. Santa Barbara: ABC-Clio Press, 1973.

Matsumoto, Valerie. *Farming the Home Place: A Japanese American Community in California, 1919–1982*. New York: Cornell University Press, 1993.

McCabe, James D., ed. *A Tour around the World by General Grant*. Philadelphia: National, 1880.

Meissner, Kurt. "General Eduard Schnell." *Monumenta Nipponica* 4 (1941).

Merk, Frederick. *Manifest Destiny and Mission in American History*. Westport, Conn.: Greenwood, 1963.

Minakawa, Saburo. *Christian Teaching and English Education in Early Japan*. Yokohama: Gakuseisha, 1953.

Miyoshi, Masao. *As We Saw Them: The First Japanese Embassy to the United States*. Berkeley: University of California Press, 1979.

More, Thomas. *Utopia.* Ed. George Logan and Robert Adams. Cambridge: Cambridge University Press, 1989.

Mori Arinori. *Education in Japan: A Series of Letters Addressed by Prominent Americans to Arinori Mori.* New York: D. Appleton, 1873.

———. "Life and Resources in America." Part 3 of *The Japanese in America,* by Charles Lanman and Arinori Mori. London: Longmans, Green, Reader, and Dyer, 1872.

———. "Religion." In *Meiroku Zasshi.* Ed and trans. William R. Braisted. Cambridge, Mass.: Harvard University Press, 1976.

———. "Religious Freedom in Japan: A Memorial and Draft of Charter." In *Mori Arinori no Shiso,* by Moriaki Sakamoto. Tokyo: Jiji Tsushinsha, 1969.

Moriyama, Alan Takeo. *Imingaisha: Japanese Emigration Companies and Hawaii, 1894–1908.* Honolulu: University of Hawaii Press, 1985.

Morris, Grace P. "Wreck of a Japanese Junk, 1834." *Oregon Historical Quarterly* 38 (1937).

Morris, Ivan. *The Nobility of Failure: Tragic Heroes in the History of Japan.* New York: Holt, Rinehart, and Winston, 1975.

Munroe-Fraser, J. P. *History of Santa Clara County.* San Francisco: Alley, Bowen, 1881.

Muragaki, Awaji-no-kami. *Kokkai Nikki: The Diary of the First Japanese Embassy to the United States.* Trans. Helen M. Uno. Tokyo: Foreign Affairs Association of Japan, 1958.

Murdoch, James. *A History of Japan.* Vol. 3, *The Tokugawa Epoch.* Ed. Joseph Longford. New York: Greenberg, 1926.

Murray, David. "Hatakeyama Yoshinari of Japan." *Japanese Student* (Feb. 1917).

Nagasawa, Kanaye. "Diaries of Kanaye Nagasawa." In *Kenkyu Nenpo,* no. 9. Kagoshima, Japan: Kagoshima Prefectural Junior College, 1980.

Nakahama, Toichiro. *Nakahama Manjiro Den.* Tokyo: Toyamabo, 1936.

———. *Nakahama Manjiro Hyoryuki.* Tokyo: Denkigakkai, 1935.

Nakane, Chie. "Tokugawa Society." In *Tokugawa Society: The Social and Economic Antecedents of Modern Japan.* Ed. Chie Nakane and Shinzaburo Oishi. Tokyo: Tokyo University Press, 1990.

Niijima Jo. "Hakodate Kiko." In *Hakodate Shishi.* Vol. 1. Hakodate: Dai Ichi Insatsu, 1974.

Niijima Jo Zenshu. Vols. 6–7. Kyoto: Dohosha, 1985, 1995.

Nordyke, Eleanor, and Y. Scott Matsumoto. "The Japanese in Hawaii: A Historical and Demographic Perspective." *Hawaiian Journal of History* 11 (1977).

Nosco, Peter, ed. *Confucianism and Tokugawa Culture.* Princeton: Princeton University Press, 1984.

Noyes, John Humphrey. *History of American Socialisms.* New York: Sentry Press, 1870.

Ogura, Takekazu, ed. *Agricultural Development in Modern Japan.* Tokyo: Fuji, 1967.

Ohira, Kimata. *Sakuma Shozan.* Tokyo: Nihon Rekishi Gakkai, 1959.

Okahata, James, ed. *Hawaii Nihonjin Iminshi.* Honolulu: United Japanese Society of Hawaii, 1964.

———, ed. *A History of Japanese in Hawaii.* Honolulu: United Japanese Society of Hawaii, 1971.

Okubo Toshiaki, ed. *Mori Arinori Zenshu.* 3 vols. Tokyo: Seibundo, 1972.

Oliphant, Margaret W. *Memoir of the Life of Laurence Oliphant and of Alice Oliphant, His Wife.* Edinburgh, Scotland: W. Blackwood, 1892.

Ooms, Herman. *Tokugawa Ideology: Early Constructs, 1570–1680.* Princeton: Princeton University Press, 1985.

———. *Tokugawa Village Practice: Class, Status, Law.* Berkeley: University of California Press, 1996.

Osada, Kenjiro. "Life of Takano Nagahide." *Transactions of the Asiatic Society of Japan* 41.3 (1913).

Pacheco, Diego. "The Europeans in Japan, 1543–1640." In *The Southern Barbarians: The First Europeans in Japan.* Ed. Michael Cooper. Tokyo: Kodansha, 1971.

Paul, Rodman, ed. *The California Gold Discovery: Sources, Documents, Accounts, and Memoirs.* Georgetown, Calif.: Georgetown Press, 1967.

———. *The Far West and the Great Plains in Transition.* New York: Harper and Row, 1988.

———. *Mining Frontiers of the Far West, 1848–1880.* Albuquerque: University of New Mexico Press, 1974.

Peterson, William. "Success Story, Japanese American Style." *New York Times Magazine,* Jan. 6, 1966.

Phillips, Clifton Jackson. *Protestant America and the Pagan World: The First Half Century of the American Board of Commissioners for Foreign Missions.* Cambridge, Mass.: Harvard University East Asian Research Center, 1969.

Plummer, Katherine. *The Shogun's Reluctant Ambassadors: Sea Drifters.* Tokyo: Lotus Press, 1984.

Potter, David M. *The Impending Crisis, 1848–1861.* Ed. Don Fehrenbacher. New York: Harper and Row, 1976.

Rei Matsuura, ed. *Nihon no Meicho: Sakuma Shozan/Yokoi Shonan.* Tokyo: Chuo Koronsha, 1970.

Reischauer, Edwin. *Japan: The Story of a Nation.* New York: Alfred A. Knopf, 1981.

Rose, Barbara. *Tsuda Umeko and Women's Education in Japan.* New Haven: Yale University Press, 1992.

Sakai, Robert. "The Satsuma Ryukyu Trade and the Tokugawa Seclusionist Policy." *Journal of Asian Studies* 23.3 (1964).

Sakamaki, Shunzo. *Japan and the United States, 1790–1853.* Tokyo: Asiatic Society of Japan, 1939; reprint, Wilmington, Del.: Scholarly Resources, 1973.

Sakuma Shozan. "Reflections on My Errors." In *Sources of Japanese Tradition.* Ed. Ryusaku Tsunoda, Theodore De Bary, and Donald Keene. New York: Columbia University Press, 1964.

Samuels, Richard. *Rich Nation, Strong Army: National Security and the Technological Transformation of Japan.* Ithaca: Cornell University Press, 1994.

Sandburg, Carl. *Abraham Lincoln: The War Years.* Vol 1. New York: Harcourt, Brace, 1939.

Saul, Norman. "Beverly C. Sanders and the Expansion of American Trade with Russia, 1853–1855." *Maryland Historical Magazine* 67.2 (1972).

Saxton, Alexander P. *The Indispensable Enemy: Labor and the Anti-Chinese Movement in California.* Berkeley: University of California Press, 1971.

Scheiner, Irwin. *Christian Converts and Social Protest in Meiji Japan.* Berkeley: University of California Press, 1970.

Schivelbusch, Wolfgang. *The Railway Journey: The Industrialization of Time and Space in the Nineteenth Century.* Berkeley: University of California Press, 1986.

Schmitt, Robert C. *Historical Statistics of Hawaii.* Honolulu: University of Hawaii Press, 1977.

Schneider, Herbert, and George Lawton. *A Prophet and a Pilgrim.* New York: Columbia University Press, 1942.

Schwantes, Robert. *Japanese and Americans: A Century of Cultural Relations.* New York: Harper and Brothers, 1955.

Sigstedt, Cyriel Odner. *The Swedenborg Epic: The Life and Works of Emanuel Swedenborg.* New York: Bookman Associates, 1952.

Silberman, Bernard. *Ministers of Modernization: Elite Mobility in the Meiji Restoration, 1868–1873.* Tucson: University of Arizona Press, 1964.

Slade, Joseph. "Historical Sketch of Thomas Lake Harris, Laurence Oliphant, and the Brotherhood of the New Life." In *Thomas Lake Harris and the Brotherhood of the New Life: A Guide to the Microfilm Collection.* Ed. Jack T. Ericsom. Glen Rock, N.J.: Microfilming Corporation of America, 1974.

Soule, Frank, John Gihon, and James Nisbet. *The Annals of San Francisco.* New York: D. Appleton, 1854.

Speer, William. *The Oldest and Newest Empire: China and the United States.* Chicago: National, 1870.

Stannard, David. *Before the Horror: The Population of Hawaii on the Eve of Western Contact.* Honolulu: University of Hawaii Social Science Research Institute, 1989.

Stein, Stephen J. *The Shaker Experience in America: A History of the United Society of Believers.* New Haven: Yale University Press, 1992.

Stelle, Charles Clarkson. *Americans and the China Opium Trade in the Nineteenth Century.* New York: Arno Press, 1981.

Stuart, Reginald. *United States Expansionism and British North America, 1775–1871.* Chapel Hill: University of North Carolina Press, 1988.

Sugiyama, Chuhei, and Tamotsu Nishizawa. "Captain of Industry: Tokyo Commercial School at Hitotsubashi." In *Enlightenment and Beyond: Political Economy Comes to Japan.* Ed. Chuhei Sugiyama and Hiroshi Mizuta. Tokyo: University of Tokyo Press, 1988.

Suzuki, Daisetz T. *Zen and Japanese Culture*. Princeton, N.J.: Princeton University Press, 1959.

Takaki, Ronald. *Pau Hana: Plantation Life and Labor in Hawaii*. Honolulu: University of Hawaii Press, 1983.

———. *Strangers from a Different Shore*. Boston: Little, Brown, 1989.

Taketa, Henry. "The Centennial Year." *Pacific Historian* 13.1 (1969).

———. "Wakamatsu Silk and Tea Farm Colony of Gold Hill: The Beginning of Japanese Immigration to America." Paper presented at the annual meeting of the California History Institute, University of the Pacific, Stockton, Calif., Apr. 28, 1989.

Toby, Ronald. *State and Diplomacy in Early Modern Japan: Asia in the Development of the Tokugawa Bakufu*. 2d ed. Stanford: Stanford University Press, 1991.

Totman, Conrad. *The Collapse of the Tokugawa Bakufu, 1862–1868*. Honolulu: University of Hawaii Press, 1980.

———. *Early Modern Japan*. Berkeley: University of California Press, 1993.

Tsai, Shih-shan Henry. *China and the Overseas Chinese in the United States, 1868–1911*. Fayetteville: University of Arkansas Press, 1983.

Tsunoda, Ryusaku, Theodore De Bary, and Donald Keene, eds. *Sources of Japanese Tradition*. New York: Columbia University Press, 1964.

Tyrrell, Ian. "American Exceptionalism in an Age of International History." *American Historical Review* 96.4 (1991).

Uchimura Kanzo. *How I Became a Christian, out of My Diary*. Chicago: Fleming H. Revell, 1895; reprint, Tokyo: Kyobunkan, 1971.

Umegaki, Michio. *After the Restoration: The Beginning of Japan's Modern State*. New York: New York University Press, 1988.

U.S. Bureau of Foreign and Domestic Commerce. *Statistical Abstract of the United States, 1930*. Washington, D.C.: Government Printing Office, 1930.

U.S. Bureau of the Census. *Chinese and Japanese in the United States, 1910*. Bulletin 127. Washington, D.C.: Government Printing Office, 1914.

———. *Historical Statistics of the United States, Colonial Times to 1957*. Washington, D.C.: Government Printing Office, 1960.

———. *Historical Statistics of the United States, Colonial Times to 1970*. Washington, D.C.: Government Printing Office, 1976.

———. *Unpublished Manuscript Schedules for the State of California, 1870*. Washington, D.C.: National Archives Microfilm, 1948.

———. *Unpublished Manuscript Schedules for the State of California, 1880*. Washington, D.C.: National Archives Microfilm, 1948.

U.S. Census Office. *Statistics of the Population of the United States at the Tenth Census*. 1880. Washington, D.C.: Government Printing Office, 1883.

U.S. Commission on Wartime Relocation and Internment of Civilians. *Personal Justice Denied: Report of the Commission on Wartime Relocation and Internment of Civilians*. Washington, D.C.: Government Printing Office, 1982.

———. *Personal Justice Denied: Part 2, Recommendations.* Washington, D.C.: Government Printing Office, 1983.

U.S. Congress. *The Congressional Globe.* 39th Cong., 2d sess. Washington, D.C.: F. and J. Rives, 1867.

———. *Statutes at Large of the United States of America.* Vol. 4, 1824–35. Boston: Charles C. Little and James Brown, 1850.

U.S. Department of State. *Correspondence Relative to the Naval Expedition to Japan.* Executive Doc. 34, 33d Cong., 2d sess. Washington, D.C.: Government Printing Office, 1854.

———. *Despatches from U.S. Ministers to Japan, 1855–1906.* Washington, D.C.: National Archives Microfilm, 1949.

———. *Diplomatic Instructions of the Department of State, 1801–1906, Japan.* Washington, D.C.: National Archives Microfilm, 1946.

———. *Diplomatic Instructions of the Department of State, 1801–1906, Special Missions.* Washington, D.C.: National Archives Microfilm, 1946.

———. *Foreign Relations of the United States.* Washington, D.C.: Government Printing Office, 1861–80.

U.S. Department of the Interior. *Ninth Census of the United States, The Statistics of the Population.* 1870. Washington, D.C.: Government Printing Office, 1872.

U.S. Senate. *Senate Documents.* Vol. 9, 32d Cong., 1st sess. Washington, D.C.: A. Boyd Hamilton, 1852.

Van Alstyne, Richard. *The United States and East Asia.* New York: W. W. Norton, 1973.

Vaporis, Constantine Nomikos. *Breaking Barriers: Travel and the State in Early Modern Japan.* Cambridge, Mass.: Harvard University Press, 1994.

Vlastos, Stephen. *Peasant Protests and Uprisings in Tokugawa Japan.* Berkeley: University of California Press, 1986.

Wakabayashi, Bob Tadashi. *Anti-Foreignism and Western Learning in Early Modern Japan.* Cambridge, Mass.: Harvard University Press, 1986.

Wakatsuki Yasuo. "Japanese Emigration to the United States, 1866–1924: A Monograph." *Perspectives in American History* 12 (1979).

Walker, Brett. "Matsumae Domain and the Conquest of Ainu Lands: Ecology and Culture in Tokugawa Expansionism, 1593–1799." Ph.D. diss., University of Oregon, 1997.

———. "Reappraising the Sakoku Paradigm: The Ezo Trade and the Extension of Tokugawa Political Space into Hokkaido." *Journal of Asian History* 30.2 (1996).

Walters, Ronald G. *American Reformers, 1815–1860.* New York: Hill and Wang, 1978.

Walthall, Anne. *Peasant Uprisings in Japan: A Critical Anthology of Peasant Histories.* Chicago: University of Chicago Press, 1991.

———. *Social Protest and Popular Culture in Eighteenth-Century Japan.* Tucson: University of Arizona Press, 1986.

Warriner, Emily. *Voyager to Destiny.* New York: Bobbs-Merrill, 1956.

Watanabe Minoru. *Niijima Jo*. Tokyo: Yoshikawa Kobunkan, 1959.
White, James. *Ikki: Social Conflict and Political Protest in Early Modern Japan*. Ithaca: Cornell University Press, 1995.
White, William. *Life of Emanuel Swedenborg, Together with a Brief Synopsis of His Writings, Both Philosophical and Theological*. Philadelphia: J. B. Lippincott, n.d.
Wilcox, Walter, and Imre Ferenczi, eds. *International Migration*. Vol. 1. New York: National Bureau of Economic Research, 1929.
Williams, S. Wells. *A Journal of the Perry Expedition to Japan, 1853–1854*. Yokohama, Japan: Kelly and Walsh, 1910; reprint, Wilmington, Del.: Scholarly Resources, 1973.
Winchell, Wallace. "The Mystical Experience of Thomas Lake Harris: The Seer as a Creator of His Own Visionary World." Ph.d. diss., Hartford Seminary Foundation, 1976.
Yamaguchi, Uji. *Kinse Shiriaku: A History of Japan*. Trans. Ernest Satow. Tokyo: Naigwai Shuppan Kyokwai, 1873; reprint, Tokyo: Naigwai Shuppan Kyokwai, 1906.
Yamamoto Ichiyo. *Wakamatsu Koroni no Ato wo Tazunete*. Aizu-Wakamatsu: Northern Japan, 1985.
Yoneda, Karl. *Zaibei Nihonjin Rodosha no Rekishi*. Tokyo: Shin Nihon Shuppansha, 1967.
Zaibei Nihonjinmei Jiten. San Francisco: Nichibei Shimbunsha, 1922.

INDEX

Abe, Yoshiya, 10
African Americans, 36–37, 44, 134
Aizawa Seishisai, 12, 19
Aizu domain, 117–24
Alta Daily News, 124–25
American Board of Commissioners for Foreign Missions (ABCFM), 16, 65, 68, 74–75, 99, 132
American Civil War, 15, 20, 37, 109
Amherst College, 55, 65, 70–73
Andover Theological Seminary, 70, 73, 74
Arai Osui, 89, 90, 91, 94
Auckland (ship), 21, 29–30
Augustine Heard and Company, 100

Battle of Shimonoseki, 46
Bellamy, Edward, 80
Biddle, James, 16–17, 27
Bolitho, Harold, 119, 120, 121
Boshin War, 120–21, 123
Brenham, Charles, 32
Brocton Colony, 86–89, 94
Brooke, John, 37, 45
Brooks, Charles Wolcott, 99, 110, 115, 128
Brotherhood of the New Life, 60, 79–96, 118, 132
Buchanan, James, 41–42

Buddhism, 28, 30, 72. *See also* Tibetan Buddhism; Zen Buddhism
Bunmei kaika ("civilization and enlightenment"), 52, 132
Byakkotai (White Tiger Brigade), 121

California, 1, 29, 122–25
Cass, Lewis, 41, 101
Castaways, 22–23, 99
Chang, Gordon, 4
Charter Oath (1868), 51
Chevaillier, Alzire, 90–91
Chinese: Chinese Exclusion Act, 2, 134; immigration and immigrants, 1–2, 59, 72, 115, 134; as perceived by Japanese, 29, 76
Chinese Exclusion Act, 2, 134
Choshu domain, 25, 46, 50, 61, 69, 70, 89, 100, 119–20, 121, 130, 134
Christianity, 53–54, 65, 67–69, 72; and Confucianism, 68–69; and Japan, 7–10, 39, 62, 72–75, 77–78, 84–86, 92–94, 132
"Civilization and enlightenment" (*bunmei kaika*), 52, 132
Coeducation, 58
Coloma, California, 118, 122, 132
Confucianism, 5, 6, 8, 14, 53, 72, 100
Conte, James, 51

Cook, James, 102
Court-*bakufu* harmony, 119–20

Daily Alta California, 33
Dekaseginin (workers away from home), 2
De Long, Charles, 100, 101, 110, 112, 113, 115, 121–22
Divine Respiration, 79, 83, 84. *See also* Harris, Thomas Lake
Dorr, Eben, 46
Doshisha University, 77
Dutch contacts with Japan, 10–12. *See also Rangaku*
Dutch Reformed Church, 49, 55–56

"Eastern ethics, Western science" (*Tōyō no dōtoku, Seiyo no gakugei*), 13–14, 48, 50, 52–53, 57, 62, 78, 119, 132. *See also* Sakuma Shozan
Eiriki Maru (ship), 28–29
Enatsu Sosuke, 87
Enomoto Takeaki, 101
Expulsion Edict (1825), 11

Ferris, John, 49, 61
Fish, Hamilton, 44, 101, 115
Flint, Ephraim, 70, 74
Flint, Orilla, 70
Fountaingrove, 89–92
Fukoku kyohei ("rich nation, strong army"), 13, 50–51, 52, 132
Fukuzawa Yukichi, 23, 52–53, 94. *See also* "Civilization and enlightenment"
Fushimi, Japan, 120–21

Gannenmono, 97–116, 132
Geertz, Clifford, 95
Gentlemen's Agreements, 135
Gold Rush (California), 1, 15, 31, 34, 98, 99, 122
Goodman, Grant, 10, 12
Gospel Society, 128
Grant, Ulysses, 15, 20, 60
Griffis, William, 54, 56, 57, 62, 63, 89
Gwin, William, 33, 41

Hall, Francis, 25, 46
Hardy, Alphaeus, 65–66, 69, 74, 75
Hardy, Arthur, 75
Hardy, Susan, 69, 72
Harootunian, H. D., 52
Harris, Charles, 111–12
Harris, Thomas Lake, 79, 82–92; and Divine Respiration, 79, 83, 84. *See also* Brotherhood of the New Life
Harris, Townsend, 20, 46, 66, 100
Harte, Bret, 76
Hatakeyama Yoshinari, 60, 84, 86, 89, 92
Hattori Ichizo, 61
Hawaii: economy of, 102; and influence of United States, 98–99; and Japan, 97–116, 132; Masters and Servants Act (1850), 109
Hawaiian Gazette, 107
Hawaii Bureau (Board) of Immigration, 102, 103, 107, 108, 110
"The Heathen Chinee" (Harte), 76
Heco, Joseph (Hamada Hikozo), 2, 21–48, 50, 76, 102, 131; becomes an American citizen, 25, 43–45; converts to Christianity, 25, 38–39; and Eugene Van Reed, 45–46, 99; formal education of, 34; meets American presidents, 26, 39–43; perception of race in America, 36–38; place in history of Japan-U.S. relations, 48; and relationship with Choshu leaders, 47; returns to Japan, 45–46
Heusken, Henry, 25, 39
Hidden, David, 70
Hidden, Mary, 70
Higashikuze Michitomi, 104–5, 106
Hine, Robert, 80
Holland, William, 70
Honolulu Pacific Commercial Advertiser, 117

Ii Naosuke, 19, 20
Immigration Act of 1924, 135
Inoue Kaoru, 47
Inoue Ryoichi, 57
Ishii Sentaro, 97, 113
Ishizuki Minoru, 51
Itakura Katsuakira, 66
Ito Hirobumi, 47
Iwakura Mission (1870–71), 20, 51, 58, 62, 74

Japan: contact with Dutch, 10–12; contact with Portuguese, 7–10; diplomatic relations with United States,

4, 16–20, 54, 131–36; economic problems of, 66, 100, 133–34; and Hawaii, 97–116, 132; seclusion edicts issued, 7, 19; travel restrictions in, 9, 27, 68; and unequal treaties, 12–13, 20
Japanese American Citizens League (JACL), 118, 129
Japanese immigrants, 2–4, 133–36; farmers, 129; as laborers, 98, 102, 105–6, 108–12, 114–16, 132–34; as "model minority," 127, 131; population of, 2–4; women, 3, 58
The Japanese in America (Lanman and Mori), 57–59

Kamehameha III, King, 99
Kamehameha IV, King, 99
Kamehameha V, King, 103, 107, 111, 114
Kanagawa Treaty, 20, 99
Kanda Naibu, 55, 58
Kasatkin, Nicolai, 69
Kearny, Denis, 1
Ke-Kuokoa (newspaper), 109
Kennedy, Paul, 13
Koin, Kido, 47
Kusakabe Taro, 55–56, 73

Labor immigration, 98, 102, 105–6, 108–12, 114–16, 132–34
Lanman, Charles, 57, 59, 95
Lee, David, 103–4, 107
Life and Resources in America (Lanman and Mori), 92
Lincoln, Abraham, 26, 42–43
Looking Backward (Bellamy), 80

Makino Tomisaburo (Saburo), 107, 108, 111, 112–13
Manifest Destiny, 15–16, 34
Manjiro (Nakahama Manjiro), 2, 22–24, 50, 118
Markham, Edwin, 91–92, 125
Marshall, James, 122
Masters and Servants Act (1850), 109
Masumizu, Carrie Wilson, 128
Masumizu Kuninosuke, 128
Matsudaira Ichiro, 129
Matsudaira Katamori, 118–23, 125
Matsudaira Tadaatsu, 62–63
Matsudaira Tadanari, 62
Matsumura Junzo, 60, 61, 84, 86, 89, 92
McCook, Edward, 108–9
Meiji Restoration, 20, 120, 122
Memoirs as historical sources, 24–27
Merchants, status of, 6
Mexican-American War, 15, 17
Missionaries, 23, 54, 59, 73, 99, 109. *See also* Christianity
Monson Academy, 60, 87, 89
More, Thomas, 80
Mori Arinori, 56–58, 73–74, 83–84, 86, 87, 88–89, 92–95, 97, 115
Mormonism, 76
Morrison (ship), 11
Murdoch, James, 26
Murray, David, 56–57

Nagasawa, Kanaye, 84, 86, 87, 88, 89, 90, 91–92, 94, 125
Native Americans, 44, 134
Naturalization Acts, 44
Niijima Jo (Joseph Hardy Neesima), 58–59, 64–78, 84, 118, 132
Niijima Tamiharu, 71
Nire Kaganori, 87
Nomura Ichizuke, 87

Okei (lived with Veerkamp family), 128–29
Oliphant, Laurence, 83, 84, 87, 88, 90
Oliphant, Margaret, 90
Opium War, 14, 53

People's Rights Movement, 134
Perry, Matthew, 13, 17–20, 23, 84, 122, 131
Phillips, Stephen, 108–9
Phillips Academy, 69
Pierce, Franklin, 39, 41
Pierce, Henry, 112
Placerville, California, 125–27
Placerville Mountain Democrat, 126–27
Portuguese contacts with Japan, 7–10
Pratt, Orson, 76

Racism: Japanese perceptions of, in America, 36–38, 59; and Wakamatsu colonists, 126–27; white perceptions of Asians and Asian Americans, 2, 44, 133–34
Rangaku (Dutch studies), 11–12, 53, 66–67

Reagan, Ronald, 129
Reagan, William, 104, 107
Reconstruction Era, 15, 20, 59
"Revere the emperor, expel the barbarian" (*sonnō jōi*), 11, 30
"Rich nation, strong army" (*fukoku kyohei*), 13, 50–51, 52, 132
The Rise and Fall of the Great Powers (Kennedy), 13
Roberts, Edmund, 16
Robinson Crusoe (Defoe), 67
Rōnin (masterless samurai), 6, 25, 50, 83, 107
Russia, 11, 32, 41, 60, 135
Rutgers College, 49–63, 73, 89, 92, 118
Ryūgakusei (overseas students), 49–63, 67, 132; from Satsuma, 79–96

Sadamoto Yuichi, 87
Sakoku policy (national seclusion), 7, 19
Sakuma Shozan, 14, 20, 52, 67. *See also* "Eastern ethics, Western science"
Sakuma Yonekichi, 106, 113
Sakurai Matsunosuke, 128–29
Sameshima Naonobu, 79, 83, 84, 86, 88–89, 92, 97
Samurai, status of, 5–6
Samurai-peasants-artisans-merchants system (*shi-nō-ko-sho*), 5–6
Sanders, Beverly C., 32–34, 38–39, 45
San Francisco, 31–34
Satsuma domain, 19, 23, 25, 50, 69, 70, 89, 100, 119, 121, 130, 134; *ryūgakusei* from, 79–96
Savory, William, 64
Scheiner, Irwin, 65, 68–69
Schnell, Edward, 123
Schnell, John Henry, 123–28
Schnell, Jou, 124, 125, 129
Scioto (ship), 104–7
Seclusion policy (*sakoku*), 7, 19
Second Great Awakening, 80
Seeyle, Julius, 70–71, 74, 76
Seward, William, 42, 106
Shima, George, 91
Shimabara Rebellion, 9
Shima Seiichi, 129
Shimazu Nariakira, 19
Shimonoseki indemnity, 46, 60
Shi-nō-ko-sho (samurai-peasants-artisans-merchants system), 5–6
Shinron (Aizawa), 12, 19
Shiroyama Seiichi, 110
Shogun's embassy (1860), 2, 20, 99
Silk production and trade, 123–24
Slavery in the United States, 20, 37
Sonnō jōi ("revere the emperor, expel the barbarian"), 11, 30
Sugar cane plantations, 97–99, 102
Swedenborg, Emanuel, 82

Takao Ozawa v. United States, 135
Takato Shioji, 58
Tanaka Fujimaro, 74
Tanimoto Hyoemon, 87
Taylor, Horace, 64–65
Tea production and trade, 123
Telegraph, 35
Terashima Munenori, 104
Tibetan Buddhism, 84
Toba, Japan, 120–21
Toby, Ronald, 7
Tokugawa history, 5–15, 17–20
Tokugawa Ieyasu, 122
Tokugawa Nariaki, 19
Tokugawa Yoshinobu (Keiki), 120, 121
Tokyo Kaiseigakko, 55
Tosa domain, 23
Totman, Conrad, 12
Toyama Masakazu, 59
Tōyō no dōtoku, Seiyo no gakugei ("Eastern ethics, Western science"), 13–14, 48, 50, 52–53, 57, 62, 78, 119, 132. *See also* Sakuma Shozan
Toyotomi Hideyoshi, 7
Trains, 35–36
Transcontinental Railroad, 1, 2, 53
Transnational history, 4
Travel restrictions in Japan, 9, 27, 68
Troy, Thomas, 32–34
Tsuruga Castle, 121

Uchimura Kanzo, 71
Ueno Keisuke, 111–12
Unequal treaties, 12–13, 20
U.S. Naval Academy, 60
Utopia (More), 80
Utopian communities and values, 80–82, 87, 89, 96. *See also* Brotherhood of the New Life

Van Reed, Eugene, 45–47, 98, 99–106, 110–13, 126

Van Reed, James, 99
Van Reed, Margaret, 100
Van Riido Kaisho, 100–101
Van Valkenberg, Robert, 105–6, 110, 121
Veerkamp, Francis, 125
Veerkamp, Henry, 127, 129
Veerkamp, Inez, 129
Verbeck, Guido, 49, 56

Waialua Plantation, 111
Wakabayashi, Bob Tadashi, 11
Wakamatsu, Japan, 118, 121, 123
Wakamatsu Colony (California), 117–30
Walthall, Anne, 6
Waring, Jane Lee, 87, 91
Welles, Gideon, 42
Whaling, 1, 98
White Tiger Brigade (*Byakkotai*), 121
Whitfield, William, 22
Wilder, Samuel, 107, 108
Wyllie, Robert, 102

Xavier, St. Francis, 32

Yamakawa Sutematsu, 121
Yokoi Daihei, 49, 61
Yokoi Saheita, 49, 61
Yokoi Shonan 49–50, 67. *See also* "Rich nation, strong army"
Yoshida Kiyonari, 60, 79, 83, 84, 86, 89

Zen Buddhism, 84–85

The Asian American Experience

The Hood River Issei: An Oral History of Japanese Settlers in Oregon's Hood River Valley *Linda Tamura*

Americanization, Acculturation, and Ethnic Identity: The Nisei Generation in Hawaii *Eileen H. Tamura*

Sui Sin Far/Edith Maude Eaton: A Literary Biography *Annette White-Parks*

Mrs. Spring Fragrance and Other Writings *Sui Sin Far; edited by Amy Ling and Annette White-Parks*

The Golden Mountain: The Autobiography of a Korean Immigrant, 1895–1960 *Easurk Emsen Charr; edited and with an introduction by Wayne Patterson*

Race and Politics: Asian Americans, Latinos, and Whites in a Los Angeles Suburb *Leland T. Saito*

Achieving the Impossible Dream: How Japanese Americans Obtained Redress *Mitchell T. Maki, Harry H. L. Kitano, and S. Megan Berthold*

If They Don't Bring Their Women Here: Chinese Female Immigration before Exclusion *George Anthony Peffer*

Growing Up Nisei: Race, Generation, and Culture among Japanese Americans of California, 1924–49 *David K. Yoo*

Chinese American Literature since the 1850s *Xiao-huang Yin*

Pacific Pioneers: Japanese Journeys to America and Hawaii, 1850–80 *John E. Van Sant*

University of Illinois Press
1325 South Oak Street
Champaign, IL 61820-6903
www.press.uillinois.edu